CHINA

CHINA

Enabling A New
Era of Changes

PAMELA C.M. MAR

AND

FRANK-JÜRGEN RICHTER

John Wiley & Sons (Asia) Pte Ltd

Published in 2003 by John Wiley & Sons (Asia) Pte Ltd
2 Clementi Loop #02-01, Singapore 129809

Other Wiley Editorial Offices:
111 River Street, Hoboken, NJ, 07030, USA
The Atrium, Southern Gate, Chichester PO19 8SQ, England
John Wiley & Sons (Canada) Ltd, 22 Worcester Road, Rexdale, Ontario M9W 1L1,Canada
John Wiley & Sons Australia Ltd, 33 Park Road (PO Box 1226), Milton, Queensland 4064, Australia
Wiley – VCH, Pappelallee 3, 69469 Weinheim, Germany

Library of Congress Cataloging in Publication Data
ISBN 0-470-82086-1

Typeset in 11.5/13 point, Times New Roman by M. G. Dorett.

Printed in Singapore by Saik Wah Press Pte Ltd.

10 9 8 7 6 5 4 3 2

Contents

The Chinese character displayed on the book cover (pronounced 'shou', in mandarin) means longevity. This book takes a long-term view honoring China's government, business and ordinary peoples' desire for continued economic growth and prosperity.

Preface

 When I first went to China in 1979, the country had few of the marks of a future economic powerhouse: no "five-star" hotels or tall buildings, no bustle of traffic on the roads, few consumer products, and a currency system which separated foreigners and locals. Despite these outwards signs, it was clear that in the country and the people lay a deep, untapped potential – for growth, industriousness, and creativity.

China's opening and development since the late 1970s is of tremendous significance to the world because it assures us of the durability of history and synthesis. By this I mean to reflect upon Deng Xiaoping's economic policies in historical light, in that they exhibit something which has been found time and again in Chinese civilization. Although it may seem inocuous, Deng's vision was to draw from conflicting schools of thought—in this case socialism that was resident in China and capitalism that had developed in parts of Asia and the west— resulting in the unique creation that became known as "socialism with Chinese characteristics". Pragmatism and the act of drawing diversity into unity are themes that have guided Chinese civilization over the past 5000 years. One sees for instance, in Chinese society, strains of the thoughts of Confucius, Mencius, Laozi, Mozi and others, despite the apparent lack of congruence between their philosophies. Certainly, if Chinese society were to reflect only one, there may be more consistency and fewer conundrums but the robusteness and continuity of society may be lacking.

The World Economic Forum's 20-year engagement with China has also evolved greatly. What began as a yearly meeting primarily among foreign investors and selected Chinese officials is today an annual point of dialogue and exchange among foreign and local business communities, together with the government, experts, and international organizations. This book is another point in the network of activities that have been spawned by the Summit.

The book attempts to capture expertise and ideas for maintaining the pace of China's growth at a critical point in the country's development. We all know that China's process of opening up began over 20 years ago, and 20 years may seem like a short time in a country's history. This may be especially true for China, with over 5,000 years behind it. But, for China, those 20 years have brought huge change and transformation in almost every aspect of life. Now the country has entered the World Trade Organization, and it is increasingly clear that its accession is just a starting point.

Each time I return to China, I am amazed again, and grateful, that I have been lucky enough to be a witness to this transformation. For my personal journey, I wish to thank Mr. Yuan Baohua and Mr. Chen Jinhua for their years of friendship and support, which I deeply appreciate.

I, together with the World Economic Forum, look forward to continuing our engagement as a forum to bring together China with the international community. We are sure that the next 20 years of China's development will be even more promising.

Klaus Schwab
President, World Economic Forum

Part 1
Introduction

Mapping China's Future:
What Scenarios, What Strategies?

A Chinese proverb says, "Wealth only lasts three generations." The first generation builds it up, the second generation consolidates and perhaps enhances it, and the third squanders it.

In retrospect, this can be a metaphor for almost all epochs of Chinese history, in terms of the rise and fall of the dynasties. We see repeatedly that dynasties came to power led by a visionary leader or reformer, but whose less charismatic successors squandered the people's goodwill in the dynasty's steady decline. China's major dynasties – the Qin, Han, Tang, Song, Yuan, Ming, and Qing – have gone through the same cycle of ruthless but hope-filled establishment, a height of glory and cultural renaissance, followed by decline due to incompetence and corruption. Dynastic endings were bloody, marked by social unrest, peasants' revolts, and a leader's catastrophic end. After a period of chaos and power shifts, a new aspiring leader would summon his forces and move into power.

The cycle seems predictable, save for the somewhat astonishing feat that throughout, the country has always been able to put its house in order and rise to catharsis and renaissance once again. In this way, China seems to be a striking exception to Paul Kennedy's proposition that great powers rise and fall.[1] Indeed – the Roman and Spanish empires fell, and the British Empire disintegrated – only China, although certainly experiencing its ups and downs, had the wherewithal to survive. Only the rulers changed.

At the end of 2002, the People's Republic witnessed the hand-over of power from the third generation to the fourth generation of leaders, and aside from much ado in the media, not much happened to mark what is supposed to be a seminal change of power. Business seemed to be as usual. Or almost.

---

[1] Paul Kennedy, *The Rise and Fall of the Great Powers* (Vintage Books, 1989).

Appearances may be deceptive. The real meaning of the proverb above lies not in the numbers, exact generations or years. Instead, it refers to the fact that Chinese history is a cycle of ups and downs, successes and failures, rises and falls. Indeed, even during the past 50 years the country has seen constant shifts, with periods both of booming growth and national austerity, of cultural freedom and tighter control. There are people who claim that China has finally broken this cycle. The past 10 years, since the post-Tiananmen years of austerity, have been one of the longest periods of sustained strong growth. Of course, in history, 10 years is nothing, but there are those who say that with WTO accession, and the winning of the 2008 Olympics for Beijing and, in late 2002, World Expo 2010 for Shanghai, there is no turning back. China's story of globalization and economic growth is now a one-way trend.

The recent collapse of the dot.coms, Enron, Arthur Andersen, WorldCom, and Global Crossing – all of which were reputed to be infallible – should make us think twice about the "unstoppable" nature of China's growth. It has become fashionable to question the "too good to be true" nature of China's economy. *Everything* is transitory; even China, the most compelling economic success story of the last 20 years, may fail.

Mao Zedong, Zhou Enlai, and their fellow revolutionaries established the People's Republic in 1949 and set the base for the country's growth. Deng Xiaoping improved on Mao's systems and trail-blazed the mixing of socialism with "outside" elements. And Jiang Zemin managed to sustain that growth, piloting the country into a widely unexpected age of seemingly unstoppable quantitative and qualitative growth. Will the fourth generation be able to continue, and even build on, this success story?

There are two overall possibilities, and a thousand in between. These two poles – "worst case" and "best case" scenarios – are overlapping subsets of truth and realism. At a critical juncture in the country's development, it is worthwhile considering these opposing possibilities for the future so as to learn how best to navigate the present. In this spirit, we map out two basic scenarios for China's evolution over the next three to five years and hope that these can contribute to our knowledge of how China can capitalize on and enhance the positive elements, while dealing with the negative.

ENVISIONING A "WORST CASE"

The "worst case" camp is led by observers such as Gordon Chang, who believe that China is headed for collapse.[2] He and others believe that China failed to complete its reformation and is currently maintaining the illusion of

---

[2] Gordon Chang, *The Coming Collapse of China* (New York: Random House, 2001).

progress on a bubble-like economy. Beneath this veneer of success, a corrupt governance system has spawned a host of problems in business, government, and throughout society, which will eventually implode under the weight of its own burdens.

Indeed, the list of burdens is long, and touches almost every facet of China's being, from the economy and politics to social issues and the environment, and every sector of society, from farmers and blue-collar workers to educated professionals, civil servants, and foreign investors. A roster could never be comprehensive, and presents a damning case for economic collapse. It would start with puncturing a hole in the myth of high growth that is predicted, falsely reported, and then trumpeted by the planners as the makings of a "natural market system under a socialist framework." That China's statistics are doctored is legendary, and could subtract anywhere from 1% to 4% a year from the country's growth.

Certainly, at the heart of the problem is the state-owned enterprises (SOEs), bloated by workers, rife with incompetence, and maligned by their shoddy products, but somehow kept alive by a financial system that continues to shovel money down the black hole of the SOEs. The scale of debt is astounding, and has been estimated at up to several trillion Renminbi – which will take years to clear and raise government debt much higher than the 13% of GDP at the end of 2002. At one point it seemed that technology offered a way out, with its promise of increasing productivity of the SOEs while providing an engine for growth through hundreds of small start-ups. Eventually, the majority of the SOEs learned that technology is great for the educated but meaningless for the uneducated and unskilled. As for dot.com dreams, China followed the way of Nasdaq, although perhaps with a bit less waste and debt.

The problems with China's industry are comparable only to the scale of its agriculture problem. China has among the lowest percentages of arable land – between 13% and 17% – for a country of its size and population. Add years of subsidies paid to farmers by bureaucrats, and even with the land reform of the 1980s which put land under the control of those who know it best, the farmers, China's agriculture sector is a huge liability. Although it employs over 50% of the country's workers, it produces only a small fraction of national GDP. Far from the cities and infrastructure, poorly educated and ignorant of their basic rights, farmers are beset with spontaneous taxes, declining commodity prices, and few options. Farmers' success stories have nothing to do with farms, and everything to do with making their way to the city to find a job in a joint venture or private factory. China's accession to the WTO only increases the bleak lot of farmers, due to the entry of high-quality, foreign-grown grains and the scaling back of subsidies.

Farmers have thus seen little of the growth of the past few years, contributing to an increasing gap between the rich and the poor, the urbanized and farmers, and the west and the coast. This disparity is increasingly resulting in social unrest, with protests by farmers and laid-off SOE workers, which has the potential to organize and escalate rapidly if picked up by the media and dissatisfied peasants in other parts of the country. Their dissatisfaction is in many ways understandable: the Party has built the country on their backs and with their support, and now, the managers and local cadres who represent the Party are able to abscond with their pensions and severance pay. The worst is perhaps that the corrupt officials and managers are then protected by those higher up, and that the wronged can get no justice in a legal system that is supposed to be protecting the rights of the masses. The glorification of the private sector and of foreign investors as the economic hopes of the country only add salt to the wound. Peasants and workers have supported their leaders for 50 years, and this is their reward?

Aside from social unrest, the world has already heard about China's burgeoning HIV/Aids problem, which is only the most visible sign of a health system that is in disrepair and constantly lacking resources. It mimics a pension and social security system that is still under construction – slowly and not so surely. In the meantime, those who have money will survive. Those without money have no options, and also no choice.

China's problems looking outward are almost as grave, though perhaps not as socially disruptive, as are those on the inside. China is being called the next great power, but which supposed power has ethnic unrest (Xinjiang), a desire for annexation (Taiwan), dreams of expansion (Spratlys), and makes friends with autocratic regimes (North Korea)? China's citizens, and especially its Internet-enabled youth, are increasingly aware of and hungry for the outside world. How will they be led by rulers who still think that the best way to manage information is to hide it?

All of these threats have been well-known for some time, but have been neglected, ignored, or suppressed in the belief that an ever-growing Chinese economy will carry the state through. China has mastered the dance of muddling through.

A Cascade of Events Leads to Collapse

But what will happen when a stick gets caught up in the spokes of the growth wheel? A whole chain-reaction could be triggered, starting with a financial crisis, leading to mass bankruptcies and lay-offs, a run on the financial system, and finally social unrest. The impetus could be anything, even something seemingly insignificant. As in chaos theory, a butterfly beating its wings may change the course of the planet. China's future may be influenced by a series of small disruptions.

Imagine that one of the four big state banks unearths a corruption case, and as a result faces a run on its deposits, which then forces it to face bankruptcy. This is theoretically a non-event, for sure, as the state stills owns the bank and will make every effort to save it. But the pain may be too much. A real Chinese "Enron," combined with a Chapter 11 scenario, might trigger an entire cascade of events that will throw the economy, starting with the financial system, into disarray. The collapse would certainly not come instantaneously, but would be marked by a series of seemingly insignificant events, in the same way that an investigation into account books and a few connected partnerships brought down the houses of Enron and Andersen.

The bankruptcy of one of China's big banks or one of its big resource or trading firms would result in large-scale unemployment, incite instability in other enterprises, and possibly cause social unrest. This would not be new in Chinese history, as the country has experienced repeated incidents of peasant unrest, not unlike the Taiping uprising of the 1850s. Often, peasant rebellions would lead to the overthrow of the ruling dynasty and the formation of a new government allying the peasants with reform-minded elements of the ruling class. Thus is formed a new dynasty. The most significant instance in which this pattern was broken was the Tiananmen incident of 1989, in which the intellectuals led the challenge to authority. The result was a new government that expelled the reformers and empowered the conservatives.

This new rebellion – by peasants, students, or workers – would not necessarily be a cry for democracy, but rather a cry for competent economic leadership that ensures that the masses benefit from the country's prosperity. Although many people in the cities are fed up with corruption, rising unemployment, and lack of social order, the upheaval is likely to start on the margins: in Xinjiang or in the rustbelt of the northeastern provinces.

Social unrest would unsettle foreign investors, for it would remind them that for all its commercial prospects, China is at base a lawless developing country. They will gauge the political and economic risks of doing business in China, comparing it with such unstable countries as Indonesia or Colombia. As many foreign investors have already failed to see profits even after years of investment and marketing, it will only be a question of time before they gauge the risks to outweigh the potential. One need only recall the siege mentality that took over in some American-owned or affiliated factories after the U.S. bombing of the Chinese embassy in Belgrade in 1999 and one can understand that multinational corporations (MNCs) have little patience for political instability. The domino effect caused by a huge MNC evacuating its staff could shake the entire foreign-owned manufacturing base in the country.

Big powers often turn to foreign policy to draw attention away from domestic problems. Although the government has relatively more control over the media than in other countries, there is no doubt that information flows enough in China so that people would become acutely aware of any threats. One could conceive of the government using a geopolitically linked maneuver, such as forcing the return of Taiwan to the motherland, in order to reunite the country under the flag of nationalism. Many Chinese claim that they are prepared to die in order to bring Taiwan back into the fold, and one does not doubt that the government would be prepared to override its military inferiority to attempt this. The toll in terms of lives and resources may be great, but when national pride is at stake, and indeed national disintegration threatens, who is counting? Not the government, and likely not the United States which by that time, or in parallel, could be preoccupied with saving its forces for the Middle East.

An exchange of hostilities across the Taiwan Strait could be disastrous for regional integration and stability in East Asia. Global supply chains would be disrupted; Taiwanese would flee, or attempt to flee, en masse from the mainland; Hong Kong would be submerged in protest and worry; and the rest of Southeast Asia would shrink from the "China as ogre" image. It is unlikely that any country in Southeast Asia – least of all ASEAN – would dare to protest, in spite of the investments that would be jeopardized, for fear that they would be denied a future slice of the China pie. Indeed, ASEAN investors, who may have more tolerance for political instability (or simply a greater thirst for a slice of the commercial pie), may end up replacing some of those Western investors who would feel compelled to withdraw either because of the unrest or because of a need to uphold certain "principles." Either way, China's economic powerhouse would be stopped in its tracks.

CREATING A "BEST CASE"

If the all-encompassing, interlocking nature of China's economic and political problems build a powerful case against the "China miracle," statistics could tell a different story. We refer not to the historically "cooked" official statistics, but to those from outside of the country: two-way documented flows of foreign direct investment (FDI), tales from Southeast Asia of the flight of manufacturing, the numbers of Chinese traveling overseas, confidence surveys of foreign business people, and the like. Non-Chinese data, as well as anecdotal and survey evidence, seem to confirm the story told by the official statistics.

That story has investment, manufacturing, and domestic demand at its center, and testifies that China's economic miracle has only just begun. The positive scenario has China moving ahead in a step-by-step fashion on all the key fronts of economic, political, and social development. Positive elements in an economy are not incited by specific incidents, but rather come into being because of a long-term solid policy and implementation which has created nurturing conditions. Thus, even in a positive scenario and as China becomes more wealthy, the country will perhaps not be able to boast of taking great strides forward but rather of making steady progress in creating an enabling framework for growth and prosperity.

Economically, this means building on investment to fund reforms in the SOEs, agriculture, and financial sector, while strengthening consumer demand and the private sector as the new engines of growth. Politically, we will see China cement a new leadership role in Asia, centered on trade with Southeast Asia, and to a lesser extent, globally. The country will also move more decisively and proactively to further develop the "soft" side of growth: education, the environment, the digital divide, and access to healthcare. The result will be not only sustained economic expansion but also a significant rise in the quality of life for most citizens.

The International Economy: FDI and Regional Trade

Foreign direct investment, which surpassed US$50 billion in 2002 (an increase of 20% year on year),[3] can be called the single most significant driver of China's economic expansion. This is especially true since FDI experienced a growth spurt starting in 1998: between 1998 and 2001, utilised FDI amounted to over US$173 billion. It has been good for the government, swelling foreign exchange reserves to over US$270 billion by the end of 2002[4] thereby facilitating ambitious capital investment programs on the back of its solid financial rating. In addition, FDI has helped to diversify and deepen the country's economy beyond the heavy industrial base that was once its core, and has also led the education of a generation of Chinese professionals in different ways of doing business.

China's FDI can be seen in two waves, linked to the economy's stage of development. The first wave, begun in the mid-1980s and already phasing out, has most multinationals making relatively finite investments into definable,

---

[3] Mark O'Neill, "China Fever Runs High Among Executives Despite Dubious Statistics," *South China Morning Post*, December 2, 2002 at www.SCMP.com.
[4] Zhu Rongji, Speech to the World Congress of Accountants, November 19, 2002, as recorded on BBC Monitoring Asia Pacific.

easily transferable industries low on the knowledge scale. These began with simple assembly plants in toys, footwear, clothing – many pioneered by or routed through Hong Kong, Taiwanese, and to a lesser extent Thai-Chinese and other Southeast Asian Chinese companies that were familiar with the terrain (Guangdong, Fujian), ways of doing business, and willing to bear the then hardship conditions.

In parallel to this first wave of Chinese-to-China investments were the first waves of Western and Japanese investment into manufacturing in China, largely along the joint venture model, in industries such as automotive, small electronics, consumer products, and chemicals. These investments have not uniformly been profitable. However, they have helped foreign companies gain a firm foothold in China's expanding markets. The importance of this should not be underestimated. While stories of Minolta and Toshiba closing plants in Malaysia and moving them to China may dominate the headlines – leading one to think that China is displacing global manufacturing bases – today over two-thirds of foreign manufacturing in China is for the domestic market. It is also true that over two-thirds of electronics exports are by foreign affiliates – the shift from global to domestic markets as the targets is an important one for China to be able to sustain growth in a global downturn.

The second wave of FDI is characterized by a two-fold shift: from low-knowledge base industries to medium and highly knowledge-intensive industries; and geographically from the coastal and southern areas of the country inward. These are two shifts that are linked only indirectly. That is, the former – scaling up the knowledge and value-added ladder – is likely to be achieved only in the developed south and coastal regions, while investment and industrialization of the so-called hinterlands can only be achieved by starting at the level of basic industries.

There is evidence that the first process is still under way. Much of the up-scaling has been led by Taiwanese companies, who, circumventing Taiwan government guidelines on investment in the mainland, saw early on the competitive advantages to be gained by manufacturing and now developing products in China. In Dongguan city in Guangdong, over 95% of parts needed in computers are available from local markets (i.e. need not be imported). The city, together with its environs, is currently the world's largest processing and export base for computer parts, with over 2,800 companies focusing on computer and IT products, including 800 from Taiwan.[5] Much of Taiwan's IT and electronics manufacturing has in the past five years gradually shifted to

---

[5] "Southern China Becomes Global Manufacturing Center for Computers," *ChinaOnline*, October 24, 2000.

China, with Taiwan's manufacturing sector now manufacturing over 56% of its motherboards, 88% of its scanners, and 58% of its monitors in China.[6]

In parallel, China is also forming an integral part of the global network for research and development (R&D) for global Information and Communications Technology (ICT) companies. In 1997, only 13% of foreign-invested firms were applying their most advanced technology to their China businesses; by 2001, over 41% were doing so.[7] Over 100 centers for R&D have been opened in China, established by global giants without regard to home country such as Motorola, General Electric, JVC, Microsoft, Oracle, Ericsson, Nokia, Panasonic, and Mitsubishi. Motorola, for instance, has over 650 research personnel with over US$200 million invested in a research center.

Microsoft has committed over US$130 million to a research joint venture and to setting up one of its five global research centers in Shanghai.[8] In mid-2002, Oracle unveiled a new software research facility in Shenzhen. By the end of 2000, 29 multinationals had set up 32 R&D centers. The growing number of foreign-invested R&D facilities has helped to reverse China's brain drain into a brain "pull," with many of its top students who went abroad and stayed there to work because of better jobs and quality of life now considering returning home.[9] Thus, most ITC multinationals' operations in China are now over 90% localized.

The concentration of electronics and technology investments in and around the major coastal and southern cities is evident from export figures and company data. While foreign trade continues to rise, the pace of growth from industrial centers such as Shenzhen and Shanghai continues to be 5–10 percentage points above the national average. For instance, foreign trade expanded 11% in the first nine months of 2002, but Shenzhen recorded an expansion of 25%, even taking into account the two-week shutdown of ports on the west coast of the U.S. in September.[10] In 2002, high-technology good account for 20% of China's total exports, but as a proportion, are

---

[6] "Taiwan's IT Hardware Producers Rush to Mainland," *ChinaOnline*, August 28, 2000.
[7] Vincent Lim, "China Set to Strengthen Impressively in Technology Product Categories," *New Straits Times* (Malaysia), September 1, 2002.
[8] UNCTAD, *World Investment Report 2002: Transnational Corporations and Export Competitiveness*, Geneva and New York: United Nations 2002, p. 5.
[9] In the past three years, Zhongguancun, China's "Silicon Valley," has attracted over 3,500 returnees from abroad, and thus far in total over 130,000 of approximately 400,000 overseas students have returned home. "China Sees Tide of Returning Talents," in *People's Daily Online*, June 28, 2002.
[10] Hong Kong Trade Development Council, *Business Alert China*, issue 11, November 15, 2002.

recording the fastest growth: in 2002, they accounted for over 40% of year-on-year growth.[11]

In parallel to the transition to a more knowledge-intensive base centered in the technology and electronics industry, China has already begun to experience and gain from investment targeted at the professional services. Foreign law firms, consultants, and financial firms first entered in order to serve their own global customers' operations in China, initially because of restrictions in some sectors such as law. Accession to the WTO, combined with Chinese enterprises' own hunger for knowledge and tools with which to meet the increasingly competitive market conditions, have already begun to change that. As a result, the large majority (over 90% in some cases) of the clients of high-profile Western professional services firms are local companies, and this has provided a fertile ground for continued investment into the widening field.

The larger economic effect of foreign investment in professional services will be felt not only by local firms in these areas – through joint ventures or affiliations as required by statute – but also by the economy as a whole as the standards of operation and the benefits of their advice and practice are dissipated. A few high-profile joint ventures or mergers in this area, such as Ogilvy's acquisition of H-Line, or Ernst & Young's merger with Hua Ming, will see a deepening penetration of foreigners into the services. The consequences of this will be a situation where essentially Chinese operations are actually meeting or mimicking international best practices in a range of services – of course, with tailoring to meet local market conditions.

This development will by necessity, and in keeping with patterns of professional service firm clustering, be focused in the wealthy urban centers along the eastern and southern seaboards. Few, if any, changes will be seen in the poorer, inner regions. Yet, these regions are the home to the majority of the population, as well as the overwhelming majority of poor, jobless and uneducated. The disparities with the booming coastal areas are stark, and quick action is needed to avert a total "disconnect" of the two areas. The government's Go West program has had high-profile press coverage and a series of high-profile investor visits – including one by the "big names" among Hong Kong's business community. Whether their participation is solely in order to curry favor with the government, or because of a genuine interest in wishing to do business in the western regions, remains to be seen; the smart money has been ostensibly betting on the former, with only a few large government-connected projects leading the way.

---

[11] Andy Xie, "The IT Export Boom," September 27, 2002.

This is changing, although only very gradually, again starting at the urban cores and spreading outwards. The Yangtze River Delta has already begun to outpace the Pearl River Delta as the primary center of growth, contributing over 20% of national GDP and over 40% in some industries such as automotive, steel, textiles and garments, and petrochemicals.[12] It is also home to four of China's richest 10 cities.[13] Even Hong Kong's "conservative" companies, who have traditionally stayed close to home in the Pearl River Delta, have plowed money into the Shanghai property market.[14]

Meanwhile, the Yangtze River Basin, centered in Chongqing, is perhaps the largest center of growth in the west, which is home to over 100 million consumers, and which has wage costs at 30–50% of those in the coastal regions. SOEs are clustered here already, with Chongqing and Wuhan playing historically important roles in the growth of heavy industry. Increasingly, domestic investment is leveraging lower wage costs in order to serve local markets.[15]

As infrastructure bottlenecks are opened up, foreign investors – led by a few Hong Kong companies and foreign investors in sectors such as automobiles and chemicals – will also be able to see this. The diversification of the inland areas will provide a pull mechanism, which will help lift these areas further out of poverty and enable them to take part in China's second wave of economic expansion. We will see the growth of the coastal areas replicated, although perhaps not with the same speed, in the inland areas.

Perhaps the most promising side of China's investment-led expansion story lies in looking toward the future. Long-term confidence in China's economy has risen significantly. In AT Kearney's FDI confidence survey, for instance, China has now displaced the United States as the world's most attractive destination for foreign investment. The key determinants driving FDI – a stable political outlook, strong underlying growth, and an improving consumer environment – all weigh positively in China. In comparison to the rest of Asia, which has traditionally looked toward the United States and Japan as their foremost trading partners, China is now the most attractive investment destination.[16]

---

[12] "Yangtze River Delta Outlook 2003," available on www.ibc-asia.com, and Xinhua, "Bright Future for Yangtze River Delta Tipped," July 29, 2002.
[13] Xinhua, "Economic Giants Mushrooming in Yangtze River Delta," October 23, 2002.
[14] Kenneth Ko, "SHKP Puts $8b into Shanghai," *South China Morning Post*, December 6, 2002.
[15] Andy Xie, "On Center Stage," November 29, 2002.
[16] AT Kearney, *FDI Confidence Index*, Vol. 5, September 2002.

In the World Economic Forum's own *Global Competitiveness Report*, China has risen significantly in 2002. In terms of current macroeconomic competitiveness, it has moved from 43rd to 38th in a ranking of 80 economies; in terms of growth competitiveness, which forecasts medium- to long-term potential, China has risen six places, from 39th to 33rd. These results are based on both an executive survey of over 4,800 business people, plus available data on a range of competitiveness inputs. Just one executive survey, completed by the Japan Bank for International Co-operation, shows that Japanese companies have consistently ranked China first in surveys of most promising manufacturing FDI. That, combined with the fact that China in 2002 became the largest recipient of FDI in Asia and the developing world, shows the robustness of China's economic growth to be not only anecdotal (that is, survey-based) but also factual.[17]

The one element that could significantly detract from China's attractiveness is currency instability: not of a global nature, which businesses have learned to expect and hedge, but rather of the Chinese currency, the Renminbi. From the Asian financial crisis through the end of 2002, the Chinese leadership and central bank have been adamant about not devaluing the yuan. However, as seen in Wu Xiaoling's chapter on monetary policy, currency convertibility is no longer a taboo topic. Indeed, it is increasingly the case that China is planning for a wider floating range as a first step toward convertibility. The fundamental conditions for currency convertibility are positive: a healthy current account, a trade surplus and reserve situation, and strong industrial output and GDP.[18] So, the issue is not so much managing the financial expectations, as managing market expectations. The sooner the central bank can publicly state its plans and give business a window of time in which to prepare, the quicker China will be on its way to ensuring that currency convertibility does not become as disruptive as it could be in other countries that are opening their fixed currency systems.

The Domestic Economy: SOE Reform, Financial System Restructuring, and the Private Sector

While foreign investment provides one engine of growth, it touches only a small part of society, focusing on the urban or industrialized areas of the east and south. The other side, almost entirely distinct from the exponential growth

[17] UNCTAD, *World Investment Report 2002: Transnational Corporations and Export Competitiveness*, pp. 44, 55.
[18] C. H. Kwan, "Time to Float the Yuan," www.rieti.go.jp, June 7, 2002.

of foreign-invested companies and sectors, is riddled with problems and inefficiencies that, five years after the start of Zhu Rongji's landmark SOE reform program in 1997, still act as a deadweight on the economy and a stranglehold on local economies. This is a crucial area needing resolution, for while the foreign-invested economy can ride on export growth, purely domestic enterprises employ hundreds of thousands of unskilled or poorly trained workers while capturing valuable state revenues in subsidies, loan non-payment, and worker services.

The cleaning up of the SOEs is inextricably tied to the fate of the state banking system. The banking system is dominated by the "big four" banks,[19] which account for over 67% of deposits and 60% of loans.[20] As detailed in the chapters by Paulson and Hu and by Xie, the banking system, beset by levels of non-performing loans that have been estimated at anywhere between 24% and 50% of total assets,[21] has become a major obstacle to corporate reform and economic growth. Certainly, the markets will have a hard time re-employing the over 30 million workers who will be laid off in the next three to five years, in addition to the 10 million new workers who enter the workforce annually. The social security system remains a point of concern, given the estimated 48 million workers who have already been laid off as a result of SOE reform. With slumping capital markets, wary investors, and revenues drying up due to an inefficient tax system that is riddled with corruption, the government has almost run out of options. Both chapters present viable ways in which the financial system can meet its commitments in the medium and long term.

Since the 1997 restructuring program was introduced, the possibility of selling SOE shares to foreigners has been off-limits. In mid-2002, this policy was changed, and it may be the first step in unlocking some of the estimated US$240 billion in shares held by the state in its enterprises. This opens the door for increased consolidation, mergers and acquisitions, and reforms, and is a major step forward in easing the industrial overcapacity and burden of SOEs on the government's books. The government must now make good on its commitment, and be willing to abide by a market-based mechanism, as it decides the fate of its enterprises.

---

[19] Agricultural Bank of China, Bank of China, China Construction Bank, and the Industrial and Commercial Bank of China.

[20] "Moody's: Chinese Banking System's Outlook Stable," *The Asian Banker Journal*, October 31, 2002.

[21] AFX News Limited, "China's New Leaders Must Tackle Significant Economic Problems," November 5, 2002.

If curing the state sector will erase the drain on revenues, supporting growth of the private sector has the potential to create a new revenue source. The private sector – together with the smaller *"minying"* hybrid cooperative enterprises – is in many ways the opposite of the state sector. It has posted growth rates consistently above the national averages, and is an engine of innovation and new job creation. In 2002, the private sector accounted for over 60% of the service industry, 50% of exports, and 24% of current GDP. At current growth rates, it will comprise as much as 40% of GDP by 2010.[22] It is also a potential source of investment into the state sector, with one recent example being the purchase of 18% of China Eastern Airlines by the private-sector Junyao Group,[23] and a continuing source of innovation. Although age-old ideologies which give preference to state enterprises or their affiliates in allocating resources (housing, health services, education, and loans) are gradually being eroded, the government will need to make a more concerted effort to embrace and support the private sector.

At the Sixteenth Party Congress, private business people were formally acknowledged as positive contributors to the nation, and one "private" entrepreneur was accepted as an alternate member of the central committee. Cynics may view Zhang Ruimin's acceptance into the inner circle as meaningless, since his company is still partly held by the government (local government). They may claim that the Party's sudden embracing of private entrepreneurs is no more than a self-interested move to remain in power while ensnaring the only source of wealth in the country. However, this is perhaps the most the Party can do to ensure continuity and stability while embracing and supporting change. Without this outward show of support from the Party, the private sector would continue to be shackled by its traditional outcast status. At the same time, the Party needed to concede that the private sector is a superior source of job creation and innovation, and by giving it equal status to state enterprises, it is freeing it to do just that.

Acceptance of the private sector by the Party is just the first step, but an important and critical one. A positive scenario for China's growth continues in this vein with the following:

· the establishment of and adherence to a clearer legal framework governing company operations and protecting private property;

· ending protectionism, which has prevented private company entry into some sectors and localities;

[22] Chao Y. Wang, "Chinese Private Enterprises and the WTO Entry: Challenges and Opportunities," ChinaEquity Presentation, November 12, 2002.
[23] "Non-state Inflows," *China Daily*, November 22, 2002, p. 3.

· proactively encouraging banks to grant more credit to private companies and establishing more venture capital sources for small and medium-sized private companies; and

· proactively seeking out the private sector as partners in and catalysts of SOE reform.

The most ambitious effort would see the government designate a specific minister or even vice premier directly responsible for the development of the private sector. Such advocates exist for all other constituencies, and development of the private sector is in many ways too important to be left to just rhetoric. The challenge here would be to accomplish this in a way that would actually create advantages and support systems within the government, without dampening the spirit and independence that drives private-sector growth. Lastly, all action is not left to the government. Private-sector companies would do well to establish more business and professional associations to enable more knowledge exchange among themselves.

Agriculture is the third stake in the domestic economy requiring immediate action. Whereas commitment, regulatory frameworks, and stricter surveillance can help solve the problems confronting the private sector and SOEs, agriculture is a different case. This sector confronts old farming methods, uneducated and beleaguered farmers, falling commodity prices, and market opening as a result of accession to the WTO. Although the sector now contributes just a small fraction of GDP, it occupies the majority of the country's population of 800 million in the countryside.

Since China's accession to the WTO, the agriculture situation has not been totally without hope. In the first three quarters of 2002, despite European Union (EU) bans on some animal products, China recorded nearly US$5 billion in agricultural trade surplus, on an 11% rise in exports.[24] Although it has prevented the initial tranche of commodity imports from the United States and other agriculture exporters by instituting strict definitions on the product composition, China has to prepare eventually to meet its commitment to lower tariffs to an average 17% from the current rate of over 21%. Admirable though it may be for a developing country – considering that after accomplishing this, China will have lower tariffs on agriculture than both the United States and Europe – drastic supports need to be put in place to protect farmers and help them make the transition to more productive, cash crop techniques.

The government's urbanization program, under which it undertakes to develop smaller and medium-sized cities especially in the western regions

---

[24] Zhu Boru, "Nation Posts Agri-trade Surplus," *Business Weekly*, November 5–11, 2002.

that house the majority of farmers, will help absorb the unemployed farmers. Local governance, to be discussed below, is another aspect that is critical to sustaining the pressures in rural areas. While containing pressures that will accompany market opening, China should use its new weight at the WTO negotiating tables, together with other developing countries, to pressure the EU and the United States to open up their markets. China is gaining more leverage on the global stage, and it should not be afraid to exercise it in protecting its own interests while it builds toward long-term sustainability in its agriculture industry.

Governance: The New Leadership, Corruption and Transparency, and Upholding the WTO Commitments

If there is a continuing thorn in the side of China's success story, it has to be governance. It is the source of farmer discontent, worker unrest, and angry stock-market and foreign investors, and it touches nearly every aspect of society and national development, from contract signing and customs approvals, to taxes, visas, investments, and even traffic violations. This does not have to do with whether the new leadership establishes its own identity. "Who is Hu?" is an issue only for foreign observers. Most Chinese citizens, whether farmers in the arid west, factory workers in the south, or professionals in the cities, know that the identity of the new Communist Party leadership will do little to change their lives in a concrete way. The change in leadership just changes the faces reported on the nightly news.

The real issue in people's lives deals with much more mundane manifestations of governance, and is a problem that every businessperson, villager, and migrant worker has confronted. While it is unrealistic to believe that the new leadership will give more teeth to the current anti-corruption drive, they are sanguine enough to realize that the rot already threatens the Party and needs to be contained and gradually wiped out. In an optimistic scenario, China will continue to cleanse its administrative ranks and ensure that at least the top-level provincial officials are clean and those with chequered pasts are neutralized. The round of provincial leadership changes during and immediately following the Sixteenth Party Congress has made clear that the criteria for advancement include political loyalty, but also, more importantly, a track record of progress in development.

In addition, the government's publicity campaigns regarding eliminating corruption – with punishment, including death in some cases, of people as highly ranked as the Vice Chairman of the National People's Congress, and governors, vice governors, or mayors from Yunnan, Guangxi, Hebei, Xiamen, Wenzhou, and Shenyang – provide some disincentive to officials who seek personal benefit. In the five-year period from October 1997 to 2002, over 37,000 government officials were punished for corruption in the courts, with 98 being at the ministry or provincial levels.[25] The media, led by magazines such as *Caijing* especially in business cases (such as the scandal surrounding the State Power Corporation), is also providing additional weight to the anti-corruption drive.

The government's delicate task is to ensure the continued cleansing and pursuit of corrupt officials – aided by the media – while also ensuring that the top leadership remain above the fray and beyond question. Foreign analysts may view this maneuver cynically, but it is the only way for the government to actually manage its way out the problem without being brought down by it. And despite the attention devoted to the prominence of Politburo standing committee members who are seen as tainted by corruption, it is important to note that neither charge is applied to the two top people, Secretary-General Hu Jintao and Premier Wen Jiabao. This distinction will be increasingly important in enforcing a clean code of conduct down through the lower levels.

Much more difficult will be the curing of poor governance that is not necessarily illegal or corrupt, but which results in a similar scale of waste and interference. The existence of administrative monopolies is one example, and, as argued by Hu Angang and Guo Yong, results in significant losses to the state, despite the fact that often the related actions are not illegal per se. Protectionism, whether based in a sector or locality, and the inability to independently adjudicate cases that may seem to threaten the entrenched interests, also have ramifications in terms of the willingness of foreign, private, and independent business people to take a long-term view in their investment planning, operations decisions, resource development, and so forth. As the economy shifts from being driven primarily by state-directed spending to independent investment – whether by foreigners, private business people, or hybrid enterprises from *outside* of a specific jurisdiction – the quality of governance will come to be felt more concretely.

Consistency and transparency in decision-making are already key components of most business confidence surveys, and China has historically ranked near the bottom in such aspects. Indeed, in the 2002 Transparency International "Corruption Perceptions Index," China is ranked 59th out of the 102 economies surveyed, below Sri Lanka, Morocco, Ghana, Mexico, Colombia, and Brazil.[26] Cleanliness is not an image that countries can build

---

[25] Xinhua, "Anti-corruption Drive in China Fruitful," December 9, 2002.
[26] Transparency International 2002, "Corruption Perceptions Index," press release, available at www.transparency.org.

overnight. However, accession to the WTO gives China a chance. It is like a litmus test. If China enforces the principles, and not just the letter, of the WTO protocols, it will have made a great stride in changing others' current perceptions of China.

After one year of WTO membership, China's performance indicates positive things for the future. Although the country has stalled on several provisions – notably, on those requiring higher levels of imported agriculture products, foreign licensing for telecommunications equipment, and foreign participation in the wholesale and distribution sectors – it has already promulgated thousands of statutes enabling the realization of WTO commitments, and has begun the training of officials, lawyers, and government functionaries. The Ministry of Foreign Trade and Economic Co-operation, as well as a number of affiliated state organs at the central and provincial levels, now have designated WTO bureaux to oversee the fulfilment of the commitments.

The other test which can effect a rapid and significant change in perceptions of China as a clean country, and can in fact give it another advantage vis-à-vis its Asian counterparts, is in intellectual property. There is perhaps no area that is critical to the success of so many sectors, from chemicals and pharmaceutical, to consumer products, to entertainment and technology. China is still considered to be a black hole in this area, with governments or the people they protect participating quite visibly in the distribution and sale of counterfeit goods. Currently, an estimated 90% of the software used in offices in China is pirated; estimates of lost revenues from piracy in movies, music, software, and books amount to about US$1.5 billion, a quarter of the total global losses in this area. The State Council's own Development Research Center estimates the value of the counterfeiting industry at around US$16 billion.[27] Most multinational consumer companies have experienced problems with counterfeit labels, whether actual counterfeits or "knock-offs" (for example, Cap for Gap, and Louis Vitton for Louis Vuitton).

A scenario in which China tackles this problem involves not only having the right enforcement forces, but also campaigns or civic education programs aimed at both the public and the government. Mounting campaigns is something China can do "almost in its sleep." With the right musicians and movie stars (who have personal stakes in this battle) involved, a lot could be done to educate the public about the benefits of adhering to intellectual property laws. China can pull ahead in this battle, but only with a concerted effort. The

---

[27] FreidlNet, "Intellectual Property: Tripping over TRIPS," available at www.friedlnet.com/news/02111004.html.

benefits are significant, not only in terms of how China is perceived abroad, especially in comparison to its Southeast Asian neighbors who have failed to eradicate the problem on a much smaller scale, but also for Chinese industries that are becoming more and more dependent on their intellectual capital for growth. This latter group includes companies that can hope to become China's first true multinationals, such as Haier, Huawei, Zhongxin Telecommunications, and Legend.

At the same time, in areas outside of the WTO, China has performed admirably in enforcing a wider code of good governance among its enterprises. The China Securities Regulatory Commission and the Shanghai Stock Exchange have together taken on very visible roles by mandating regular reporting, cracking down on non-disclosure and trading violations, and professionalizing their own staff. This has dampened the market and affected the government's plan to disinvest from SOEs through the stock market, although it is debatable whether it is the only cause of the market slump and may, in the long term, result in a more vibrant capital market. In addition, the State has made significant efforts to upgrade its accounting sector, starting with new training institutes in Beijing, Shanghai, and Xiamen. These are just small steps, but taken together they have the potential to reverse the current trend in China's corporate governance.

Professionalization has also taken place in other areas of the government, within the confines of the "iron rice bowl" system which still guides staff placement and retrenchment. Almost all government departments at the central, major municipality, and provincial levels have overseas training programs for officials. These programs take place both at the high-profile level, at institutions such as the Kennedy School of Government and the University of California, and at "ordinary" institutions, such as the University of Maryland and the Nanyang Technology University in Singapore. Government workers are urged to take study sabbaticals abroad in order to improve their own skills, and also as a tool for staff retention. In the Shenzhen Municipal Government, staff at even the deputy director or lower levels have attended one-year study abroad programs at the Columbia School of International and Public Affairs and at Stanford University. For those who are not funded to go abroad, China's own universities are making rapid advancements in starting government training programs along the lines of those which exist in the developed world. The professionalization of the Chinese civil service is under way, and it is only a matter of time before the civil service becomes upright across the board, instead of only in some elements.

Regional Relations and Geopolitics: Oil, the U.S. relationship, Taiwan, and Asian Trouble Spots

The new leadership enters at a time of relative global instability and transition in the system of global alliances and trading relationships. Although it is a contentious time, it is also a time of opportunity on the key fronts of China's geopolitical stance.

Perhaps the most significant relationship that is open to definition is the one with the United States. With Europe unable to define a united policy stance, China is the only country that could imagine providing a counterweight to the U.S. at a global level. Although it has not exerted its weight in forceful manners, the Chinese insistence on a United Nations (UN)-based agreement on invading Iraq was one of the major factors convincing the U.S. to seek the Security Council's approval. In time, the Chinese leadership will begin to exercise its power in a less reactive, more proactive manner.

It has already done so on two issues over which it has relative control: vis-à-vis its central Asian neighbors, with the launching and then the continuation of the Shanghai Co-operation Organization, and vis-à-vis North Korea. This latter issue could be one that brings China and the U.S. closer together as they work for a peaceful way to bring the perceived renegade state into the global embrace. The Chinese search for oil security will continue to play an important role in its relations with the Middle East and Southeast Asia. During the 1990s, China's average annual oil output rose 1.7 % annually, while consumption rose 7.3% annually, resulting in the country being a new importer of oil since 1993. Conservative estimates state that China will need to import 120 million tonnes of oil per year by 2010, and by 2015 it will need to import at least half of its requirements. Although China's economy is seen as more resilient to oil shocks than other more oil-dependent economies such as the United States, the country is already starting a strategic reserve in 2003 which will be built up to 15 million tonnes by 2010.[28]

To this end, China has been advancing its relations with Iraq and other Middle Eastern countries, and one notes that at the end of 2002, it had already invited the Iraqi Foreign Minister to Beijing to underline its opposition to any military action being taken against Iraq by the United States. 2002 was also the first year in which China's major oil companies reached out to secure strategic reserves and contracts with Southeast Asia, with PetroChina and CNOOC both cementing deals in Indonesia. China will continue to build up a buffer against the possibility of oil price spikes or crises by building up ties, if

---

[28] Mark O'Neill, "Iraq Crisis Raises China Fears over Oil Security," *South China Morning Post*, September 19, 2002.

not allying itself directly with key oil-rich countries in Southeast Asia and the Middle East. Instead of using these ties and its increasing global weight, China will see that it stands to gain most by continuing to advocate for multilateral or UN-based solutions to regional conflicts in areas such as Southeast Asia. It will not directly counterweight the United States in its own relations with those same countries, despite the increasing opportunities to do so. This will have the effect of building a reserve of trust vis-à-vis these countries in particular, and globally in general. These allies will be useful, especially when "push comes to shove," perhaps over Taiwan.

The Taiwan issue is the only issue in the world where conflict may be inevitable. All other regional and domestic disputes have high chances of being resolved, or at least of having the potential for conflict reduced. Why is this so, and how would a "positive" scenario for the Taiwan situation play out?

Conflict is inevitable because China insists that Taiwan must eventually revert back to the motherland as a province, while Taiwan has consistently refused to do so. There are fundamental differences in perceptions of how "independent" Taiwan is at present. Although the government of the Democratic People's Party (DPP) is more adamant and extreme in its language, one should not regard the Kuomintang (KMT) party as being any more willing for Taiwan to return to the mainland than any other province. Both political parties would require significant provisions giving the territory probably more independence than is given to Hong Kong. No other issue so inflames Chinese on both sides of the Taiwan Strait, both within government and among ordinary people. It is also an issue that is thoroughly interwoven with economic stakes for both sides. Taiwan investment in the mainland is now conservatively valued (that is, not counting investments appearing as being from Hong Kong, because of routing) at US$100 billion. Manufacturing based in China, which is crucial to the survival of Taiwan's technology industries, accounts for over 25% of Taiwan's GDP and workforce and is its most important foreign exchange earner.[29] Discussions between China and Taiwan over future relations always leave noticeable marks on Taiwan's stock market, one indicator of confidence.

A positive scenario for China would not necessarily see the province revert back to the mainland. Indeed, in the current situation, this would happen only by force, as outlined above, with deep consequences for both sides and for the region as a whole. The positive story would see the current stalemate inch toward a resolution, marked by Taiwan's acceptance of a date – or at

---

[29] The Republic of Taiwan Yearbook 2002, available at www.roc-taiwan.org.

least a horizon – for reunification, and the mainland's acceptance of a degree of autonomy or independence of at least their economic and domestic affairs for the Taiwanese people. Neither side wants to come to blows, but it is perhaps more China that is itching for this last vestige of its imperial past to be resolved sooner rather than later. The challenge for China is to tame its belligerent or nationalistic impulses within its government and among its people, and to accept that Taiwan deserves, and will accept nothing less than, a voice in its own future. Thought revolutions are not new for China, and this one will see China achieve nothing less in order to avoid bloodshed on its own soil and, worse, foreign intervention in what is resolutely seen as a domestic issue.

While the Taiwanese may like to think that the United States would come to its aid in a situation of stress with China, they would do well to have a more realistic picture of the extent to which the U.S.'s political interests are determined by its commercial stakes. U.S. businesses have as much as, if not more than, Taiwanese businesses invested in the mainland, and have deeply integrated their operations and sales with China. American businesses have been, and will continue to be, a staunch force against any further escalation of U.S. commitment to military intervention in Taiwan, and the U.S. government knows that its interests lie first in protecting U.S. commercial interests and only secondarily with enforcing policy.

For China this is good news, since conflict with the U.S. would benefit neither side. Instead, China's evolving relationship with the U.S. will continue to be shaped by the twin poles of the ideology of the U.S. leadership and U.S. commercial interests. Since the EP3 incident[30] and the bombing of the Chinese embassy in Belgrade, China's savvy in the international arena has increased significantly, just in time for its rise to become the only country capable of confronting the United States at a global level. A positive outlook for U.S.– China relations sees China gradually stepping into this role, with no major actions or outbursts, and avoiding conflict until it is more certain on its feet as a global power.

In a positive scenario, China will not intervene in any major conflict – it has neither the firepower nor the resources to do so. In some senses, its rhetoric will continue to be bound by its lack of military prowess and professionalism, and the country will continue to build up both of these in the

---

[30]EP3 is a type of plane, and the incident refers to the case in April 2001, during which gunfire was exchanged between a Chinese jet and a US EP3 surveillance aircraft in the South China Sea. The Chinese claimed that the EP3 spy plane was within Chinese airspace and that the Chinese plane was justified in forcing it to land. The plane landed on Hainan Island, and together with the pilot was held for a standoff period of over one week before resolution of the issue was achieved.

near term. Certainly in the longer term, China will be able to surmount its material obstacles and take its place at the global geopolitical table. Until then, the new leadership will continue to study and observe international relations, exercising its power in multilateral terms, and never belligerently unless it is provoked first. This will give it time to build up both confidence and industrial strength for its entrance as a global power by the time its economy is truly of comparable size and sophistication to the other industrial giants.

Quality of Life: Education, the Environment, the Media, Urbanization, and Health System

Disparities pervade any description of the quality of life in China today. Whether in income, housing, basic utilities, access to education or technology, or politics, China can be seen as not one country but over a dozen, and foreign media have been quick to point this out in an effort to deflate the China "myth." It is true that disparities are wide and present the government with steep challenges as it seeks to better distribute the gains of development. As could perhaps be expected with government projects, progress has been more forthcoming in some areas than others. To its credit, though, China has, at least on a policy level, begun to address the consequences of uneven development, through a range of declarations, legal improvements, and spending programs. A positive scenario for growth would see these programs all move ahead on the basis of uninterrupted funding flows, government's increasing openness to addressing the problem publicly, and more professionalism and consistency in program implementation.

China's income gap is its Achilles heel. While Beijing, Shanghai, Guangzhou, and other eastern cities boast urban per capita GDP levels approaching or in excess of US$3,000, the average peasant – representing over 600 million people – still scrapes by on less than US$900 per year. Over the past 10 years of industrial growth, the situation has become worse rather than better, as China's Gini coefficient measuring the severity of income disparity increased from 0.35 to 0.4 in the decade from 1988 to 1997. The situation is deteriorating, due to losses sustained by farmers as a result of China's accession to the WTO, and the increasing numbers of state enterprise workers who will be laid off (already over 40 million, with no clear end in sight).[31] At the current rate, China's Gini coefficient is set to place China on a par with some countries in Latin America in terms of income disparity. The

---

[31] "Beijing Forms Software Alliance to Beef up Industry," *ChinaOnline*, December 21, 2001.

income gap is a potent source of social unrest, since it cuts to the heart of the government's claim to be creating an egalitarian society in the socialist tradition. Already, groups of farmers and laid-off workers have organized protests large enough to warrant central government intervention and foreign news reports.

How can the government navigate this potentially explosive situation? The best case scenario would rely on the government's clean-up of local cadres and village officials as the first step, and the increase of resources allocated to easing the burdens of farmers and laid-off workers. Part of the local anger results from peasants and workers feeling that they have been "had" by corrupt managers or cadres. As long as this corrupt group is ostensibly representing the State, the State becomes the target of anger. Once the central government exercises more direct control over local representatives and makes clear efforts to rectify and improve the situation of poor people, their tolerance will increase and the potential for unrest will also dissipate. Progress is being made gradually, and the positive scenario would see a much faster rate of this local cleaning-up process.

HIV/Aids has been called China's other ticking time bomb. Although different voices within the government estimate that 60,000 to half a million people are HIV positive, the UN and international agencies claim that as many as one million may already be infected. A UN report in June 2002 predicted that without drastic action, China would have 10 million infected people by 2010. Whether one believes the foreign or government statistics, it is certain that the Aids problem will be significant and requires action immediately. Again, to its credit, the government is addressing the problem, although not in the same manner and perhaps not with the same banners and speed as international organizations might like.

From a climate where Aids activists could still be arrested for anti-government actions, by the end of 2002 the country had come around to a situation where government officials were marking World Aids Day with support for prevention programs, and where public awareness efforts are being staged openly and with government support. Although neither the government nor the country's budding civil society organizations are likely to undertake highly public campaigns, the increasing awareness work – through the media, public advertisements, government pronouncements, and talk shows – will do much to increase public understanding of the issue. Indeed, the fact that United Nations Secretary General, Kofi Annan was able to address this issue when he received an honorary degree from Zhejiang University in Hangzhou in 2002 shows how far the government has come in opening up.

Another key area that is urgently in need of progress is education. While China has largely solved the problem of illiteracy, poverty in rural areas is already threatening to undo the country's gains. The positive scenario sees China step up funding at the primary school level, to ensure that families have free access to primary education without additional expenditures. At the tertiary level, China is well known for having some of the brightest students in the world, but it remains a fact that university education is available to only a small percentage of students; moreover, that education is still woefully under-funded compared to many other developing nations. It seems that the single biggest factor preventing faster expansion of research and development in China is the country's limited ability to produce more engineers and scientists. Currently, the government estimates that over 600,000 engineers and scientists are needed annually, but it can only supply around 180,000 from all sources, including its own universities and technical institutes.[32] Easing this strain is mostly a question of funding additional universities and upgrading facilities.

More difficult will be changing the culture of learning in the schools, regardless of level. Currently, the Chinese education system scores well on producing brilliant scientists and mathematicians, but scores miserably on producing critical thinkers and questioners who become the bedrock of continual innovation and renaissance. This requires a whole turnaround in mentality that will not be achievable while "taboo" subjects exist. Students will follow teachers' leads and teachers will follow administrators' leads. It is unrealistic to think that teachers would change on their own or mount movements against the administrations. The best case would have the leadership and the Ministry of Education launch a campaign promoting "free thinking" and "free questioning," under which there are few, if any, taboos. This may sound a bit like the Hundred Flowers Movement of 1957[33], but this time the government must be prepared to "eat bitter" in order to reap the long-term gains that will be made possible through the generation of entrepreneurs and economic productivity.

Anecdotal evidence shows that China's top universities are already doing this. Students at the top universities in Beijing and Shanghai already pose questions that are as rigorous as any in the developed world, which is increasingly where more professors are spending time either being educated

---

[32] An example of this would be Shanghai, where private cars (owned by the rich) but not taxis (used more by the middle-class and non-car owners) are allowed to use the tunnel linking central Puxi and Pudong at rush hours.

[33] The Hundred Flowers movement was an attempt to inject new thinking and energy into society and government, by letting "a hundred flowers bloom, and a hundred schools of thought contend." This resulted in widespread criticism of government policies, which then caused the government to crack down by purging or jailing those who spoke out.

or in special training. Exposing faculty to outside ways of educating yields positive results and will be continued, along with teacher exchanges that bring foreign professors to Chinese universities for a year or more. The elite universities set the trend, but the ministry and school administrations must take more proactive stances for freeing up thinking, in order for the true intellectual prowess of Chinese students to be harnessed.

The environment and urbanization conundrums are linked for China, and also do much to determine the quality of life for Chinese citizens. In as much as China may publicly state that it, as a developing and industrializing nation, should be allowed to continue to pollute at its current levels, the government knows that a development program which sacrifices the environment for progress is no progress at all. To its credit, the government has already taken strides to move polluting industries out of city centers and to begin the transition from coal-based fossil fuels to cleaner forms of energy. Although its hands are to some degree tied by its need to fuel its development with available resources, it is also aware of the health consequences. Thus, it is very much a case of paying today, in terms of developing more "expensive" forms of fuel, or paying tomorrow though health consequences.

The government has, as a top-line policy, chosen the former. It is developing natural gas reserves, establishing energy supply lines from Russia and Southeast Asia, and gradually closing down its own coal mines. At the same time, China has moved with much haste to develop mass transport in its cities, with respectable subway systems already existing or in development in the major cities. It has done less, however, to contain the growth of automobiles in cities, and has in some instances even privileged car drivers above public transport or taxi users.[33] China has signed the Kyoto Protocol, which has done much to increase its stature internationally. At home, it must not promote car ownership, despite the fact that the automotive industry has been targeted as one of eight key growth industries. Promoting mass transport and keeping the streets safe for bicycles could do much to contain China's thirst for foreign oil.

CONCLUSION: READING BETWEEN TWO TRUTHS

By this point, it will be evident where our bets lie: we see our view as positively realistic. We believe that China's growth story is full of thorns and weeds, but that, overall, the roots are strong and the trend is undeniably upward.

The chapters in this book are part of that story. The core chapters, on the primary economic and political facets of China's growth, illustrate that the country's development continues to face challenges and difficulties, in addition to opportunities. Fundamental aspects must change, whether one examines an aspect of governance, as Hu Angang and Guo Yong do, or the misallocation of capital detailed by Andy Xie. No observers will deny that fixing the banking system is indeed a "mission critical," as outlined by Fred Hu and Hank Paulson. These tasks are made all the more difficult by the increasing globalization of China's economy, something pointed out by Fan Gang in his analysis. Great change remains possible, in the same way that Zhu Rongji transformed China, as discussed by Laurence Brahm, but one senses that the change will henceforth be slow and perhaps not even be noticeable.

Geopolitically, China's difficulties are equally steep, especially in the increasingly complex international environment detailed by Philip Bowring, or in seeking a new relationship with an old foe, Japan. Southeast Asia poses another new terrain, as China seeks leadership befitting its economic pre-eminence, while trying not to dominate like a modern-day colonial power. Zhang Yunling explores a way forward for East Asian regionalism.

Government will always provide a clear policy direction, whether in economy, business development, monetary structure, or urban development. This is clear in the policy voices which comprise the third part of the book: each covers a field in a succinct and no-nonsense manner that is the way of governing in the People's Republic today.

The final section is meant to be the third leg in this triumvirate leading the economy. While experts will wean truth from facts and government will set frameworks for operations, the business community drives day-to-day reality. Thus, the executive roundtable, bringing together a uniquely diverse group of CEOs – from state-owned and private companies, Chinese and multinational, companies from a variety of sectors, and corporate giants as well as small start-ups – aims to highlight the panoply of concerns and perspectives which drive firms' actions in and toward China today.

Of course, the extent to which business people can really change the economy, beyond their immediate operating environment, is debatable. The government still determines the basic regulatory and operating framework and enacts wide-scale restructuring of key industries by internally decided decree instead of public consultation. In addition, business continues to need government approval for all but the smallest maneuvers. However, even in this environment, the leadership has accepted a greater role for the business community.

One of the landmark decisions during the Sixteenth Communist Party Congress in November 2002 was that of allowing private entrepreneurs and business people into the Party ranks. This reverses a fundamental view within the Party that it should be comprised of laborers and farmers, or the masses. Now, perhaps in view of the increasing number of economic drivers, the

Party has ended the ideological limbo for the private sector and even admitted them to the inner circle of the Standing Committee, even if only as an alternate member. The increased participation of private entrepreneurs also symbolizes a growing middle-class, the new rich who until recently had to "jump into the sea" (in Chinese, "*xiahai*"), or swim in the rough seas beyond government protection and legislation, who now find themselves in new positions of privilege.

At the same time, much of the rhetoric about the economy that came out of the Congress concerned ways in which the business operating environment could be strengthened and improved. Among the proclamations were items that the business community has been pressing for, or at least complaining about: protection of property rights, market access, land use, unfair taxation, access to credit, foreign investment rights, and fair competition between the private and state sectors. Many of the imbalances which marked the economy prior to WTO but which continue to raise problems for companies are fated to end, according to the proclamations.

The shift in which the state valorizes a group previously disdained – in this case, the business community in general and the private sector in particular – exemplifies a pattern that is repeated throughout Chinese history and increasingly in the move toward a "socialist market economy." This is a tendency toward pragmatism, at the expense of rhetoric and ideology. If the Western world tends to base decisions on ideology and dogmatism, the Chinese prefer an evolutionary understanding of history. The Chinese marry differing principles and experiences so as to achieve a final outcome of progress.

It is impossible to predict where ideology and pragmatism will lead to next. The only guidance we can take is to study the past, observe the present, and place our hope in a future that is increasingly multilateral, multi-stakeholder, and diverse. And yes, this can even be true in the case of China.

Part 2
Perspectives:
Economy

Reform and Development:
The Dual-Transformation of China

*Fan Gang**

 China has been one of the fastest-growing economies in the world over the past 20 years. During that time, it has also made remarkable progress in the institutional transformation toward a market system. However, at the same time, two questions have been raised: (1) Where is China headed in both the short term and the long term? (2) Is China's progress at risk as a result of the country's current economic, social, and political problems?

This chapter attempts to answer these questions by analyzing the "dual-transformation" process.

THE PROCESS OF "DUAL TRANSFORMATION" IN CHINA

China differs from the transition economies in Eastern Europe, in that it is a low-income, rural society-based developing country. At the same time, it differs from other developing countries in Southeast Asia, because it is a transition economy, with problems similar to those experienced by Russia and the Eastern European countries, such as problems of state-owned enterprises and government control. And China's population of 1.2 billion makes its problems all that more difficult to resolve.

This argument means that, while other countries may have one set of problems arising from their being either "developing" or "transition" economies, China has both. It is undertaking both to transform its rural economy into a modern society and to transform its planned economy into a market system. It is this "dual" nature of its problems that makes the transformation process in China so difficult, as the two sets of problems complicate and amplify each

* Fan Gang is Professor of Economics at Peking University and the Graduate School of the Chinese Academy of Social Sciences, and a Director of the National Economic Research Institute, China Reform Foundation.

other. For instance, legal reform in China is not just a matter of replacing one set of laws or rules with another, but is also a process of building up the whole concept and whole set of institutions based on the"rule of law" from an initial condition of a rural, even "medieval," society with a long and complex history. Even once the laws have been promulgated, it will take many years, and much testing of them in the courts, for the legal framework to reflect the new realities.

It will unavoidably take a long time for China to build an orderly, functioning market system. In general, institution building is a long-term process, anyway. Seventy years may not be an unrealistic estimate for transforming China from a medieval economy to a modern market economy, given that countries in the West have been undergoing the same process since the 17th century and given that China has not experienced colonialism.

Such a historical, long-term perspective is necessary if we are to understand the current situation. We must expect that there will be problems; the real question is: are the necessary changes being made that will gradually see the present gap between China and the advanced market economies narrowed tomorrow? For instance, although the banking sector is still very poorly organized, it has achieved significant progress in the last five years. The overall political stability that has puzzled many observers is fundamentally based on the fact that most interest groups in Chinese society today are better off, in many senses, than they were 20 years ago, or even five years ago, and have expectations of being even better off in the future, no matter how poor is their current situation.

Development of the non-State Sectors and Reform of the State Sector

It has been pointed out by many that the most serious economic problem in China has been that of the state-owed enterprises (SOEs). Inefficient SOEs have increasingly become a burden on economic growth. The unemployment of state employees is the major cause of some local incidents of social unrest. The mounting non-performing loans (NPLs) owed by the SOEs to the state banks have caused a credit crunch that has contributed to the ongoing deflation. And reform of the large SOEs seems not to have achieved any real progress. It is these problems that have led some analysts to predict that China's growth will cease and its economy will collapse. But China's economy has *not* collapsed, and its growth looks set to continue for the foreseeable future. The key to understanding this puzzle is the fact that economic growth in China is now supported mostly by the non-state sector, rather than the state sector.

The non-state sector, which consists of private companies, self-employed businesses, shareholding corporations, joint ventures with foreign investment, and community-owned rural industries, a great part of which are actually private undertakings, now contributes 74% of industrial output, 62.2% of GDP, and more than 100% of the increase in employment. This means that, even though the state sector's problems have worsened, the importance of the SOEs has lessened in terms of the overall economic growth and development of the market economy.

The most important feature to date of China's "gradual" or "incremental" approach to institutional transformation has been the development of the market-oriented, non-state sectors, not the reform of the state sector.[1] The low level of industrialization and nationalization (the number of state employees has never exceeded 20% of the total labor force) enabled China to rely on its vast rural and "non-state" labor force to grow the new sector without first having to reform the old sector. (By comparison, Russia has had to release all the resources tied up in the state sector in order for a new system to grow.)

The reform of the SOEs has been long delayed, compared with the radical approach to reform taken in some other countries. But one of the key elements of the incremental approach to reform is that the development of new sectors and changes of economic structure will create and improve the conditions for reform of the old sector:

- The growing competition from the non-state sector reduced the monopolistic profits of the SOEs, resulting in their experiencing financial difficulties. Without such difficulties, they would be unlikely to accept the reform programs.

- The jobs created by the non-state sector laid down some pre-conditions for the "mass lay-off" of the state sector. The overall economic growth, supported by the growth of the non-state sector, has made it possible for the government to mobilize some resources to compensate the unemployed state workers. As a result, over 15 million state employees have been laid off in the past five years, without causing major social instability.

- The growing private capital and entrepreneurial capacity are making the "reforms" more akin to "takeovers." As the non-state companies are still not big enough to take over the large-sized SOEs, privatization so far has been mainly taking place in the small and medium-sized SOEs,

---

[1] Fan Gang, "Incremental Changes and Dual-track Transition: Understanding the Case of China," *Economic Policy,* December 1994.

except in a few cases of joint ventures between large SOEs and foreign investors. Some reports indicate that in some regions over 70% of small SOEs have been privatized in one way or another, including being sold to employees and managers and converted into so-called employee shareholding companies, as the first step in the process of reform.

Although many large SOEs are still not ready to be reformed, the conditions for reform will improve with the further development of the non-state sector.[2] The recent reform policies adopted by the central government have not only reconfirmed the direction of "restructuring the property rights," but have also taken more concrete steps toward the "diversification of ownership" by offering "executive stock options" and further reduction of state shares of the listed companies, which were previously untradable.

THE DYNAMIC EVOLUTION OF CHINA'S MODEL FOR TRANSFORMATION

Some questions may emerge from the above discussion of reforms about where China's economic system is heading and what are the real meanings of the officially defined reform objectives of a socialist market economy.

To answer such a question, it may be useful to look back at how the official line was drawn from time to time during the past 20 years. Table 2.1 shows that the official "objective formula" has continued to change and evolve during that time, from a "planned economy supplemented by some market elements" in 1979 to, in 1999, a "socialist market economy," with the withdrawal of the SOEs from competitive industries and mixed ownership.

From this point of view, it seems not very meaningful to spend too much time clarifying what is the current official objective model. What is more useful is to analyze when and why the objective has changed, and in what direction. Such an analysis reveals that nothing is accidental and the logic of political economy prevails. For instance, a major policy shift took place in 1993 when the term "socialist market economy" (replacing the term "planned economy") was first adopted by the CCCCP. The previous year, for the first time, the non-state sector accounted for in excess of 50% of industrial output (see Table 1). In 1996, the state industrial sector as a whole suffered a "net loss" for the first time. Then, in the following year, the Chinese

---

[2] The author once wrote in a syndicated article published in some European countries' newspapers that: "In some sense, a Western Germany is emerging in China in the process of reforming the Eastern Germany."

Communist Party (CCP) adopted policies of "diversifying the ownership" and "developing the private sector together with the state sector." In 1998, the Constitution was amended by the addition of: "Private ownership should be equally protected and promoted." In short, the contents and definition of "socialist market economy" have changed over time according to the needs of the economy. With the further growth of the private sector and the private business community, which serves as the main support of China's economic prosperity and social stability, the CCP has recently started inviting private-business "millionaires" to join the Party (see Table 2). There is no doubt that the official "objectives" will continue to change further in the same way.

Table 1: The gradual evolution of the official "formula" of reform objectives since 1978

Time	Formulation of reform objectives
1978 - 1984.10	Planned economy supplemented by some market elements
1984.10 - 1987.10	Planned commodity economy
1987.10 - 1989.6	"State regulates the market and market regulates enterprises"
1989.6 - 1991	"Organic integration of planned economy and market regulations"
1992	Shareholding system and security market (started) can be used by socialism
1992.10	Socialist market economy
1994	"Corporatization of SOEs and reform of property rights"
1997	Developing the state sector together with all other kinds of ownership; "holding on to large SOEs while letting small ones go to the market"
1998	Constitution amendment: private ownership should be equally promoted and protected
1999.10	SOEs withdraw from competitive industries; diversification of ownership of corporate and "mixed ownership"; executive stock options for SOEs
2001.7	"Three representative functions of the Party"; allows owners of private and individual enterprises to be Party members; further develop various ownership forms

Source: *Various official documents of the Central Committee of the Chinese Communist Party (CCCCP)*

It may be correct to say that reform without clear-cut objectives is a major weakness of China's transformation. But focusing on what is achievable and acceptable without clarifying a "final destination" may have the virtue of pragmatism and may lower political costs.

CAN THE REFORMS AND GROWTH CONTINUE FOR ANOTHER 20 YEARS?

Why 20 years? First, it takes no time to destroy an institution – it can be done overnight; but building an institution takes time. For a country like China, it may take some time to build modern market-based institutions, including all the necessities for the rule of law. Second, it may take 20–40 years for China to complete its industrialization process, during which more than 400 million rural laborers will have to find new jobs in non-farming sectors in the current global environment of technology revolution and oversupply.

There are many obstacles and potential problems that may hinder the process of transformation and economic growth. Some of the major economic problems include:

- huge non-performing loans and financial risks;
- high unemployment, leading to social unrest;
- income disparity in general, and regional disparity in particular;
- rural poverty;
- challenges of globalization; and
- corruption and government reform.

The discussion of these issues will show that, despite the great difficulties in dealing with these problems, there is cause for optimism.

Financial Risks

China is famous for the high percentage of non-performing loans in its state bank system. Official estimates have put the ratio of NPLs to total credit in the major state banks at around 26% in 2000, and 24% in 2001, equivalent to about 25% of GDP. If we add those NPLs that have been transferred to the asset management companies (AMCs) that were specially designed to deal with NPLs, the total NPL/GDP ratio might be as high as 40%. This may be one of the highest in the world.

In some sense, a domestic financial crisis has already occurred in China. Indeed, the high level of NPLs held by the SOEs with the state banks has caused a kind of credit crunch since 1996. In response, the monetary authorities and the banks must tighten their financial discipline and make risk control their first priority. This response is already becoming evident, with new loans to SOEs having been reduced and, since October 1997, some kind of monetary contraction which has contributed to ongoing deflation. It is the high level of NPLs and the insolvency of the banks, when compared to some other Asian countries, that have led to predictions that China is headed for a financial collapse.[3]

However, one of the major reasons for China's high level of NPLs is that, since the mid-1980s, the government has shifted all its fiscal responsibilities for the SOEs to the state banks. Since that time, it has neither invested in or nor provided subsidies to the SOEs, all of whose needs have been met by loans made by the state banks. From this point of view, the NPLs between the SOEs and the state banks are actually quasi-government deficits. But one would be mistaking the overall financial risks if the government budget is not taken into account. The reality is that while the NPL level is extraordinarily high compared to other countries, including some Southeast Asian countries, China's government debt has remained extraordinarily low in world terms. At the end of 2001, it was equivalent to less than 16% of GDP. Such a comprehensive picture[4] explains why China still enjoys some financial stability despite the high level of NPLs, and why the Chinese government is still able to mobilize resources to stabilize the economy, including using debt-financing as its expansionary fiscal policy in order to deal with deflation. It also explains why China is still managing to keep its growth and reform policies going.

China's external balance is also quite manageable. Both the current account and capital account are in surplus, and foreign exchange reserves have risen to US$220 billion. Foreign debt has been well served so far, and the short-term debt/GDP ratio is also extraordinarily low, accounting for only 1% of GDP. In addition, China's capital account is not yet opened, and portfolio investment is minimal. Therefore, it seems safe to say that, for the foreseeable future, there will be no financial crisis in China similar to what happened in some Asian countries in 1997–98. The solution to the NPL problem and to China's long-term financial stability lies in, of course, reform of the SOEs and the banking sector, which transformation will take some time to accomplish.

---

[3] See Nicholas R. Lardy, *China's Unfinished Economic Revolution* (Brookings Institute, 1998)

[4] We may define the sum of government debt, NPLs, and total foreign debt – the "government's comprehensive liability" for China – as an indicator of the financial risk of the economy. Based on this calculation, China's overall liability is about 50%, while that of other countries in Southeast Asia ranges from 73% to 114%. See Fan Gang, (1999).

The good news is that a kind of consensus has been built up among policymakers and bankers at all levels, that concerted efforts are needed to stop the growth of the NPLs.

Unemployment

It should be noted that there are three kinds of unemployment and under-employment in China.

The first type is the unemployment of urban labor, reflected by the official "urban unemployment rate" (annually about 3.5% of the urban labor force in recent years). This class refers mainly to new entrants to the urban labor force, people in the transition phase between jobs, and people who have been laid off by the private sector. The formally registered urban unemployed are covered by unemployment insurance managed by the social welfare department of the government.

The second type is rural under-employment. There are around 600 million rural laborers, around 200 million of whom have engaged in non-farming activities (about 100 million have already settled in the cities); 70% of the rest are actually under-employed on their own land. However, the rural population is never considered to be totally unemployed, because every household is entitled to a plot of farming land, no matter how small that plot might be. Therefore, they should be categorized as "under-employed." The high level of under-employment drives rural people out of rural areas or out of agriculture in search of better-paid jobs in other places and other industries. If they find a new job, they will be better off; if not, they may return to their plot of land as a last resort to provide the means of life (or "security"). But the employment of rural people has never been the responsibility of the government. The rural population have never been covered by government-run social-security programs, even under the previous socialist welfare system. From this point of view, rural under-employment is, in principle, not a short-run political issue and, in fact, rural people do not look to the government to solve their problem of finding suitable jobs.

In the long run, say 40 years, with the growth of the population, up to 400 million rural laborers may need to be reallocated in non-farming industries. Otherwise, the increasing urban–rural income disparity may cause great social instability.

The third type of unemployed workers are laid-off former state employees. This is a real political problem, because the previous socialist "social contract" implied that state workers were guaranteed lifetime employment by the government. The reforms have changed all that. However, for the time being, laid-off state employees are still provided with some protection under a special arrangement that gives them the status of "off-post workers" (*Xia-gang Zhi-gong*). With this special status, they are entitled to receive a certain amount of minimum payment (higher than the unemployment insurance payment), retraining programs, and several job offers during the first two to three years after being laid off. Between 1997 and 2001, more than 24 million state workers were laid off, perhaps the largest lay-off in human history over that amount of time. So far, the situation seems to be manageable in terms of social stability, as those people who have lost their jobs are relatively well-protected by the government. Under the best scenario, their number will be reduced in the near future. But no one assumes that this should happen overnight.

While the first two kinds of unemployment (under-employment) may change with the macro-business cycles, the third is mainly an institutional issue and independent of business cycles – some people must be laid off only because the reforms proceed. The more important difference is that the first two kinds of unemployment seem not to be politically troublesome, but the mass lay-off of workers may be dangerous with regards to social stability. However, over the past years and in the context of changing overall economic conditions, the laying-off of workers has become politically more acceptable, for the following reasons:

- Many SOEs are experiencing financial difficulties and many of them are not able to pay their workers, anyway. Most protests by workers in the past years have resulted not from being laid off, but from delays in receiving their wages (sometimes up to 10 months). Given that there is little chance of the situation at the SOEs improving, people are realizing that they can no longer rely on the SOEs for job security and a steady income. In short, remaining with an SOE has become a less attractive choice.

- Meanwhile, after 20 years of development, the non-state sector is now providing many more jobs. The possibility of finding a new and better-paid job in the non-state sector, or of becoming self-employed in one's own business, is increasing, and should continue to do so if the overall growth continues. In other words, it may be a better option to leave one's job with an SOE to join the non-state sector.

- The severance packages for laid-off workers normally enable them to keep some of the benefits they enjoyed in the SOEs. In addition, the government has increased its expenditure on the so-called Urban Re-employment Center in recent years, which has improved the financial situation of unemployed people.[5]

---

[5] In 1998, the central government introduced a new program called the Urban Re-employment Center (URC). The key new element of the URC is that lay-offs and re-

In conclusion, it would appear that China will be able to manage the situation where three to five million people are laid off each year for the near future without running into major social unrest. The real problem for China, however, is how to create jobs for the 400 million rural laborers in the coming decade. Obviously, this same issue will be important if China can continue its growth for the next 40 years.

Income Disparities

The increasing income disparity between groups, regions, and rural and urban populations has become a major socio-economic problem since the beginning of reform. Consequently, there are increasing concerns and increasing complaints about the disparities, although there has been no major social unrest or conflicts caused by such disparities. But the following facts should be kept in mind:

1   China's economic and social transformation started from an over-equalized society under the former socialist regime. The introduction of a market system itself means the introduction of larger income differentials; without these, China would still be operating under the old system. From this point of view, the disparity is pursued and is "good." For example, there must be lay-offs, and consequently a relative decline in the income of state employees, in order to reform the SOEs and develop the private sector at the same time.

2   In the past 20 years, the large majority of the population, including those in the poor rural areas, have been better off in real and absolute terms, although some people may be relatively worse off. This is a situation fundamentally different from one where a large proportion of the population are absolutely worse off. Those people that are worse off are mainly state employees aged 40–45 years who have been laid off and are having difficulty in finding new jobs. As the generation who lived through the shortages and difficulties of the Cultural Revolution in the 1960s and 1970s, however, they seem more tolerant of their current difficulties (compared to the younger generations who have benefited the most from the reforms and growth) because of the feeling of overall improvement, although they may have initially resisted the reforms and, in so doing, slowed the reform process.

employment should be financed by three parties – the central government, the local government, and the company – instead of only by the company, as formerly. This apparently has improved the situation of people who have been laid off. According to a report of the Ministry of Labor, the percentage of workers who were paid on time increased to 97% in 1998, from the previous year's 12%.

3   With a population of 1.2 billion, most of whom are still in the countryside hoping for better-paid jobs in non-farming industries, China's wage level for blue-collar workers could remain very low for a long time. At the other end of the scale, with the growth of the financial markets and high-tech industries, a small group of white-collar workers may soon catch up to international income levels. Therefore, the problem of income disparity may be a long-term problem that China has to face as long as it wants to pursue economic development. It is hard to see how the government can do much about it if it commits to market-oriented reforms and economic growth.

The key policy issue here is not how to make a government "income policy" in order to narrow the gap, but how to ensure that the majority of the population are better off in absolute terms along with the overall economic growth. In this regard, the further promotion of labor-intensive industries, together with the development of high-technology, could be a necessary policy that will increase the incomes of the vast majority across the board.

Regional Disparities and Mass Immigration

As a result of the rapid opening up and growth of the coastal regions, regional disparities have become one of the most sensitive political issues in China. The problem should not be exaggerated, however. The decentralization of the government and the enlargement of regional economic differences does not necessarily lead to attempts to "split up" the country, as speculated by some observers.[6] China is now much more integrated than ever before, as market forces are bringing benefits to all. The poor regions depend more on the rich regions' labor market, capital flows, and technology transfers; and the rich regions (such as Guangdong) rely more than ever on the markets and resources of the other regions. Every region has its own reasons to complain about the disparities, but it is clear that progressing toward an integrated national market is in everyone's interest.

Meanwhile, there are other factors that are contributing to narrowing the gap of per capita income between regions:[7]

---

[6] We do not discuss ethnic factors in this chapter.

[7] It should be noted that part of the problem of regional disparities is institutional. For example, the slow growth of the northeast regions has been mainly due to the concentration of SOEs in those regions. From this point of view, the problem will not be solved until the reforms are more advanced.

- As living standards and labor (and land) costs have continued to increase in the coastal regions, in recent years, investment, both foreign and domestic, has started to move inward to central China, along the Yangtze River. Growth in those regions (such as in Anhui and Hubei) since 1998 has already exceeded that of the coastal regions.

- The government has started to increase the transfer of funds and investment in the interior regions, although it is still very limited. Recently, the central government has announced a plan of further "exploration" of the western regions that will be a major part of its Tenth Five-year Plan covering 2001–05.

- Immigration plays an important role. People have started to move out of the poorer regions to the richer regions, looking for better-paid jobs. Over 200 million of the working population have migrated to places such as the coastal cities. In the long run, migration may be the only way for some regions to increase their per capita income, given their resources and geographical conditions. It can be expected that China will experience even bigger mass domestic immigration, and that the distribution of the population will be significantly changed along with the economic transformation.

In conclusion, it would seem that regional disparities are not a big "negative" for the continuation of economic growth, nor a major potential "explosive factor" leading to social instability.

Rural Development and Urbanization

China has suffered an oversupply of grains in recent years, so the question of "who will feed China?" has been fading. However, the low productivity of agriculture and the low incomes of rural people remain challenging problems at present and for the near future.

The key issue here is that there are too many people working on the small amount of cultivable land, and therefore the ultimate solution to the problem is industrialization and urbanization, which move people off the land. Studies show that the marginal product of labor in agriculture is so low as to be almost negligible, and that only a reduction in the number of people who rely on the land as their source of income can make it feasible for modern technology to be used in China's agriculture. Furthermore, only an increase of the amount of land cultivated per head can lead to a meaningful increase in the per capita income in the agricultural sector.

The rural industries over the past 20 years have played an important role in improving the income levels of rural people and supporting the country's overall economic growth. As a result, the industrialization of the Chinese economy progressed significantly, with non-farming employment[8] accounting for 54% of the total labor force in 1997. More than 100 million rural laborers have found new jobs in non-farming sectors. This process has slowed in recent years, demonstrating its own limitation, as it has not been accompanied by urbanization. At the end of 1998, only 32% of the total population lived in cities and towns. Such a disproportion between industrialization and urbanization is one of the major bottlenecks for further growth.

The government is adopting policies aimed at speeding up urbanization More large cities, or groups of cities, are planned for the coastal areas. However, in the foreseeable future, China's agriculture will still be highly labor-intensive and any increase in rural incomes will be very limited.

Challenges of Globalization

There has been a growing consensus among the Chinese people that globalization is a process that requires their participation, lest they become marginalized. People have realized that the country's opening-up has been one of the main impetuses for domestic reforms, which are the only way for China to catch up with the developed world. China's accession to the World Trade Organization (WTO) is just another step in the globalization process.

On the other hand, it became apparent with the Asian financial crisis that domestic reforms and globalization are full of risks and bring great challenges. Being handicapped with serious domestic institutional problems, an over-speedy transformation could be devastating. Therefore, domestic reforms and market liberalization should be pursued together in a compatible way and "pre-matured market liberalization" avoided. It can be predicted that the further opening of China's market will continue to be a gradual process in general in order to minimize the costs. Nothing dramatic or radical should be expected. In particular, the opening up of the financial market and the capital account convertibility of foreign exchange will not happen soon.

With the WTO accession, China may be able to enjoy a high level of foreign direct investment (currently in excess of US$47 billion per year, but hopefully over US$60 billion by 2003) for years to come. The trade surplus

---

[8] This includes the workers in rural industrial enterprises and rural self-employed non-farming individuals.

will decline due to deflationary pressures on the international market and the further opening of China's market. This may not be a bad thing, because the previous high-level surplus of the balance of payments and the high level of foreign exchange reserves are not economically efficient for a developing country such as China. But in the foreseeable future, China's international accounts will remain balanced and no debt crisis should be expected.

Corruption and Government Reform

There has been some progress in government reforms in recent years: the restructuring of the administration has been under way since 1998; the anti-corruption campaign has been hiked up; village elections are now a nationwide practice; and the People's Congress now plays a bigger role in balancing the powers of the administration. But there is no doubt that China's economic transformation requires further acceleration of government reforms.

A great part of the problem of corruption is tied to the existence of big state-owned economic sectors, not only the government bureaucracy and political structure. Therefore, the privatization of the SOEs and reforms of other state-owned institutions will be one of the key factors in reducing corruption. The ongoing development of the private sector and the fast growth of the middle-class are laying the foundation for a political transition toward a constructive, rather than a destructive, democracy.

A very important fact is that there seems to be a consensus among most Chinese people that China should not go back to the chaos and civil wars that stopped the country's development in the last century. For most people, nothing is more important than the continuation of economic prosperity and catching up to the international market. This fear of civil war and social chaos will facilitate compromises being made among conflicting groups. This, plus the perception of being better off than in the past, are the fundamental bases for political stability.

The examples of a relatively peaceful and gradual transition to a constructive democracy in some newly industrialized Asian economies (such as Korea and Taiwan) give people confidence that China may be able to do the same.

CONCLUSION

There are many problems and difficulties in the Chinese economy, each one of which could lead to some kind of crisis or "collapse." When China enters a new stage of development and transition under its WTO membership, many scenarios could be applied with equal probability. But according to the analyses above, it seems unlikely that China will suffer a financial crisis, political turmoil, or vast social unrest in the near future. The government still enjoys some room to maneuver policy, both financially and politically. Growth will continue at a level lower than in the past but still as high as 7–8%. The reforms will continue in all aspects, although still in a gradual manner. No dramatic changes are predicted in the next five years, but the gradual accumulation of small steps of evolution can be very meaningful. However, of course, the question remains: Is the progress being made at this stage sufficient to lay the foundations for further development, or is it too small to avoid a crisis in the next stage?

Banking Reform in China:
Mission Critical

Hank M. Paulson and Fred Hu

As China moves into the next stage of economic reform and development following the Sixteenth Party Congress, the country's new generation of leadership must respond with utmost urgency to a critical challenge – that is, the restructuring of its ailing banking system. With 190% of GDP in total assets, the banking sector plays a dominant role in China's financial system. However, government-directed credit allocation (policy-lending), lax supervision, and mismanagement in the central planning era have left China's banking sector burdened with massive bad loans, with the non-performing loan (NPL) ratio likely to be as high as 40%. As we have learned from financial crises around the world, including the 1997/98 Asian crisis and Japan's decade-old economic malaise, problems in the banking sector have grave macroeconomic consequences. Monetary policy is likely to lose effectiveness when the banking sector is in distress, and an ensuing credit crunch could severely depress private consumption, corporate investment, and foreign trade, thus choking off economic growth and exacerbating deflationary pressures. If the banking system ceases to function properly, fiscal policy will have to assume the full burden of stimulating demand and growth, leading to widening budgetary deficits and higher long-term interest rates. Moreover, the required NPL resolution and recapitalization will entail massive fiscal costs, imposing a severe burden on the government budget and public-sector balance sheet.

While China has made substantial progress in economic restructuring and has recorded impressive GDP growth rates in recent years, its vast economic potential will not be fully realized unless it rapidly tackles its banking

* Hank M. Paulson is Chairman and CEO, Goldman Sachs Group, and Fred Hu is Managing Director, Goldman Sachs Group, Hong Kong.

sector woes. China must build a modern, efficient financial system if it is to continue to fuel its dramatic economic take-off. Among the myriad of risks China still faces today, nothing poses a greater threat to its macroeconomic stability and long-term growth prospects than the fragility of its banking sector. As such, banking restructuring constitutes China's single most important macroeconomic and structural reform challenge ahead. To use a military metaphor, for China's new generation of reformist leadership, banking reform is mission critical.

What has China accomplished so far in its efforts to reform its troubled banking sector? How large a risk is there that China will succumb to a systemic banking crisis? Can China afford a gigantic bank bailout with fast-paced NPL clean-up? These are the central questions we attempt to address in this chapter.

STILL ON THE BRINK
The 1997/98 Asian crisis provided a wake-up call to the Chinese leadership, reminding it that China's own weak banking system makes the country vulnerable to crises similar to those that engulfed its neighbors in the late 1990s. Premier Zhu Rongji has moved swiftly to stabilize a rapidly deteriorating banking sector and taken strong measures to maintain investor confidence. The government issued RMB270 billion in special national bonds in 1998 to recapitalize the four biggest state-owned commercial banks ("the Big Four") – Industrial and Commercial Bank of China (ICBC), Agricultural Bank of China (ABC), China Construction Bank (CCB), and Bank of China (BOC) – which at the time together accounted for nearly 70% of the banking sector's assets and were the most important pillars of China's banking industry. A year later, the government established four specialized agencies, called asset management companies (AMCs) – Huarong, Great Wall, Cinda, and Orient Asset Management – which were modeled after the Resolution Trust Corporation set up in the United States to deal with bad loans following the U.S. Savings and Loans crisis in the 1980s.

Between 1999 and 2000, the AMCs carved out and took over a total of RMB1.3 trillion of NPLs in face value from the Big Four banks, setting in motion the process of bad loan resolution through collections, debt-equity swaps, restructuring, and asset sales. Meanwhile, China has stepped up its efforts to stop government interference, at both the national and regional levels, in bank lending decisions. The government established three new public-funded "policy banks" – China Development Bank, Agricultural Development Bank, and the China Export-Import Bank – to separate policy lending from commercial lending, and launched a radical reorganization of the nation's central bank, the People's Bank of China (PBOC), in a bid to reduce unwanted government influence over the banking sector and enhance the operational autonomy of both the central bank and commercial banks. In particular, the PBOC, as the country's primary bank regulator, has striven to improve its supervisory standards and practices.

Despite these efforts over the past five years, China's banking system remains hobbled by a high level of NPLs, low profitability, unsound lending practices, poor credit culture, and endemic governance problems, as shown by the seemingly endless revelation of bank fraud and corruption cases. China's banking system, while slowly improving, has not yet left the danger zone, and fragility of the banking sector continues to pose the single biggest threat to China's macroeconomic stability and long-term growth prospects.

Assessing the financial health of China's banks has proven to be difficult due to poor disclosure, questionable accounting standards, and inconsistent accounting practices. While the Chinese government has been rightly focused on the bank NPL problem for some time, to date no reliable NPL estimates are available to accurately capture the true scale of the problem.

Bad NPL definition is mostly to blame. For a long time, China employed an outmoded, four-category system of loan classification, consisting of performing, overdue, idle, and bad loans. The official estimate on this basis put the NPL ratio at 26% in 1998,[1] a figure widely disputed at the time by private-sector economists. Bottom-up evidence, as indicated by the overall dismal financial performance of the state-owned enterprises (SOEs) that made up almost all the borrowers of the banking sector at that time, strongly suggests the official estimate may have grossly understated the NPL problem.

Most Chinese banks have by now replaced the antiquated four-category system and migrated to a new, five-grade loan classification system that is closer to the international standard. This new system promises a more rigorous assessment of loan quality, and hence represents a big step in the right direction. According to the PBOC, currently the NPL ratio stands at 22.3%. Unfortunately, neither the PBOC nor commercial banks themselves have publicly released NPL estimates based on the old and new loan classification systems consistently for the past five years. The NPL ratio based on the new system typically ranges from 19% to 29% for the Big Four banks as at the end of 2001, but no effort has been made to use the new criterion consistently to re-grade loan books going back for several years, thus rendering it difficult to monitor changes in NPLs over time.

The PBOC has provided an updated NPL ratio for the Big Four banks of 25.4% (the old definition) as at the end of 2001. This estimate reflects the average asset quality of the Big Four banks post the NPL carve-out in 1999–2000. The carve-out, at RMB1.3 trillion, amounted to 18% of total loans outstanding at the Big Four banks at that time. Therefore, the overall NPL ratio at the end of 2001 would be 43% if we add back those bad loans already transferred to the AMCs. This implies either that the original 26% figure for 1998 (pre-NPL transfer) was a gross underestimation, or, more disturbingly, that NPLs, at least in monetary terms, have continued to increase at an alarming pace post the NPL transfer. Using the new definition, the PBOC's official NPL estimate for the Big Four banks is 29.4% as at the end of 2001. The NPL ratio under the new definition would then be around a whopping 47% if we include the bad loans that have already been carved out from the Big Four banks. The figure below gives further details

Figure 1 China NPLs: National average and at selected banks

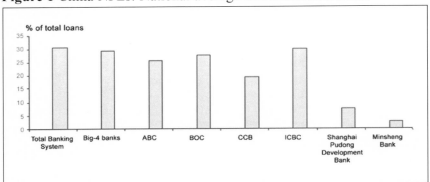

Note: *NPLs under the five-category loan classifications as at the end of 2001, except for ABC which is an estimate under the old four-category loan classifications.*
Source: *PBOC, company reports; Goldman Sachs Research estimates.*

Aside from the four publicly listed banks on the domestic stock exchange – Minsheng, Pudong Development Bank, Shenzhen Development Bank, and China Merchant Bank – most other Chinese banks – including the Big Four – produce their financial statements in-house, rather than relying on an external auditor to conduct an independent loan review and audit. Given the general lack of transparency and poor accounting and reporting standards, such in-house-produced NPL estimates by Chinese banks unfortunately inspire little public trust.

The official figures almost certainly still understate the level of NPL ratios. Independent academic and private-sector economists have put the NPL ratio at a much higher level, ranging from 30% to as high as 50%. Based on results from regional loan reviews for branch offices, such as those in Guangdong and Hainan provinces, which have been undertaken by individual banks using the more stringent new loan classification criteria, with the technical assistance of agencies such as the International Monetary Fund (IMF) as well as the bottom-up analysis of operating income for sample borrowing companies – typically SOEs – our own best NPL estimate, admittedly backed up by educated guesses and informed judgment calls, put it at 40% (excluding the 1999–2000 carve-out) for the Big Four banks.

The government has set a numerical target for the Big Four banks to reduce their respective NPL ratios by 2–3 percentage points each year, to 15% by 2005. But this target is meaningless without a consistent, reliable yardstick against which to measure NPLs and track their changes over time.

Whatever the true figures for NPLs, few would dispute the fact that China has one of the worst banking systems in Asia, or even in the world. As Figure 2 shows, only Indonesia and Thailand at the peak of the Asian crisis recorded NPLs at or above China's level. While to varying degrees the Asian "crisis" countries have so far managed to bring their NPLs down to a more sustainable level, for China the systematic effort to dispose of bad loans has just begun. Owing to the sheer scale of China's banking problems, banking reform will represent a mammoth challenge to the Chinese leadership.

Figure 2 China has one of the highest NPL ratios in Asia

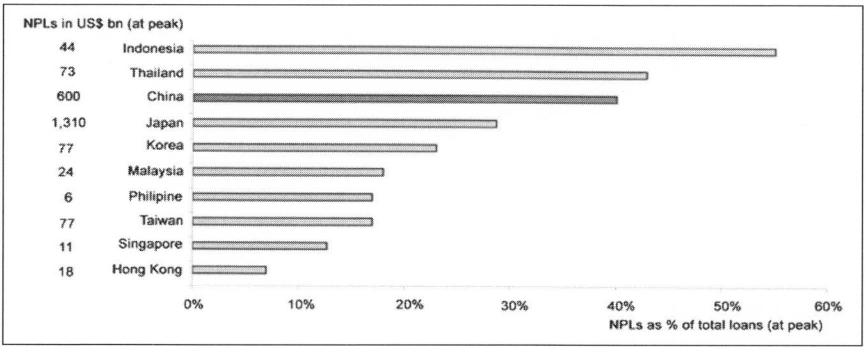

Source: Goldman Sachs Research estimates.

BABY STEPS FORWARD

The good news, though, is that China has taken some encouraging initial steps in the right direction. Instead of denial and delay, the government has embarked on a program of banking reform since 1998. Partial recapitalization, NPL carve-outs, asset sales, debt restructuring, and write-offs, combined with early efforts to strengthen credit appraisal and risk management systems, have succeeded in fending off a full-blown banking crisis and in maintaining public and investor confidence.

Following the Big Four bank recapitalization of RMB270 billion in 1998, the government has attempted to formulate a cost-effective and comprehensive bank restructuring plan. The establishment of AMCs specialized in bad loan disposal is the centerpiece of the government's NPL strategy. As mentioned above, a total of RMB1.3 trillion in bad loans has been carved out from the Big Four banks and transferred at face value to the AMCs. The Big Four banks, in return, received Ministry of Finance-backed AMC bonds. This sizable carve-out has provided an enormous, if temporary, relief to the Big Four banks and improved their balance sheets. Since their inception, the four AMCs have used debt-equity swaps, debt restructuring, and loan collection to recover bad loans. However, aside from a number of high-profile debt-equity swap deals with the large SOEs, the fledgling AMCs have not established themselves as an effective clearinghouse instead of simply as a warehouse for bad loans.

Nevertheless, since the asset auction pioneered by Huarong Asset Management Company at the end of 2001, asset sales to domestic and foreign investors have gained momentum. International institutions such as Goldman Sachs, Lone Star, and Morgan Stanley have been invited for the first time to actively participate in bidding for China's bad loans. Public auctions and structured deals with the involvement of experienced foreign investors can help jumpstart from scratch a secondary market for distressed assets in China. But the Chinese government should quickly put in place regulations and policies to facilitate foreign investors taking part in China's disposal of its NPLs.

So far, the four AMCs have achieved a respectable 30% in average loan recovery rate. However, the recovery rate is likely to decline going forward, as loans already resolved tend to be the easiest to work with – the "low-hanging fruits." Remaining NPLs are progressively harder to tackle and the final asset recovery rate will likely be much lower.

A low recovery rate in itself does not suggest the failure of China's banking reform. The AMCs' efforts in NPL resolution will likely yield a number of intangible benefits. In particular, they have a positive impact on China's credit culture. Growing pressures on debtors for loan collections should go a long way to improving the borrower payment culture, breaking a tradition fostered under decades of central planning when loans extended to SOEs by state-owned banks were typically regarded as merely a transfer of "free funds" that need not be repaid.

A leading cause of the slow progress in NPL disposal in many countries around the world has been political opposition. Government-funded agencies such as AMCs are vulnerable to the allegation of selling assets too cheaply to domestic and foreign "vulture funds." Furthermore, swift actions in loan recollection could cause a surge in bankruptcies and unemployment, contributing to wider social and political risks. The Chinese government has so far shown pragmatism in its willingness to let bad loans be disposed of at market-clearing prices.

China's under-developed legal system, ineffective bankruptcy and foreclosure procedures, and the absence of a liquid secondary market for distressed assets are all formidable obstacles to quick NPL resolution. In addition to bad loans taken over by the AMCs, substantial NPLs remain on the books of the Big Four state-owned banks, second-tier banks, and other deposit-taking institutions, including small city banks, not to mention rural credit cooperatives most of which are moribund. Cleaning up the staggering stock of US$600 billion in bad loans remains a daunting challenge for China.

To speed up the NPL resolution process, the government has changed tax rules in favor of increased loan provisioning and write-offs (see Figure 3). But the sheer size of the problem of NPLs means it would take too long for the banks to repair their balance sheets if they are solely reliant on internal operating profits for NPL workout.

Figure 3 Increasing loan provisioning at China's Big-4 Banks

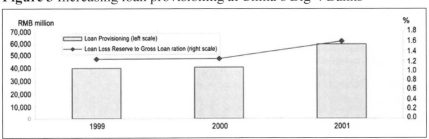

Loan provisoning includes BOC, CCB and ICBC only, ABC's loan provisioning information is not available. Loan Loss Reserve to Gross LoanRatio includes all Big-4 banks.
Source: PBOC, company report, Goldman Sachs Research estimates.

Perhaps the most encouraging development to date is that the average quality of new loans has shown some tentative signs of improvement. Reduced government interference with banks' lending decisions, growing awareness of credit risks, greater management accountability and, most importantly, tighter lending standards for SOEs and increased exposure to the private and household sector via mortgage and consumer financing, have raised hopes that the flow problem (quality of new lending) has been brought under better control despite the overhang of the massive stock of bad loans from the past era. For example, the NPL ratio for new loans reported by ICBC, China's largest bank, is well below 1%. While this ratio is likely to rise as the life span of recently extended loans increases, it seems unlikely to repeat the same degree of asset quality problems as in the past, given that (a) the composition of new credit is more tilted toward the household sector in mortgage and consumer loans as opposed to the SOE sector in commercial loans; (b) there is a whole new credit process in place with the separation of loan originalization and authorization functions and centralized loan approval procedures; and (c) a marginally better risk management system.

As a key component of China's banking reform strategy, the government has been actively pursuing privatization of its largest state-owned banks. Bank of China, the country's premier foreign exchange bank, and one of the Big Four, has successfully launched an initial public offering (IPO) of its Hong Kong-based operations, under extremely challenging global market conditions. The IPO, following a lengthy process of internal restructuring and changes in governance and management, has helped strengthen the equity capital base and laid the foundation for establishing Bank of China as a better-run, globally competitive bank. Importantly, this landmark transaction has paved the way for privatization of other large state-owned banks in China. In the coming two to five years, the Chinese government will likely accelerate privatization of its large financial institutions.

BANKING SECTOR OPENING POST-WTO ENTRY: A CURSE OR A BLESSING?

China's 15-year-long arduous negotiations on World Trade Organization (WTO) membership culminated at the WTO ministerial meeting in Doha in November 2001 in its final accession to the global trading body. China's entry into the WTO was an important milestone in the country's transition to a free-market economy. Sweeping trade liberalization and market opening measures will have a tremendous impact on China's modernization and integration with the global economy.

As part of its WTO accession commitments, China will open up the domestic banking sector to foreign competition. Foreign banks such as Citibank, Hongkong & Shanghai Banking Corporation (HSBC), and Standard Chartered can provide local-currency corporate banking services in China two years from the date of accession, and retail banking services such as deposit-taking, mortgage loans, credit cards, and consumer loans to Chinese households five years from the date of WTO entry. In other words, the Chinese banking industry is expected to be fully open by 2007.

Foreign competition unleashed by China's WTO accession will certainly impose enormous pressure on domestic banks struggling with mountainous bad loans. But gradual and orderly opening up of the banking industry, far from triggering a domestic banking crisis, could actually help strengthen China's banking sector by transferring technology, new products and services, and risk management expertise, hence raising the standards of banking service in China.

The Chinese government has been encouraging foreign strategic investment in domestic banks. HSBC has purchased 10% of ownership interest in Bank of Shanghai, and Newbridge, a U.S. investment fund, has acquired from the government a controlling stake in the A-share-listed Shenzhen Development Bank, not only becoming the largest shareholder of the bank but also obtaining rights of managerial control. Other institutions, such as Minsheng Bank, Shanghai Pudong Development Bank, and Bank of Communications, are also actively exploring opportunities to forge strategic relationships with foreign banks. The Big Four banks, on the other hand, have been focused on internal restructuring to improve their balance sheets, operations, credit appraisal, and risk management systems. These large domestic banks, though badly affected by past mistakes, stand a chance of competing with well-established foreign giants in China's growing banking market, provided they are successfully restructured within the five-year grace period provided by the WTO timetable.

Foreign entry need not be the death toll for the Big Four and other Chinese banks given the sector's enormous growth potential. International banks are set to increase their market share steadily to 10% within a decade, but domestic banks most likely will be able to maintain a dominant market share. The key thing to watch here is whether there will be fast-paced reforms. Without meaningful reform, Chinese banks will find it hard to survive, with or without foreign competition.

A Full-Blown Banking Crisis Remains a Low-Probability Risk

While China's banking system continues to face a host of fundamental challenges, the probability of a full-blown banking crisis, characterized by panic bank runs, widespread bank failures, and a severe economy-wide credit crunch, remains fairly low. National ownership of large banks, abundant liquidity, a high domestic savings rate, substantial foreign exchange reserves, and, above all, profitable new lending opportunities offered by China's fast-growing economy are all factors that could allow China to address its banking sector problems methodically, rather than in a crisis-driven panic.

Efforts undertaken by the Chinese government to date clearly have not yet succeeded in turning around the banking system, but they have helped maintain public confidence. While state ownership has been the root cause of China's banking woes, the irony is that in times of distress, such public ownership has offered a sense of safety for depositors as people believe, rightly or wrongly, that the state banks will not fail and that, with an explicit or implicit government guarantee, their savings are not in jeopardy.

Public confidence and a high savings rate have contributed to strong inflows of deposits to China's banking system. With deposit growth far outpacing loan growth, the banks are flush with liquidity, providing a strong cushion against bank runs if they were to occur (see Figure 4).

Figure 4 Abundant liquidity in Chinese banks

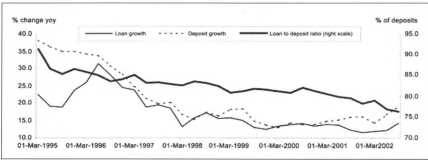

Source: CEIC

In recent years, a large number of countries, particularly in the emerging market world, have experienced the so-called twin crises, which refers to a banking crisis combined with a currency crisis. The catalysts for these twin crises are typically severe current account imbalances, an excessive build-up in external debt, particularly short-term debt, a weak banking sector that misallocated credit on a massive scale, and grossly inadequate foreign exchange reserves. In contrast to these cases, China has enjoyed an exceptionally sound external position, with persistent current account surpluses, strong foreign direct investment inflows, modest external debt, and, most notably, hefty foreign exchange reserves at US$258 billion as at the end of September 2002.

China's dynamic economy has provided a most favorable business environment for the otherwise beleaguered banks. Strong economic growth and prospects have fueled robust demand for bank loans. Credit demand from the emerging private businesses, multinational corporations operating in China, and households is especially strong, providing banks with profitable lending opportunities at potentially a much lower level of credit risk compared to past lending to state-owned banks. A particular bright spot is residential housing financing, which has boomed in the past few years as private home ownership starts to take off across urban China. ICBC, China's largest bank, has also emerged as the country's largest mortgage lender, with housing loans skyrocketing 32 times in four years, reaching 8% of its total loans outstanding.

Healthy expansion in credit to the most dynamic sector of the Chinese economy, while unlikely to allow Chinese banks to "grow" out of all the problems they have, will certainly provide a breathing space for banks to restructure and rehabilitate. This is perhaps the biggest difference between China and Japan, as both countries grapple with their troubled banking sectors. These factors – public confidence in part stemming from state ownership of banks, strong liquidity, substantial foreign exchange reserves, and significant fresh opportunities for quality loan growth – should help the Chinese banking sector escape the worst of the possible outcomes. Barring an unexpected, sharp macroeconomic downturn, China appears likely to be able to avert a full-blown banking crisis within a five-year horizon.

THE GOVERNMENT'S CENTRAL ROLE IN CHINA'S BANKING REFORM

This does not mean, however, that China can afford to relax and just shrug off its banking sector problems. Despite favorable conditions, one cannot hope that Chinese banks can just grow out of their bad loan problems. Furthermore, it is unlikely that these staggering problems can be addressed sufficiently quickly by banks on their own. The Chinese government, for its part, has been less than forthcoming in promising new fiscal injections lest further government bailouts would weaken the incentives of banks to make their own efforts to clean up NPLs, potentially causing a moral hazard problem.

However, this approach could prevent a quick resolution of China's NPLs and risk, prolonging the woes of the banking sector. While there is some legitimacy in this concern about "moral hazard," the scale of the NPL problem in China is too large and time is too pressing for the government to rely on the banks to get the job done on their own. As shown in Table 1, existing own equity and loan-loss reserves (LLRs) together cover only 40% of the bad loans for the Big Four banks. In other words, these banks are all technically insolvent. It would be unrealistic to simply count on banks themselves to write off all of their bad loans. Sooner or later the government must step in to assume the bulk, if not all, of the clean-up costs.

Table 1 Banks' own equity and loan-loss reserves inadequate to cover potential NPL losses, 2001 (RMB billion)

	Big Four banks	Total banking system
Equity	655	766
Loan-loss reserve	117	179
NPL (ex AMC)	1,931	3,679
Loans transferred to AMC	1,394	1,394
Total	3,325	5,073
LLR as % of NPL (ex AMC)	6.1%	4.9%
LLR as % of NPL (total)	3.5%	3.5%
Equity + LLR as % of NPL (ex AMC)	40.0%	25.7%
Equity + LLR as % of NPL (total)	23.2%	18.6%

Sources: PBOC; Goldman Sachs Research estimates.

Since banking sector problems tend to have a systemic impact on the broad economy, government and related regulatory authorities typically play a proactive role in driving banking reform, with taxpayers bearing a substantial part of the costs, even in market economies where banks are mostly privately-owned corporations. In the case of China, banks are mostly state-owned, and a principal cause of bad loans is policy-lending in the past when banks functioned as a quasi-fiscal instrument to fund priority public investment projects or to bail out loss-making SOEs on behalf of the government. Naturally enough, the government must play a central role in cleaning up China's banking messes which it itself helped to create.

Estimating Bank Restructuring Costs
China's banking problem, then, simply boils down to a fiscal problem, at least from a cost perspective.

The first order of business is to get a handle on the likely costs to the government budget. Because of enormous uncertainty as regards the precise amount of NPLs – both initial NPLs and peak NPLs – in China's banking system, and the prospective loan recovery rate, a sensible approach is to construct different scenarios and estimate associated costs under each of these alternative scenarios (see Tables 2 and 3).

Table 2 Estimates of bank restructuring costs — recap needs of the Big Four banks (RMB billion)

Different assumptions

Scenarios	Best	Likely	Worst
Capital/reserves to cover losses:			
Equity (as at end of 2001)	665	665	665
Loan-loss reserve	130	130	130
Total	795	795	795
Memo: Loan-loss reserve ratio	1.6%	1.6%	1.6%
Memo: Equity/total loans (%)	8.2	8.2	8.2
Total loans, gross (as at 2002Q3)	8,112	8,112	8,112
x Peak NPL ratio (%) (ex AMC)	23	40	50
= Total NPLs (ex AMC)	1,866	3,245	4,056
x Assumed NPL loss ratio (%)	50	70	90
Estimated loan-losses (ex AMC)	933	2,271	3,650
1 Capital surplus (deficit) after NPL losses	(138)	(1,477)	(2,856)
(US$bn)	(16.7)	(178.4)	(344.9)
Surplus/(deficit) as % of GDP	-1%	-14%	-28%
Amount needed to recap to minimum CAR			
Total loans, net of provisions	7,982	7,982	7,982
Required CAR (8% of loans)	639	639	639
Less: existing surplus capital	-	-	-
2 Equals: required new capital (local currency)	639	639	639
(US$bn)	77.1	77.1	77.1
3 Total bank recap cost (1 + 2) (local currency)	777	2,115	3,494
(US$bn)	93.8	255.5	422.1
As % of GDP (ex AMC)	8%	21%	34%

Scenarios	Best	Likely	Worst
Loans transferred to AMC	1,394	1,394	1,394
Assumed NPL loss ratio (%)	50	70	90
4 Estimated AMC loan losses	697	976	1,255
(US$bn)	84.2	117.9	151.6
As % of GDP (AMC)	7%	10%	12%
5 Total bank recap + AMC loan losses (3+4) (local currency)	1,474	3,091	4,749
(US$bn)	178.0	373.4	573.6
As % of GDP	14%	30%	46%

Source: Goldman Sachs Research estimates; central bank bulletins; China Economic Information Centre (CEIC)

Under the "likely scenario," we assume that the NPL ratio would peak at 40%, and the most likely NPL recovery rate at 30%. For the Big Four banks, the total bill to the government, including both offsetting loan losses and rebuilding the minimum required regulatory capital, would be US$373 billion, or 30% of 2002 GDP, after netting out existing equities and loan-loss reserves. For all deposit-taking financial institutions, the total net cost would be US$549 billion, or 44% of 2002 GDP. Undoubtedly, these numbers are mind-boggling.

Since the official NPL estimate has been generally considered to underestimate China's NPL problems by a wide margin, we take it as the lower-bound estimate for the NPL ratio. The PBOC's NPL estimate for the Big Four banks is 23% as at the end of September 2002. This lower-bound NPL ratio, together with an optimistic assumption of 50% as the loan recovery rate, make up our "best scenario." For the Big Four banks, the total net cost would be US$178 billion, or 14% of 2002 GDP. For all deposit-taking financial institutions, the total net cost would be US$263 billion, or 21% of 2002 GDP. The simulation results even under the "best scenario" are quite sobering.

Under the "worst scenario" – the peak NPL ratio at 50%, and the expected NPL recovery rate at 10% – the net cost to the government for the Big Four banks would amount to US$574 billion, or 46% of 2002 GDP, and for all deposit-taking financial institutions, the total net cost would be US$842 billion, or 68% of 2002 GDP. In this scenario, the numbers are simply eye-popping.

These simulation results under various plausible scenarios all point to the massive costs associated with cleaning up and recapitalizing the Chinese banking system. So, the next big question is …

Table 3 Estimates of bank restructuring costs — recap needs of total banking system (RMB bn)

Different assumptions

Scenarios	Best	Likely	Worst
Capital/reserves to cover losses:			
Equity (as at end of 2001)	766	766	766
Loan-loss reserve	202	202	202
Total	968	968	968
Memo: Loan loss reserve ratio	1.6%	1.6%	1.6%
Memo: Equity/total loans (%)	6.1	6.1	6.1
Total loans, gross (as of 2002Q3)	12,640	12,640	12,640
x Peak NPL ratio (%) (ex AMC)	23	40	50
= Total NPLs (ex AMC)	2,907	5,056	6,320
x Assumed NPL loss ratio (%)	50	70	90
Estimated loan-losses (ex AMC)	1,454	3,539	5,688
1 Capital surplus (deficit) after NPL losses	(485)	(2,571)	(4,720)
(US$bn)	(58.6)	(310.6)	(570.1)
Surplus/(deficit) as % of GDP	_5%	_25%	_46%
Amount needed to recap to minimum CAR			
Total loans, net of provisions	12,438	12,438	12,438
Required CAR (8% of loans)	995	995	995
Less: existing surplus capital	-	-	-
2 Equals: required new capital (local currency)	995	995	995
(US$bn)	120.2	120.2	120.2
3 Total bank recap cost (1 + 2) (local currency)	1,480	3,566	5,715
(US$bn)	178.8	430.8	690.3
As % of GDP (ex AMC)	14%	35%	56%
Loans transferred to AMC	1,394	1,394	1,394
Assumed NPL loss ratio (%)	50	70	90
4 Estimated AMC loan losses	697	976	1,255
(US$bn)	84.2	117.9	151.6
As % of GDP (AMC)	7%	10%	12%
5 Total bank recap + AMC loan losses (3+4) (local currency)	2,177	4,542	6,969
(US$bn)	263.0	548.6	841.9
As % of GDP	21%	44%	68%

Sources: Goldman Sachs Research estimates; central bank bulletins;CEIC.

Can the Government Afford it?

Since it is inevitable that the bulk of bank restructuring costs in China must be absorbed by the government, many investors and economists, both within and outside China, have been concerned about the medium- and long-term fiscal implications of a bank bailout on a scale as massive as China's.

Efforts to assess medium- to long-term fiscal sustainability are hampered by the uncertainty surrounding China's interest-rate outlook and GDP growth prospects. These variables may be endogenously affected by the health of the banking sector. Bank fragility may lead to excessive tightening of credit conditions, deflation, and higher real interest rates, thereby likely bringing down the rate of growth in real GDP to below the underlying potential growth rate. Clearly, banking restructuring will be more expensive, and the corresponding fiscal burden heavier, in an economy with sluggish growth than in a fast-growing economy.

To simplify our simulation analysis, we match the "likely scenario" with trend GDP growth and gradually falling real interest rates, the "best scenario" with an above-trend GDP growth rate and rapidly falling real interest rates, and the "worst scenario" with a below-trend GDP growth rate and gradually rising real interest rates. We also assume that the primary deficit as a percent of GDP in the first five years of banking reform will be the average of the past five years – that is, we rule out any significant fiscal adjustment measures such as spending cuts or tax hikes until after 2007. The poor profitability of the SOE sector and remaining obstacles to collecting taxes from the fast-growing private-sector businesses suggest that China would encounter difficulties in relying on tax revenue to finance the bank restructuring program, at least in the short to medium term. Therefore, we assume that the government will principally use debt financing to fund the bank bailout.

Tables 4 and 5 show the assumptions of the simulation exercise and the resulting public debt profile. Table 4 shows the debt profile if the costs of bank restructuring are met in one year – 2003. Table 5 assumes the costs are uniformly distributed over 2003–07 – that is, an equal amount of public resources, raised by long-term government bonds, are spent on bad loan write-offs and follow-on recap every year over a five-year period between 2003 and 2007. The results in Figures 5 and 6 indicate that China's fiscal position will deteriorate sharply as a result of government-supported bank restructuring, but that the banking woes may not necessarily translate into a severe fiscal crisis ahead.

Table 4 Bank restructuring and public debt dynamics in China
(assuming the costs occur within one year in 2003)

		2002	2003	2004	2005	2006	2007	2008	2009	2010	2011	2012
1. Likely scenario												
Bank restructuring cost	RMB bn		4542									
Total debt/ GDP	% of GDP	30.3	72.4	71.5	70.6	69.8	69.0	66.4	63.9	61.5	59.2	57.0
Assumption												
Real interest rate	%	4.0	3.5	3.0	3.0	3.0	3.0	3.0	3.0	3.0	3.0	3.0
Real GDP growth	%	8.0	7.2	7.0	7.0	7.0	7.0	7.0	7.0	7.0	7.0	7.0
2. Best scenario												
Bank restructuring cost	RMB bn		2177									
Total debt/ GDP	% of GDP	30.3	50.7	50.4	49.7	48.5	47.4	44.5	41.9	39.4	37.0	34.8
Assumption												
Real interest rate	%	4.0	3.0	3.0	2.5	2.0	2.0	2.0	2.0	2.0	2.0	2.0
Real GDP growth	%	8.0	7.2	7.5	8.0	8.5	8.5	8.5	8.5	8.5	8.5	8.5
3. Worst scenario												
Bank restructuring cost	RMB bn		6969									
Total debt/ GDP	% of GDP	30.3	94.6	94.6	95.5	97.3	99.1	99.1	99.1	99.1	99.1	99.1
Assumption												
Real interest rate	%	4.0	4.0	4.5	4.5	5.0	5.0	5.0	5.0	5.0	5.0	5.0
Real GDP growth	%	8.0	7.2	6.5	5.5	5.0	5.0	5.0	5.0	5.0	5.0	5.0
Memo												
Primary fiscal deficit		2.5	1.8	1.8	1.8	1.8	1.8	0.0	0.0	0.0	0.0	0.0

Note: *Assume zero inflation in the banking reform period.*

Table 5 Bank restructuring and public debt dynamics in China
(assuming the costs are uniformly distributed over 2003–07)

		2002	2003	2004	2005	2006	2007	2008	2009	2010	2011	2012
1. Likely scenario												
Bank restructuring cost	RMB bn		908	908	908	908	908					
Total debt/ GDP	% of GDP	30.3	39.4	47.4	54.6	61.1	67.0	64.5	62.0	59.7	57.5	55.3
Assumption												
Real interest rate	%	4.0	3.5	3.0	3.0	3.0	3.0	3.0	3.0	3.0	3.0	3.0
Real GDP growth	%	8.0	7.2	7.0	7.0	7.0	7.0	7.0	7.0	7.0	7.0	7.0
2. Best scenario												
Bank restructuring cost	RMB bn		435	435	435	435	435					
Total debt/ GDP	% of GDP	30.3	34.9	38.9	42.2	44.6	46.6	43.8	41.2	38.7	36.4	34.2
Assumption												
Real interest rate	%	4.0	3.0	3.0	2.5	2.0	2.0	2.0	2.0	2.0	2.0	2.0
Real GDP growth	%	8.0	7.2	7.5	8.0	8.5	8.5	8.5	8.5	8.5	8.5	8.5
3. Worst scenario												
Bank restructuring cost	RMB bn		1394	1394	1394	1394	1394					
Total debt/ GDP	% of GDP	30.3	43.9	56.8	69.3	81.9	93.9	93.9	93.9	93.9	93.9	93.9
Assumption												
Real interest rate	%	4.0	4.0	4.5	4.5	5.0	5.0	5.0	5.0	5.0	5.0	5.0
Real GDP growth	%	8.0	7.2	6.5	5.5	5.0	5.0	5.0	5.0	5.0	5.0	5.0
Memo												
Primary fiscal deficit		2.5	1.8	1.8	1.8	1.8	1.8	0.0	0.0	0.0	0.0	0.0

Note: *Assume zero inflation in the banking reform period*
Source: Goldman Sachs Research estimates.

Figure 5 Likely scenario: Public debt dynamics (costs occur within one
year in 2003)

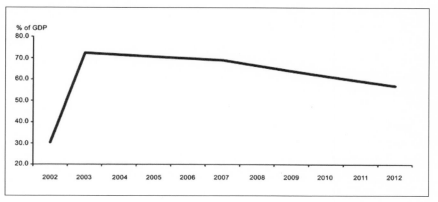

Figure 6 Likely scenario: Public debt dynamics (costs uniformly distributed
over 2003–07)

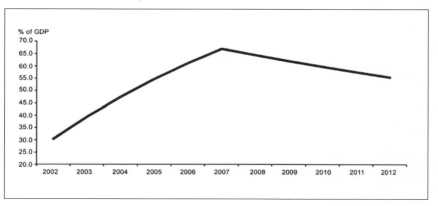

Source: Goldman Sachs Research estimates

Under the likely scenario in Figure 6, the public debt to GDP ratio will
more than double to 67% of GDP by 2007, from the 30% of GDP at the end
of 2002. After peaking in 2007, however, the debt to GDP ratio starts to
decline, implying a sustainable path for public debt. These results support a
central role for the government in China's bank restructuring and allay concerns
that the resulting fiscal burden may be too onerous to bear, triggering a fiscal
crisis akin to those in Argentina and Brazil.

We have so far excluded the implicit public pension liability in our discussion. Government pension debt estimate is highly sensitive to assumptions about demographics, target income replacement rate, and the modalities of ongoing pension reform. Estimated pension debt by the World Bank and other organizations ranges from 30% of GDP to as high as 80% of GDP for China. Our own best estimate puts the unfunded pension liability for the state sector at 65% of GDP. If this number is added to the peak debt/GDP ratio shown in Exhibit 5.6, the consolidated public debt will be 132% of GDP.

This is clearly a high ratio, but it is by no means unusual by international standards. As one can see in Figure 7, many OECD countries, including Japan, have implicit public debt well in excess of GDP if unfunded pension liability is included. The combined fiscal challenge to China is not substantially greater than that to many other countries around the world. In fact, the challenge may be somewhat easier to meet in the case of China, given the size of the state-owned assets, potential privatization proceeds, and, importantly, the favorable GDP growth outlook.

Figure 7 Implicit public debt in selected countries (2001)

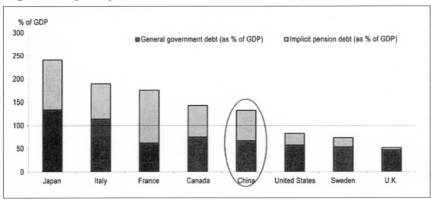

Sources: *OECD; IMF; Goldman Sachs Research estimates.*

In conclusion, the fiscal costs of China's bank clean-up, while massive, are likely to be manageable, and China's medium-term fiscal outlook is not as grim as is widely claimed.

THE ROAD MAP

The Chinese leadership has clearly recognized the challenge and has embarked on a reform program since 1998. Yet, performance to date has been rather mixed. China's greatest achievement so far has been containing its banking problem and preventing it from becoming much worse, thereby successfully maintaining public confidence. By gaining temporary financial stability, China has bought itself precious extra time in which to undertake reforms.

But the clock is ticking. China's WTO market-opening schedule provides a grace period of five years for the domestic banking industry before the onslaught of full foreign competition. China must aggressively tackle the mounting NPLs, repair its banks' balance sheets, and put the banks on a stronger financial footing before the closure of the five-year window of opportunity.

Speedy resolution of the NPLs and recapitalization will require a massive injection of fresh public funds and inevitably generate pressure on China's fiscal position. But China has the capacity to mobilize the resources needed to meet the fiscal challenge posed by banking reform. A healthy and well-functioning banking sector also requires drastic changes in ownership, management, transparency, credit culture, and corporate governance. Privatization of state-owned banks will be a key part of the reform program.

To forestall future banking crises, China must also strengthen its supervisory standards and practices, including a thorough and comprehensive loan review based on a more stringent loan classification system. To allow for efficient pricing of credit risks, China should also speed up interest-rate liberalization.

Banking reform in China is a race against time. While China's commitment to banking reform is beyond doubt, its current plan is inadequate to fix its banking woes in a sufficiently compressed time frame. The real danger for China is not necessarily succumbing to a full-blown banking collapse, as seen in some neighboring economies during the Asian crisis, but going down the same path Japan has taken, with missed opportunities and, ultimately, far greater collateral damage to the economy.

China should avoid muddling through its banking reform. It is time for a Big Bang – substituting the piecemeal measures taken so far with a more aggressive, more comprehensive, and accelerated reform strategy. Accelerated banking reform is critical to sustaining China's economic success.

REFERENCES

Dai, Xianglong, "China's Banking Sector Outlook Post WTO," Speech at the Hong Kong General Chamber of Commerce, Hong Kong, 2002.

Hu, Fred, "Probing Weaknesses in China's Banking System," *Asian Wall Street Journal*, February 1999.

——, "China's Banking Reform: A Long March," Global Economics Paper No. 28, Goldman Sachs, London, September 1999.

——, "China's Banking Reform: Pitfalls Ahead," *Asian Wall Street Journal*, November 24, 1999.

——, "China's Banking Reform – a Race Against Time," *Asian Wall Street Journal*, February 11–13, 2002.

Lardy, Nicholas R., *China's Unfinished Economic Revolution* (Washington, D.C.: Brookings Institution, 1998).

Lindgren, Carl-Johan, Gillian Garcia, and Matthew I. Saal, *Bank Soundness and Macroeconomic Policy* (Washington, D.C.: International Monetary Fund, 1996).

People's Bank of China, *China Financial Statistics Quarterly Bulletin Q1–Q3 2002*, Beijing.

Zhou Xiaochuan, "Non-performing loans in China's Banking System," *Capital Markets Journal*, Beijing, 1998.

Zhu Rongji's
"Managed Marketization" of the Chinese Economy

Laurence J. Brahm[*]

 From the moment he assumed the role of Vice Premier in 1992, through his term as State Council Premier (1992–98), Zhu Rongji managed China's transformation into a market economy over the critical decade of the 1990s. Unabashedly combining the tools of command and market economics, Zhu has brought inflation down from 21.7% in 1994 to 1% at the time of writing in mid-2002, while maintaining an average 8% growth rate over this same period. He has streamlined and rationalized China's banking and financial systems, taking on and closing down the investment and trust companies, old bastions of an unregulated system in the early stages of transition. He steered China through the Asian financial crisis without devaluing the Renminbi, strengthening the currency in the process. The reforms Zhu has overseen as Premier have involved reengineering the state-owned enterprises, cutting government bureaucracy by half, and replacing the "iron rice-bowl" system with the framework of a modern social-security and insurance-based healthcare and pension system. Such reforms have involved more than structural changes and institutional capacity building. They have required the reengineering of Chinese society as a whole.

The execution of any International Monetary Fund (IMF) or World Bank reform measures in Russia, Eastern Europe, Central Asia, Mongolia, Indonesia, South Korea, or any other transitional economy has received praise from Washington, D.C. and the predominantly pro-Western international media. However, one must ask honestly: how many of these reforms have been successful in carrying out economic structural capacity-building, raising lifestyles, invigorating these economies, and establishing social and political stability in these countries?

[*] Laurence J. Brahm, CEO of Naga Group, is a political economist and lawyer by profession.

China has crossed the same period, as Deng Xiaoping put it, like crossing a river one step at a time, on the rocks. None of the fancy voodoo economic formulas rattled off by academic gurus from think tanks in Boston or Washington, D.C. were applied. China's economy nevertheless grew at an average of 8% per annum during the 1990s, and, with the exception of a single critical period in 1993–94, witnessed low, and often negative, inflation. The old "iron rice-bowl" system was melted and replaced with insurance, pension funds, and commercialized education and housing. The banking system, cluttered with woes, was overhauled – an ongoing process still unfinished – to meet the new demands of commercial life in a market economy. Private business has flourished in the shadow of the restructuring and downsizing of state enterprises. Lifestyles have generally improved across the board for most people, although, undeniably, there are some who have fallen between the cracks of such dramatic change.

It is hard to imagine the leader of any other country daring to take the political risks inherent in tackling economic and financial challenges on such a scale as China's. Yet, Zhu has done so and, arguably, succeeded. In doing so, he has ignored the formulas and sacrosanct IMF prescription for developing countries. Many of those who accepted the economic panacea proffered by Western academics have lived to regret it. Zhu, however, developed his own practical model suited to Chinese realities, his own theory for the "managed marketization" of China's economy. And China's economy is all the stronger for it today.

OPPORTUNITY IN CRISIS

During the Asian financial crisis, China did not follow the IMF's prescription. Premier Zhu Rongji refused to devalue the Renminbi. Those nations that did follow the IMF's prescription witnessed, first, economic and then political meltdown. Meanwhile, China's foreign exchange reserves soared, reaching US$230 billion at the time of writing, the second-largest in the world. Following its own course, China emerged from the crisis stronger than ever. China's new export economy is booming, drawing manufacturers from the West and from throughout Asia to relocate production in China. Meanwhile, a brisk new pattern of domestic consumption has arisen, tilting the economy away from an overreliance on exports, which proved to be the Achilles heal of the other Asian tiger economies. The Chinese have a saying: *shuiluo shichu* – "When the tide goes out, you can see the rocks."

The Asian financial crisis was a real crisis for China. In charting his own course to cope with the crisis, Zhu was in fact breaking new ground.

Many government economists were less sure and wondered whether China would survive the crisis. Wang Shuilin, one of the leading economists of the State Council Economic Systems Reform Office and now serving as a senior economist to the World Bank, has perhaps summarized the situation best: "It was as Deng Xiaoping described our early reforms, 'cross the river by feeling the stones'; we were not sure whether we would survive or not." Wang has noted, "[Twenty] years of reform and open economic policy created resilience and the ability to absorb negative economic impact."

The Asian financial crisis brought into focus the question of what kind of economic model China should adopt. Before the crisis, China was seeking to develop a Japanese-style market economy based on the success of Japan and South Korea during the 1980s. But this view was dropped after the meltdown of these models in 1997. Zhu Rongji's view was that the market should play the major role, with corporate governance under law taking a stronger, firmer position. China's state-owned enterprises could hardly be protected forever. Enterprise group mergers completed through administrative means could only be pursued so far. The lessons learned from the Asian financial crisis would become the inspiration for Zhu to push against domestic political opposition protecting certain industrial sectors in aggressively seeking entry to the World Trade Organization for China.

At the back of Zhu's mind were memories of the hardships of the 1950s and 1960s. But China had managed to pull through those times. Belt-tightening could work. It would be better to look inward than to become an IMF colony and have to pay back Western debts forever. Although the decision not to devalue the currency was basically Zhu's, it received the repeated public backing of Jiang Zemin and the Politburo. Not to devalue the Renminbi was a move calculated to maintain 8% growth targets, to show capacity to support Hong Kong, to provide the psychological effect of financial stability, and to demonstrate the government's willingness to enforce its decision to maintain stability and serve in its own capacity as a rudder and model to the rest of Asia. This last factor most likely irritated the IMF and the so-called Washington Consensus the most.

In fact, China's successful handling of the crisis directly challenged the vision of the Washington Consensus. What would have been the cost of addressing the crisis if China had had a so-called American-style democracy like Taiwan or Japan can only be imagined. Because the government was being run like a tightly held family business, Zhu was able to make decisions quickly, react appropriately, and mobilize all resources toward one target. If a government is weak and cannot reach consensus, it cannot enforce policy. The unity within the Chinese Communist Party and the ability to mobilize unified action at all levels of the system enabled the leadership to implement its decisions and keep China on course.

On March 15, 1999, at the close of the second year of the five-year term of the Ninth National People's Congress, Premier Zhu Rongji received questions from the foreign and domestic media. Journalists queried his view of, and response to, the Asian financial crisis. Zhu's response in a way summarized both the linkages between his various policy measures at critical financial crisis points during his years at the helm, and his own view of where the IMF's models stood against his own macro-control model.

> In 1993 China adopted the system of "macro-controls"... to hit real estate and other factors using inflation to reach 21.7% in 1994 ... Within two years China solved the problem of economic overheating, Zhu explained. "The fact that China last year was able to go through the Asian financial crisis ... was due to the experiences of 1993. American funds overflowed into Asia ... followed by the monetary policies of certain institutions ... economic development and financial opening must have macro-controls which are according to each country's specific situation, and extreme demands to rapidly open capital markets can easily destroy a nation's economy."[1]

Economic Crossover

By summer 2000, China had clearly emerged unscathed from the Asian financial crisis and, in some ways, with a stronger, more solid economy than before. The shattered economies of Thailand, Indonesia, South Korea, and Russia stood as stark monuments to the failure of IMF policies. That China had been able to ride out the financial storm was, in large part, due to Zhu's own macro-control policies and his refusal to take advice from the IMF. Zhu was prepared to make this point to the European Union leaders. It certainly wasn't what the Washington Consensus wanted to hear.

Zhu, whose own background was rooted in state planning, was simultaneously applying the tools of traditional socialist state intervention alongside those of classic fiscal and monetary policy of a market economy. With no qualms over theoretical conflicts, he managed these apparently opposite mechanisms of economic leverage to guide and, at times, force China's transitional economy on to the market path. The end result was more than hybrid economics. A fresh strategic model of macro-control (*hongguan tiaokong*) market management evolved from Zhu's practical application of all measures at his disposal to manage the emergence of the world's fastest-growing developing mega-market. It was Zhu's intention to allow the market, which by that stage already offset the prices for over 92% of all consumer commodities and 80% of all industrial production, to grow yet further, albeit within the framework of macro-controls.

In guiding China through the economic storm that had hit Asia in 1997, Zhu Rongji was playing economic crossover, creating his own brand of fusion economics. While the theorists in Boston and Washington, D.C. were busy arguing over rules of how emerging economies should develop, Zhu was making the rules for running the largest developing economy in the world, and making it the world's fastest-growing economy at that. By background an electrical engineer and not an economist, Zhu was making China's economic machine work, while others were theorizing as to how it should work. Fundamental to his success was a deep understanding of China's industrial–social conditions and the psychology of its people.

Understanding the reality of this situation is critical to an understanding of the foundations of Zhu Rongji's macro-control policy. Western academics and think tanks have called repeatedly for China to adopt market mechanisms in line with the standards proselytized by the Washington Consensus. In fact, the nature of China's economy – indeed, the nature of China's society and the psychology of the Chinese masses – are factors which may often impede successful application of those monetary intervention tools recommended by Western economists, academics, the IMF, and the World Bank. The reason for this is simple: the often complex conditions that exist in China are outside the collective experience of Western institutions. Their models fail to consider the everyday realities of life in China.

Zhu's managed execution of his program of reforms was influenced by his grasp of both successful and failed measures adopted by China in handling economic and financial predicaments during the 1980s, and by his understanding of the reactive psychology of China's overall population. Moreover, Zhu understood at a remarkably deep level how this psychology was evolving and changing over this period. In turn, his policies were adapted to the reactions of such psychology. In short, he understood the resistance points of popular sentiment; how far reforms could be pushed without sparking unnecessary social reactions which might otherwise put these very reforms off course.

"One Guarantee"

Underlying the aim to sustain 8% growth in 1998 was a policy to keep the retail price index below 3% and the consumer index below 5%. This objective would come to be known as part of Zhu Rongji's "one guarantee," expressed at his inaugural press conference on assuming the position of Premier in March

1998. Zhu boldly promised to maintain 8% GDP growth while restraining inflation within 3% for 1998. Many questioned whether this could be achieved. Zhu's optimism was predicated in part on his ability to use both administrative planning and market intervention tools in tandem.

China adopted a framework of moderately tight fiscal and monetary policies, inflation controls, and measures designed to "prevent financial risks." While growth had fallen somewhat short of expectations, it remained high and inflation low, presenting a healthy economic picture for the year, despite the financial carnage already affecting the rest of Asia. Zhu continued to enforce price-control mechanisms while an oversupply of products eased the chronic supply shortages of the past. The result was not only an easing of inflationary pressure for 1998; it also led to negative inflation – while growth for that year fell short of the anticipated 8%, coming in at 7.8%, inflation was –3.6%. This had never been achieved before in any transitional, developing, or developed country in the world.

One critical factor underlying Zhu's success was a crystal-clear understanding that food was the first necessity of the majority of China's population. He was determined to maintain sufficient staples to sustain anticipated demand at low prices – a policy that was to become a pillar of his reform program. Three consecutive years of bumper grain harvests before 1998 provided the basis for a steady supply of surplus foods. This, in fact, gave him the leeway he needed to push forward structural reforms of China's state-owned enterprises and social-welfare system without fear of a backlash.

The impending massive lay-off of workers required by Zhu's reforms carried the threat of social instability. However, for most of the population, food was the bottom line. Three years of grain surplus was to prove a critical factor for ensuring macroeconomic stability. By 1998, more that 13 million workers had been laid off. But Zhu had taken to heart Mao Zedong's key adage: "Grain is the most important link." Like Mao, Zhu was born in rural Hunan and understood where China's "masses" would draw the line.

To counter the slowdown, Zhu shifted toward what some observers characterized as a Keynesian approach. At the beginning of 1998, the central committee determined to increase investment in domestic fixed assets by 17% over the preceding year, with the intention of building growth to a level above the 1997 figures. With a glut of surplus goods perpetuating a buyer's market, however, analysts expected consumption to drop well below the 1997 level. Interest-rate cuts had failed to turn up China's growth engine.

There appeared to be two key reasons for the slowdown. The first was a drop in the added value of agriculture due to readjustments in the maize acreage and drought in northern China. The second reason was excessive over-production of redundant products, mostly by collectively owned industries, including the much talked-about "township enterprises." This had forced many to stockpile goods, rolling back production and slowing growth.

The recommendation of these economists was that China would have to beef-up investments in fixed assets in order to sustain a relatively high rate of growth. In Zhu's analysis of the situation, China needed to readjust its existing industrial structure to optimize capital layout and usage. The problems of slack consumption and slow enterprise growth were linked, in large part, to over-production of shoddy, repetitive goods and poor quality control, without regard to what the market actually required.

The inability of enterprises to sell their goods was, in turn, linked back to complications in collecting receivables and paying back loans. To turn this situation around would effectively require an entirely new injection of capital. In short, it was easier to start building anew than to tinker with an antiquated machine. Huge capital outlays would be required for the task, calling for fresh injections of new start-up funds as investments in fixed assets.

So, while Zhu attempted to adopt classic Western monetary and fiscal tools, the nature of China's economy during this stage of transition also required the simultaneous use of administrative intervention – effectively, the tools of planned economics – to coordinate the disparate and uncoordinated aspects of China's economy. The incredible irony of Zhu's crafted macro-control model was that tools of command economics were being used to build a market economy.

MANAGING A MEGA-MARKET

By 1999, the Asian financial crisis had magnified difficulties. So did growing unemployment at home, which further cramped consumer spending, especially in the cities. Premier Zhu Rongji faced the dilemma of how to stimulate China's domestic market. In the countryside, those with electricity had all the consumer goods they needed. However, many areas lacked electricity supplies altogether and did not constitute a market. Parallel falls in investment and consumption pointed toward a general downward slide in the economy. A number of critics blamed the downslide on the diverse policy objectives of Zhu's administration, arguing that the effect of such widespread simultaneous reforms had, in fact, been to undercut their own predicted effects.

The multiple objectives of Zhu's monetary policy were also viewed by some as self-neutralizing. Zhu's mopping up of the investment and trust sector, the standardization of the inter-bank lending market, the guided merger of city cooperative banks, and the centralization of loan-approval authority all had the effect of tightening up credit sources badly needed by the non-state sector for business expansion. Zhu's countervailing logic was that the negative impact of short-term contraction of credit to the non-state sector would be offset by the long-term healthy development of the financial sector.

So, Zhu and his economic strategists were confronted with the challenge of stimulating demand amid economic contraction and rising social uncertainty. The Premier's reforms were breaking the iron rice-bowl, taking away long-guaranteed amenities such as housing, education, medical care, and retirement benefits. This, in turn, shattered all the social assumptions underpinning the remarkable economic transformation of China in the 1980s and the record growth of the 1990s. The problem was coming full circle. In the end, it would be up to the State to spend the funds needed to create the social conditions to realize consumer demand.

Zhu adopted a series of financial, monetary, and price policies aimed at fueling investment and consumption demand. When the Western-style interest-rate cuts failed to take effect, Zhu resorted to aspects of the old state-planned system, making massive state-designated investments in infrastructure. The later measures had some effect in lifting real-estate investments, with property prices picking up by 2.1% in the second quarter of 1998. Most significant in this regard was the lift given to key building materials. At the same time, in line with Zhu's grain circulation reforms, the State purchased back large amounts of grain from farmers, lifting farm commodity prices. Simultaneously, Zhu launched a massive crackdown on smuggling, which had the effect of cutting some product redundancy out of the markets, albeit mostly at the high end. However, the measure that proved most effective was government spending on public utilities and urban infrastructure.

The government invested heavily in infrastructure. Some RMB260 billion was earmarked for roads to open up backwater provinces; RMB270 billion was set aside to modernize the national railroad system; RMB130 billion was invested in agricultural irrigation projects; with a further RMB100 for public utilities (such as theaters, cultural centers, and hospitals). By 1999, it looked like the 1930s' New Deal of U.S. President Franklin D. Roosevelt had come to China. The objective was to create jobs to absorb the growing numbers of laid-off workers. The logic was straightforward: if roads and railways were built, cement and steel would be required, reviving those industries. Jobs would be created, and savings would grow again, stimulating renewed consumer spending.

These infrastructure developments were to be financed by government bond issues. The government's expansionary fiscal policy kicked off with a RMB100 billion Treasury bond issue in 1998, which it managed to offset to a great extent through a tough tax-collection drive. Zhu's objective was to increase the proportion of fiscal receipts to 20% of GDP for the coming three to five years. In 1999, an additional RMB370 billion-worth of Treasury bonds were issued. Zhu's strategy was to invest in basic infrastructure throughout the underdeveloped central and western provinces, making them attractive to investment from enterprises in the wealthy coastal regions. State investments into these regions would lock in itinerant labor and boost savings, turning the vast rural hinterland into a future marketplace for the developed industrial coast. This would alleviate the country's overall reliance on exports for growth. China had the potential to become a self-sustaining market, an economic universe unto itself. That, at least, was Zhu's vision.

In 1997, the Fifteenth National Congress of the CCP had identified a need to develop the country's small cities as a keystone to opening up the interior. Zhu pushed this agenda. By 1999, China had 2,600 counties, each consisting of between 10 and 20 townships. That meant anywhere from 30,000 to 50,000 townships nationwide. The plan was to develop them through infrastructure investments by the central government, matched by financing at the local level. The construction of modern towns would mean job opportunities for rural labor. The aim was to raise the quality of living for China's farmers. If rural families could move into modern areas with water and electricity, their lifestyle would change and consumer demand would rise, stimulating production in China's vast consumer-goods industrial sector. Authorities estimated that anywhere from 10 to 20 years would be necessary to build all the townships required to become the backbone of China's next growth wave.

Initially, the government would pick up the tab, spending on infrastructure over a two- to three-year period to provide the critical basis upon which commercial investments could be made in the interior. In the mid-term, coastal enterprises would be expected to invest in the interior, taking advantage of both the government-financed infrastructure and the newly created conditions for stimulating consumption there. The corresponding overhaul of the financial sector would enable commercial banks to provide the necessary financing to support commercial investments being made in the hinterland.

Managed Marketization

Where shock-therapy advocates and the Washington Consensus had called for all transitional economies to follow a model of immediate privatization, Zhu's model called for nurturing the private sector alongside the state sector, not a wholesale dismantling of one in favor of the other. Countries such as Russia and Mongolia had suffered from the shock-therapy system, leaving a vacuum between one system and another. Unlike the shock-therapy advocates, Zhu was not talking Cambridge chalkboard economics. He was managing a country of 1.3 billion people. The question of economic transition could not be simplified down to doctoral thesis formulas to please prattling scholars in academic institutions. Zhu had to deal pragmatically with the demands of building an efficient economy for the world's most populous country with the tools and systems on hand.

"Deepening of state-owned enterprise reform will involve insisting on the basic economic system in which public ownership and mixed ownership will develop together," Zhu once explained in calling for coexistence between the state-owned and private-sector industries. He called for "further opening of the market and [a] relaxation of prices [that] will break up the departmental and professional monopolies and regional protectionism [and] establish a fair, unified and regulated market system as soon as possible." In doing so, Zhu insisted on the application of his own macro-control formula to dismantle state monopolies and encourage private enterprises to create a level playing field.

Zhu described his objectives: "People's livelihood based on basic comfort must progress to *gengjia fuyu* [affluence]. The major change is to expand employment and increase income, to continuously increase the people's livelihood and increase the urban and township income, especially for those on a low income. The responsibility for social protections must be passed on to society as a whole." Zhu's model of economic reform has involved "managing" an economy rather than free-floating it; adopting a series of often unrelated tools of economic intervention and guidance; leading a closed market in the direction of an open market; evolving, not dismantling, institutions; and allowing private enterprise to grow alongside state-owned enterprise, not replacing one with the other. Like so many things Chinese, Zhu's model sought a middle road. It was neither capitalist nor socialist; in fact, in its application, such ideological terms became irrelevant. Zhu's model was practical, applied to each situation, but with vision to keep a certain momentum, always moving the economy closer toward a market-based system, without worrying about the theoretical baggage. At times, this meant commanding the economy to move toward a market-based system, giving rise to Zhu's own economic model of managed marketization.

All of this, of course, flies in the face of the mainstream economic formulas taught at universities in Boston and adhered to like a religion by the Washington Consensus. We have seen the results of "shock therapy" and the "IMF's prescription." We have also seen the results of Zhu Rongji's macro-control policies. In putting these policies into the context of a new framework of economic-development theory, they could best be explained and understood as a model of managed marketization.

From his position as Vice Premier and then Premier of the State Council, Zhu Rongji oversaw the formulation and implementation of policies which converted China from what was still a command economy in the early 1990s to a largely market economy by the close of the century. Zhu had systematically tackled economic crises – from the triangle debts of 1992 to the super-inflation of 1994 to the Asian financial crisis. Where necessary along the way, he had adopted the heavy hand of old-style state intervention to keep China on the path to a market economy.

During this period, China's economy had taken a sharp upward turn led largely through a program of state spending on infrastructure projects. Zhu's policies – which he often described as a macro-control system – had worked. This system can be best understood as a model of managed marketization. That is, "Boss Zhu," as he is known in government circles, literally "managed" the emergence of China's market economy like a tough corporate boss, orchestrating, at times intervening, and even interfering at a macro level to steer the market in the direction perceived necessary for the long-term interests of the economy. Zhu's style involved literally "managing" China's economy, bringing it out from the framework of planning into the operations of a market system. China's transformation throughout the 1990s is testimony to the successful application of Zhu's formula of economic fusion. Maybe it is about time that Zhu Rongji's reforms are recognized in their own right, in the context of contributing to economic-development theory a new and fresh model for developing and transitional economies.

The tools of the market are essential to open up the arteries of free-flowing capital, prices, goods, and the financing required to make an economy grow. But the hand of the central government and, with it, the old tools of planning or command economics have been required to make capital and goods flow. Zhu's macro-control model of managed marketization of China's economy has involved:

- introducing the tools of monetary and fiscal intervention accepted and applied in developed-market economies, while at the same time using the old command tools of planning to make the new tools work;

- anticipating "mass-movement economics" – the patterns of enlarged social reaction to opportunities that characterized China's political mass movements of a previous era – and applying "signal economics" at the critical time to send the hard messages required to make the masses shift direction;

- setting often overly ambitious objectives, knowing that while standards cannot be met, this is necessary to motivate people to achieve the results desired; and

- maintaining a vision, observing changes in the situation carefully, moving consistently toward critical objectives, and having change as a constant, though not disruptive, force in the system.

Controlling inflation, rationalizing the banking and financial sectors, steering China through the Asian financial crisis, shifting the export-based economy toward a growth model that will rely also on domestic consumption – these are all clear achievements of Zhu Rongi. However, there are critics who say that his reforms in restructuring state-owned enterprises, in debt-conversion clearance, in grain circulation, in social-welfare services, and in capital raising have not been completely carried through. Some have said that social and political factors have impeded the completion of these reforms, rendering them incomplete or only partially successful. While perhaps merely serving to underline the restrictions imposed on the visionary by existing social and bureaucratic systems, such criticisms may have some substance. However, the fact that Zhu has changed the overall direction of the Chinese economic system – and, with it, the social structure as well – is an achievement in itself. Zhu has set China on a new course. By pushing for China's entry into the WTO, he has given momentum to a new and irreversible reality for China's future.

Zhu's contribution has been in seeking a middle road for economic reform to achieve marketization of the world's fastest-growing mega-economy, and doing so while maintaining political cohesiveness and broad-based social stability. His model of managed marketization is one that can be adopted and reapplied to other developing or transitional economies. It provides a practically proven alternative to the holy writ and shock-therapy theories coming out of U.S. universities and Washington think tanks. For China, Zhu Rongji's legacy has been the transformation of this nation's economy from a planned to a market system while maintaining high growth and broad-based political and social stability. The world should give due recognition to Zhu Rongji for the successful application of a new economic-development model of managed marketization. His name should be remembered alongside that of Keynes.

Zhu has provided a practical demonstration of how fusion, crossover economics can prove to be a viable option, and has brought economic theory into a new epoch. As Deng Xiaoping once said to Zhu in Shanghai, "Planning and market are both tools to accompany the use of resources, but are not in themselves standards of socialism or capitalism." The world community of economists should finally give credit where it is due.

Financial Sector Reform:
Competition Must Drive Capital Allocation

*Andy Xie**

 China no longer limits competition in the goods market. The service sector is also becoming more competitive, with barriers to entry breaking down in most industries. However, the financial sector remains largely under government control. Introducing market forces into capital allocation remains the last hurdle in China's transition toward a full-fledged market economy.

CAPITAL COMPETITION IS AT THE HEART OF CORPORATE GOVERNANCE

Corporate governance has become a major concern for economic development in China. The emphasis in solving this problem has been on strengthening administrative supervision of both listed and unlisted companies by government agencies. I believe that the main focus should be on enhancing competition for capital. Regulations and administrations can only complement, but not substitute for, the role of market competition in fostering good corporate governance. More than anything else, what is missing in China is genuine competition for capital.

Corporate governance has become a global issue. The Asian financial crisis exposed the dearth of good corporate governance in East Asia during the boom years. Global attention is now focused on the United States, due to the corporate scandals of Enron, WorldCom, Tyco, and so on. Bad corporate governance can take two forms: (1) corporate management continues to run a company despite poor performance; and (2) management hides poor performance through manipulation. The first type may be caused by a dysfunctional market. For example, family-controlled companies often can

* Andy Xie is Managing Director and Chief Economist for Asia-Pacific, Morgan Stanley.

totally disregard corporate governance because they, as insiders, control the company.

China has been comparing its problems in corporate governance with those in other countries, but I believe that this is not addressing the main issue. In established market economies, problems in corporate governance often derive from management tactics that circumvent market forces. Family control, for example, is used to keep away the force of the capital market discipline. Accounting manipulation is intended to fool the market into rewarding an under-performing company.

There is no genuine competition for capital in China, and thus it is difficult to attribute China's problems with its corporate sector to corporate governance issues per se. Government banks control most of the capital in China, and institutional constraints and government decisions heavily influence their lending decisions. Often, they lend on need or directive, rather than on the basis of performance. Despite the recent reforms, this tendency has not fundamentally changed.

The stock market is large in terms of market capitalization but is actually quite small in terms of mobilizing capital. In 2002 it raised a mere 1% of GDP in funds for companies, compared to around 5% in countries with mature capital markets. The main story in the stock market is really about wealth redistribution: through manipulation, insiders can fool generally small retail investors into buying worthless stocks. Hence, the stock market is really a social justice issue, rather than a corporate development issue. It does not play a significant role in promoting corporate development.

Hence, it is not appropriate to compare China's problems with those in other countries. The foundation for a genuine capital market is far from complete. China's challenges are much more fundamental and primitive than what mature economies are facing.

THE DUAL TRACK SYSTEM

China has adopted a dual track system in its gradualist approach in both the real and financial economy – that is, the state-owned track exists along with a foreign or private one. In the case of capital formation, the government has been aggressively promoting foreign direct investment. Rules and regulations are often modified to satisfy the needs and requirements of foreign investors. Joining the World Trade Organization is the ultimate step in attracting foreign investment, by promising to turn China into a market economy based on international norms.

The other track takes place through state-owned banks that control most of the domestic savings. They guide capital to the state-sector entities or government-sponsored projects. Three-quarters, or more, of the credit in China goes to the state sector. Many companies that are considered to be non-state-owned are controlled by local governments and state-owned enterprises. Foreign-invested enterprises have been receiving working capital loans from the banks and, in a few cases, even term loans for investment. Nevertheless, a negligible portion of the credit in China is in the genuine private sector. The dual system has created a two-tiered capital structure. The state sector is highly capital-intensive but has low returns. The non-state sector is much more profitable. The institutional barrier keeps capital from flowing between the two, unless illegal incentives are introduced. The performance gap between the state and non-state sectors has been widening as a result.

The capital returns on foreign investment appear to be robust and improving. One good indicator is the ratio of net factor income outflow relative to net foreign direct investment. In the 1990s, this rose from zero to over 50%. In other words, for every dollar of foreign investment inflow, half a dollar is taken out as profit. Factor income outflow reached US$29 billion in 2001, compared to the foreign capital stock of about US$400 billion. A rough estimate puts returns on foreign capital at above 10% and improving. Although the private sector is small and data are scarce on capital returns in this sector, it is quite rare to find an entrepreneur willing to put capita into a project without an expected return of 25% per annum or higher.

The state sector, on the other hand, has been experiencing low and declining returns. The listed state-owned companies in the Hong Kong market have been experiencing 3–5% returns on capital, even though they are among the better companies in the sector. The state-owned companies in the domestic market have been reporting about 5% returns on capital, although the numbers are not reliable. Three percent is likely to be the average return on capital in the state sector.

LACK OF MEANINGFUL CREDIT INTERMEDIATION

Institutional and policy biases have turned domestic savings into capital accumulation in the state sector. China's financial institutions do not have incentives to take risks outside of the state sector because, under the current structure, if a loan to a state-owned enterprise turns sour, the loan officer bears no responsibility. Usually, some government official has left some evidence of promoting the loan. On the other hand, if a loan to a private company turns sour, the loan officer may be severely punished, while if the loan is profitable, the loan officer is unlikely to get a bonus or promotion. The risk and reward ratio is totally skewered against taking initiative by lending to parties outside of the state sector. The anecdotal evidence from private entrepreneurs, who count "access to capital" as among their largest problems, bears this out. Indeed, the strongest incentive for lending to a private company is the kickback for the loan officer. It makes one automatically suspicious if a loan officer makes a loan to a private company. Such a vicious circle has made the banking system not quite relevant to the non-state sector.

Further, not long ago, the state banks were really government agencies and did not go through massive personnel changes in order to adapt to a market economy. The ranking system for personnel power carries great weight in the banking system. A local government holds sway over the branch of a state bank in a county, since its officials tend to have a higher rank than the officers at the bank branch. Such personal dynamics have made bank loans in most poor countries quasi-fiscal debt. By law, only the central government can borrow money. In reality, local governments have been financing their expenditure through loans to enterprises under their control. A substantial chunk of the non-performing loans is of such a type.

To rein in bad credit, the state banks have been lending to the central government directly or to projects that are sponsored either by the central or provincial governments. As a result, exposure to the government has risen to 9.1% of their total credit in 2002, from 1.3% in 1993. While it is difficult to assess how much quasi-government lending has increased, it is quite possible that most of their bank loan increase has been of such a nature since 1997.

One significant improvement is in the creation of the mortgage market for the banking sector. The extremely low interest rate and rapid income growth have triggered a boom in the demand for property. The rapid increase in mortgage demand has created an opportunity for the banking system to improve its asset quality. Even though mortgages as assets still account for less than 10% of the total, they offer a source of income independent of the state for banks.

A STIR-FRY STOCK MARKET

The stock market could have made a change to this system of biased lending. Reforming the state banks is difficult and slow everywhere, and examples are rare of rapid transformation of state banks into competitive commercial entities. The stock market is an intermediary used to match investors with companies directly. If harnessed properly, it could dramatically improve the efficiency of capital allocation.

Instead, the stock market became a source of funds for companies that have good connections but have difficulty in obtaining bank loans. Preferential access to the stock market was given to companies in financial difficulty, and the program of selling shares of state-owned enterprises on the stock markets, though now stalled, did not help this. It is not surprising that the average quality of companies listed in the market is quite low and that the fundamental demand for stocks issued by these poorly performing companies is also low.

This is why China's stock market tends to swing wildly. Investors have a very short horizon, as most stocks are not worth holding for the long term. Only the expectation of quick gains attracts investors and, as such, the stock markets become vulnerable to speculation. Organized rackets have manipulated the market in order to attract and sucker in retail investors. However, retail investors' enthusiasm eventually wanes after losing again and again. With improving market supervision and regulation, manipulators now have more chance of being caught. One way or another, the funds for market speculation tend to come from banks. The exposure of the banking system to non-monetary financial institutions has risen above 11% of total credit, from 3.7% in 1997. A considerable portion of this exposure probably ended up in the stock market. Also, state-owned enterprises lent and invested in the stock market a considerable amount of funds that they borrowed from the banks.

The total market capitalization of the stocks in the domestic A-share market is about US$500 billion, of which about one-third is free float. It is virtually impossible to estimate how much of the free float is really held by retail investors with their own money. I suspect that most of the funds in the market are not from Chinese households.

CONSEQUENCES OF CAPITAL MISALLOCATION

Why should China worry about its financial efficiency? Even with all the problems described above, the country has achieved robust growth. There are three reasons why China should not let the problem simmer.

First, China could have done much better. The country has a massive army of surplus labor. It has allowed some companies to mistreat workers, which is a serious threat to social stability. If China could grow by one or two percentage points more, this problem could be much reduced. Each additional percentage point of economic growth could create two million additional jobs. This would make a massive difference to the labor market over one decade. At 7–8%, China's growth rate is below its potential, as its labor productivity achieved this level of growth over the past 20 years. Without some reduction in labor productivity, China could not sustain this rate of job creation. Its potential growth rate could be easily at 10%. If China can fix its financial sector and use its capital more efficiently, it may indeed reclaim a 10% growth rate.

Second, China is giving away the opportunity for competitive domestic firms to emerge in the global market. Despite two decades of rapid growth, China has not created meaningful global companies. This is very much a result of the inefficient financial sector. China's capital does not flow from bad to good companies, but instead gets locked up in bad companies. To prevent their bankruptcies, the State funnels more capital into such bad companies. The capital allocation process in China is not a process of searching for good companies that can use capital more efficiently. This is one reason why no genuine global companies have emerged out of China in the past two decades.

At the same time, China's weakness has created an opportunity for foreign capital. Multinational and overseas Chinese companies have taken advantage of China's inefficiency and have established strong positions in both its domestic economy as well as the export sector. In many consumer sectors, multinational companies are competing against each other, and home-grown Chinese companies are relatively absent. Foreign ownership is not necessarily bad; in fact, it is a constructive force in the global economy. China has benefited tremendously from foreign technology through foreign investment in the past two decades. However, the country's financial-sector problem has unnecessarily hampered the potential of Chinese companies. The large outflow of income in China's balance of payment is one cost.

Third, a bad financial system increases the risk of a major crisis. When growth is down, the problems in the financial sector may erupt. We saw such incidents during the Asian financial crisis. China has continued to grow through the ups and downs of the global economy. Low wages and high savings have made this possible. However, one could never guarantee that China's growth will never be disrupted.

The U.S. economy is probably entering a decade of slow growth and this, combined with increased geopolitical instability, has made the global economy more fragile as a result. China's growth is still very dependent on gains in export market shares, rather than on an expanding domestic market. The tension in the global economy is bound to rise as a result. Geopolitical forces could disrupt China's growth process at some point. Fixing the financial system would make China much more resilient and able to cope with a potential economic downturn.

THE CASE FOR A FINANCIAL BIG BANG

There are three schools of thought on how China's financial sector may and should evolve. First, China could grow out of its problem. The economy could double in 10 years, making the problem half as big in relative terms. Second, a crisis may be inevitable, and China will fix its problem only after a major crisis has erupted. The third option is for China to fix its financial system with a big-bang approach.

The first school of thought is quite popular among a large number of influential people in China. It may indeed succeed. Small regional and local banks could grow big. They may become efficient institutions and, hence, increase the overall efficiency of capital allocation over time. The state sector is shrinking under the reforms mandated from joining the WTO. Hence, the proportion of the economy that may waste capital is declining. The surplus funds in the banking system could be diverted to the low-risk mortgage market. Foreign and private investment can keep up the capital formation in the productive sector to sustain economic growth.

A good example is Taiwan. Even with a bad financial system, it has continued to grow for decades and has yet to experience a major crisis. Meanwhile, its current per capita income is US$12,000. It may take two decades for China to reach the same level of per capital income. Why cannot China keep growing for another two decades in the same manner?

There are two conditions for this approach to work, in my view. First, growth cannot be seriously disrupted. If it is temporarily disrupted, the currency must adjust quickly to absorb the blow. A bad banking system does not present an immediate threat as long as liquidity is plentiful. For export economies like China's, good liquidity can only be sustained by continuing export growth. It can be cushioned by currency adjustment during a temporary downturn, but a protracted downturn would have dramatic consequences. Second, the system must keep the amount of bad financial assets from growing faster than the economy. This was not the case for a number of East Asian economies, and what resulted was the Asian financial crisis. China has to undertake significant institutional changes to ensure that the financial sector would not deteriorate during economic growth. The most important step is to put risk management at the core of the banking system. This may conflict with the existing system, which places political loyalty at the core of the management system.

The second school of thought is popular among foreign observers. It presumes that the power of inertia overwhelms all other forces in the system. Hence, a systematic change, which is what China needs, will not happen without a major crisis. This has indeed been the case for all other transition economies in Eastern Europe. Japan is a counter example, in the sense that it has not pursued painful financial reforms for 12 years. This is so because Japan has skillfully avoided a major crisis, many would argue. Korea, on the other hand, pursued much more dramatic restructuring after a major crisis.

Should China be different? One could have made the same argument two decades ago. Two strengths have allowed China to avoid a major economic or financial crisis. First, the concentration of political power has allowed China to make difficult decisions just in time to avoid a crisis. It has happened and may happen again. This emergency brake is absent in all economies that have experienced a crisis in the last two decades.

Second, Chinese people accept low wages. China's competitiveness in trade largely derives from this fact. After two decades of rapid growth, the average urban wage remains at US$100 per month, while the quality of labor has improved dramatically. This has allowed China to cut export prices continuously in order to gain market share. This super-competitiveness makes China's exports especially resilient. Hence, the Chinese economy can weather global cycles much better than many other countries. However, past success hardly provides a guarantee for the future. Circumstances may change. China's systemic capacity for avoiding economic or financial crisis is particularly impressive and it is quite probable that it may continue to be so in the future. A more likely scenario is a period of low growth, if the global economy does not perform for an extended period of time. China's financial inefficiency constrains it from generating smooth growth of domestic demand.

The big-bang scenario presumes forward-looking leadership that is both powerful enough and willing to remove the risk of a future crisis, enhance the growth potential to solve unemployment problem, and mobilize the state resources to underwrite the restructuring cost associated with joining the WTO.

China must address the financial sector, and its consequences in the real sector, at the same time. Otherwise, there would be too much resistance. There are two issues in the real sector. The workers who lose jobs must be taken care of. Equally important, the vested interest groups need to walk away better off. The government has the ammunition to engineer such a transformation. Public assets are worth over 100% of GDP, probably more than the government's contingency liabilities that include the losses associated with the non-performing loans in the banking system, unfunded pension liability and payments to the laid-off state-sector workers.

Move from an Approval to a Registration System for the Stock Market

The government could swap its assets for household savings to solve the stock problem in the financial sector. The more important task is to make institutional changes that will prevent the accumulation of bad financial assets in the future and ensure that capital goes to efficient companies.

The first and foremost task is to remove the government as the final arbiter in capital allocation. Instead, the government should focus on establishing sound rules for the process and focus on enforcement. In the case of the stock market, for example, the government should move from an approval system to a registration system for initial public offerings or follow-on issuance. As long as a firm sends in the registration forms and claims its fulfillment of all the state requirements, it should be allowed to proceed with fundraising without ever walking into the regulator's office or waiting for "approval" from the regulator. Of course, the firm will assume legal responsibilities if its claims later turn out to be false.

This change would do more for China's capital market development than anything else. It puts investors on notice that there are no restrictions to supply. If speculators want to stir-fry the market to create momentum, they must risk being swamped by new issues, as companies take advantage of high valuations. This forces investors to look at fundamentals more carefully when making an investment decision.

The soundness of a stock market ultimately rests with market forces. If the government tries to protect investors or companies with a complicated system, it is bound to achieve the opposite effect. Government rules and regulations must complement, but absolutely not replace, market forces. Timely and accurate information disclosure, for example, enhances market efficiency. The government should institute and enforce rules to achieve this. However, it would be totally wrong for the government to go a step further and attempt to control the quality of the listed companies.

A competitive stock market would probably make the biggest difference to China's corporate development. If China wants to see its domestic companies succeed in the global marketplace, it must ensure that a competitive process governs the capital allocation process in the stock market. If the government continues to influence who gets money in the market, China may not see globally successful companies for another 20 years. That will be a terrible waste for the country.

Decentralize the Banking System

China's four state banks take in three-quarters of the country's deposits. China is a continental-sized economy and cannot afford to have such a concentrated banking structure. There is no evidence to suggest that the economies of scale for the banking business are so high. An optimal structure may well involve 20–30 large banks and 100 or more local retail banks in China.

The transition toward the optimal structure must be based on market competition. Otherwise, it could lead to another wave of non-performing assets forming in the system. One approach is to split the four state banks into eight or more banks. While their separation may be based on geographical or business lines, they must be allowed to compete against each other in all areas. Strategic investments by global banks could be introduced to inject modern technologies and risk management skills into these entities. Regional and local banks could be allowed to expand into more provinces, or even nationally. These banks have small balance sheets and are more adaptable. They could focus on consumer finance and mortgage-business lines that are simple and carry a low risk. They could replay what has happened in the real sector. If the state banks fail to change dramatically, these banks could replace the state banks as the pillar for China's banking system in a decade or so.

Non-bank financial institutions should be allowed to compete against banks in more businesses. For example, there is too little competition in the mortgage business. The margins on mortgages are much wider than in other markets, while the services are not first class and the range of products is narrow. This is largely due to the deposit concentration in the state banks. Insurance companies should be allowed to participate in the business first. They have long-term funds and are better positioned than banks to provide fixed-rate mortgages. This one change would dramatically enhance the efficiency of China's financial sector.

Specialized financial entities should increasingly be encouraged for consumer and corporate services. Credit card companies, for example, should be encouraged to compete against banks in the card issuing business. Auto financing is another business that finance companies can participate in efficiently. With so much concentration, decentralization could significantly improve China's financial sector.

Establish an Efficient Bond Market

China's bond market is underdeveloped. While the market for government bonds is sizable and liquid, the market for non-sovereign bonds is virtually non-existent. This is understandable in light of the inefficiency in enforcing property rights. Hence, other bonds (for example, bonds issued by banks, large state-owned enterprises, or infrastructure bonds) are priced off their support by the sovereign. The market guesses how likely it is that the sovereign will come to the rescue of an issuer, if it faces the risk of bankruptcy. The state development banks, for example, face the lowest spread between their bond yield and treasury bonds of similar maturity. State banks are next lowest. Other large state entities follow.

A genuine credit market has yet to emerge in China. The court system and reliability of financial data are the two main reasons. Recent cases of enforcing creditors' rights have not turned out well. The pace and transparency of the process cast serious doubts on a viable credit market. Further corporate financial data are not reliable, to begin with. The market is simply too inefficient to be viable. A genuine credit market carrying the existing problems would make the capital too expensive for good companies. The basic conditions for a viable credit market for the corporate sector are quite stringent. It will likely take a long time before the reforms are advanced sufficiently for a genuine bond market to emerge. However, a bond market could be established for the consumer sector first.

Securitization is an efficient instrument for reducing the cost of capital for the household sector, especially for mortgages. It can provide long-term fixed rate mortgages that banks couldn't provide by themselves, as their funds are relatively short-term in nature. Low-cost and fixed rate mortgages will dramatically enhance the efficiency of financing for the household sector.

A bond market for securitization of household debt is far less dependent on the legal reforms that are critical to a corporate bond market. The household demand for credit will rise if the financing cost comes down and the terms become more attractive. It will improve significantly the overall efficiency of capital allocation. The banks also can reduce the need for capital in expanding their businesses. Recapitalization of the banks is widely considered a heavy burden for the government.

A mature securitization market for household debt can lay the foundation of a corporate bond market. For example, securitization of corporate physical assets could follow the mortgage securitization. As the rest of the system becomes more in tune with the bond market, a full-fledged bond market could be established in this decade.

GOOD TIMING FOR A BIG BANG

The net foreign assets in China's banking system (including foreign exchange reserves) have risen by US$4.5 billion per month in the past year (2002). In addition, foreign currency deposits are also rising substantially. Both of these suggest that China is experiencing high demand for its assets and, indeed, joining the WTO has made it more attractive. As China follows through with reforms that come with joining the WTO, the funds inflow is likely to rise rather than decline.

The liquidity condition in China could remain quite robust. Indeed, it is possible that it may experience some sort of asset bubble under the combination of a currency peg and strong capital inflow. Hence, a big-bang approach to China's financial reforms would have far less consequence for economic growth than might otherwise be the case. Indeed, it may just be in time to prevent an asset bubble. Hence, this approach may well be in China's best interest, no matter from which angle one may judge its effectiveness.

A big-bang approach may involve monetizing US$50 billion of state assets in either the stock market or through direct sales. Chinese households have increased their savings to levels approaching US$200 billion in 2002; at current rate of growth rates, this figure could exceed US$300 billion within the next five years. Foreign direct investment has passed US$50 billion in 2002 and could reach US$100 billion within five years. Liquidity appears not to be a problem at all enabling the government to monetize its assets. Whether this approach succeeds or not will depend on what the government sells and at what price. The quality of the companies in the market today is not high, and household demand for their stocks is quite low. This is why the market falls whenever the government mentions selling down its holdings in the listed companies.

If the government sells high-quality assets, the demand is likely to be high. For example, the dual listing of SinoPec in the domestic market attracted massive demand and was priced at a much higher valuation than it received in the Hong Kong market. Several other Hong Kong-listed companies have successfully listed their stocks in the domestic market at a higher valuation than in Hong Kong. One of the most valuable assets is what the government holds in foreign joint ventures. Multinational companies dominate China's consumer market. These franchises are highly valuable. Local governments or state-owned enterprises own a big chunk of these franchises. Sometimes, these franchises have different partners in different provinces. The government could realize a huge amount of funds if its holdings through various entities were consolidated and sold to Chinese households in the stock market. The demand for such stocks would be extremely high, in my view.

Local and regional banks are other valuable assets. Even though these banks may not be very profitable, investors would pay a high price for them if they were restructured properly to capitalize on the ongoing consumer finance boom. If foreign strategic investors are introduced into these banks, they could be sold at two to three times their book value. The government could realize a massive windfall to pay off its debts.

At the heart of the issue is whether the government is willing to risk its current portfolio in order to undertake the multiple transformations required to erect a sustainable and efficient capital allocation framework. It is as large a task as any it has had to approach until now, including entry to the WTO. With China now on center stage and undergoing a deep globalization process that is changing both its own manufacturing makeup and impacting global production chains, the final task is to develop the service sector and enable the growth of world-class indigenous enterprises. Financial system reform is the basis for both of these.

Administrative Monopoly, Corruption, and China's Economic Transformation

Hu Angang and Guo Yong[*]

INTRODUCTION

Corruption is a manifestation of the failure of institutions. In the course of economic transition, as old institutions are undergoing transformation, new mechanisms have not yet taken shape. In this gap, many opportunities and temptations may arise, leading to corruption. Corruption not only absorbs huge economic resources, but it also results in serious societal pollution and may cause the legitimacy of the governing regime to be questioned. Logically, and also examining primary evidence, it is not difficult to understand why corruption in transition economies has been called a serious concern by governments and experts all over the world. In addition, many have suggested that corruption in transition economies is more rampant and endemic than in developed market economies.

The purpose of this chapter is to address a new category of corruption in transition economies, which has not been fully elaborated by many of the current corruption studies. In the context of rent-seeking theory, we examine a unique phenomenon of corruption in China – the administrative monopoly (AM) – and try to outline its causes, forms, and features, the scale of the rent it has created, and how the rent has been dissipated. We then project a vision for future reforms. We find that AM is one of the most endemic types of

[*]Hu Angang is a professor in the School of Public Policy and Management (SPPM) and Director of the Center for China Study (CCS) at Tsinghua University, Beijing, China. Yong Guo is a Ph.D candidate in the SPPM and CCS at Tsinghua University, as well as in the Chinese Academy of Sciences. The authors wish to thank Ran Liao from Transparency International (Berlin), Minxin Pei from the Carnegie Endowment for International Peace, Daniel Kaufmann and Joel S. Hellman from the World Bank Institute, and Ping Liu from Tsinghua University.

corruption in China in that it has brought about huge economic loss to the state, as well as arousing extensive public resentment. This must be changed if the government is really serious about fighting corruption. The most important aspect for achieving this would be reorientating the roles played by the government in the economy and regulating the domestic market in accordance with the norms and rules of the World Trade Organization (WTO). China must scrap the current doctrine of an omnipotent government and make a paradigm shift to good governance characterized by openness, transparency, efficiency, and integrity.

This chapter first discusses administrative monopoly as a unique phenomenon pertaining to China's gradual economic transition, looking at the mechanisms, causes, performances, and features of AM in the present stage. Then we estimate the economic losses caused by AM and how these losses were dissipated. We then summarize the progress of reform in curbing AM, and project a vision for future reform.

ADMINISTRATIVE MONOPOLY

In the context of rent-seeking theory, corruption is regarded as rent-seeking in kind.[1] As defined by Gordon Tullock, rent-seeking is the expenditure of scarce resources to capture an artificially created transfer from the political process, which is higher than that which a competitive marketplace would allow, but less than the damage that it brings to the others.[2] What is most important to bear in mind in this case is that the government is not only an object for "being captured" during the course of rent-seeking; it is also a subject, which has strong incentives to create rent.

According to Wei He's analyses, rent-creating behaviors can be divided into three types according to the role played by government: the government's unintentional rent creation, the government's passive rent creation, and the government's active rent creation.[3]

Unintentional rent creation is mainly an outcome of the government's interference in and regulation of the economy. An example of this may be found in the early stages of economic reforms in China, with the government's decisions to relax the control of commodity prices and to adopt a "dual-track" interest rate and exchange rate. With the development of a market economy

---

[1] Not all rent-seeking activities are illegal. However, rent-seekers do often indulge in illegal activities, such as bribery, smuggling, or black-market operations.
[2] See Gordon Tullock, *Rent Seeking* (Chengdu: Xinan Finance and Economics Press, 1999), p. 27.
[3] See Wei He, pp. 206–38.

and reduction of the government's direct control, this type of rent creation has been decreasing.

Passive rent creation refers to a situation in which the government, under the influence of interest groups, uses its power to provide a comparative advantage to a particular sector. Rent-seeking occurs, in part, because interests groups receive concentrated benefits through government actions. The interest groups would seek regulatory policies that will carve out niche markets or obstruct competition by offering illegal payments or exerting influence to induce or compel government to promulgate more biased or favorable regulatory standards. It is in such a process that a rent is created and which is commonly referred to as corruption.

Active rent creation involves different departments of government that will try their best to design regulations aimed at creating rents, to increase the benefit accrued by their own industrial sectors or local enterprises affiliated with them. In return, the latter must provide them with profit, which is in fact a portion of the rent created for them by the government officials.

Research by Joel Hellman and Daniel Kaufmann and others has shown that in Eastern Europe and the former Soviet Union, the government's passive rent creation behaviors, such as state capture and influence, are prevalent. These states' pace of transition – essentially, "shock treatment" – is in sharp contrast to China, which has chosen a gradual path. This difference has impacted the types of corruption that have arisen. In the former Soviet Union and Eastern European transition economies, the shock treatment has broken the pre-existing links between the government and enterprises overnight, greatly curtailing the government's ability to regulate the economy. This situation has also given interest groups less room in which to maneuver. Research has shown that only large-scale enterprises that have maintained close relationships with the bureaucracy and which have more resources at their disposal can exert a strong influence in the process of public policymaking. Meanwhile, new and emerging entrepreneurs can only use buying-off to seek regulatory policies. This is referred to as state capture.

In countries such as China, where a gradual transition has been adopted, active rent-seeking by the government is common because of the mixed functions of the government in terms of regulation and enterprise management. Before the central government became more streamlined in 1998, there was much interference by ministries and commissions in the economy, especially by those that were responsible for supervising one or more industries. Since the "umbilical cord" between some government departments and their affiliated enterprises has not been cut, the former often seek to ensure treatment that favors their own interests or those of their affiliated enterprises by resorting to regulatory policies such as restricting entry to competitors, imposing tariffs, establishing various licensing procedures, and so forth.

In China, the close links between the State and the state-owned enterprises (SOEs) have been relaxed gradually. In many sectors, the interests of state monopolies are well taken care of. China's protection of those SOEs and monopolistic enterprises, which we refer to as AM, is distinguished by the fact that the initiative is taken by the government – that is, it is active rent creation by the government to protect the interests of those SOEs. We can thus suggest a re-division of the types of corruption in transition economies based on the following criteria: whether an illegal payment or interest is offered; and whether influence is exerted on the process of policy/regulation formulation or implementation (see Table 1).

Table 1 Types of corruption in transition economies

Types of corruption	Offering direct and illegal payment	Not necessarily offering direct and illegal payment
Exerting influence on the process of regulatory policy formulation	State capture Administrative monopoly	Influence
Exerting influence on the process of regulatory policy implementation	Administrative corruption	Connection[4]

---

[4] We regard "connection" as an important form of corruption in transition economies, in that it is a common practice in China. Connection means that people try to influence the implementation of policies without offering a direct and illegal payment. How well a connection can work also has a lot to do with social customs. One of the most commonly seen practices of connection is when public officials abuse their entrusted power for the personal gain of their family members or friends. We need to bear in mind that there are few relationship that do not involve an exchange of interests. Therefore, we have treated connection or relationship as one type of corruption, or at least as potential corruption. According to C. Simon Fan and Herschel I. Grossman ("Incentives and corruption in Chinese Economic Reform, Brown University Department of Economics Working Papers 98-8, available online at http://ideas.repec.org/s/bro/econwp.html "connection" was a key factor in China's central and planned economy, and continues to play an important role in the dual-track economy. It is "personal connection" between government officers

Our re-division of corruption in transition economies challenges the long and widely accepted definition of corruption as "a public official abusing public power for private gains." Our study shows that the subjects of corruption, whether occurring in a situation of state capture, administrative monopoly, or influence, are all collective- and enterprise-based. Furthermore, we find that the economic loss created by corruption mainly takes place in those areas where group corruption and sector corruption are the most common manifestations. This is a typical example of systematic corruption. Clearly, one of the important manifestations of grand corruption in China today is administrative monopoly, which emerges from the active rent-creating practices of the government.

THE CAUSES, FORMS AND FEATURES OF ADMINISTRATIVE MONOPOLY

In our study, we would like to define AM as an outcome of the government's regulatory policies by which various government departments try to ensure a monopolistic status for a particular sector or enterprise or group affiliated with them, in order to secure their own interests. An AM could also be called a statutory monopoly, since its manifestation is commonly in the imposition of regulatory barriers to competition or for rent-seeking.

Differences Between AM and Other Types of Monopoly

We should first distinguish AM from other types of monopoly. According to N. Gregory Mankiw, monopoly can be classified into three categories: market monopoly, natural monopoly, and administrative monopoly.[5]

Market monopoly accompanies market competition, when a few enterprises establish their monopoly status by means of their superiority in capital, technology, or advanced management. Market monopoly is a kind of "structural monopoly" – that is, market shares are established via fair competition. Such a market monopoly can play an active role in promoting the efficient allocation of resources.[6] It is only when those who have dominated

---

have to maintain very good connection with the relevant government officers and managers of other enterprises, in order to obtain the necessary resources of production (such as electric and water) and to duly deliver materials and semi-finished products as needed. This indicates that "connection" plays an active role when the system is not flexible.

[5] See N. Gregory Mankiw, *Principles of Economics* (Beijing: Peking University Press, 1999), pp. 314–43.

[6] Therefore, sometimes it is even welcomed by consumers. But the market dominants cannot afford to push the monopolistic profit up too high, for fear of encouraging their

the market try to restrict market competition by illegal means such as price-fixing, supply manipulation and discrimination, market carving-out, conspired blockage, illegal mergers, and so on, that consumers' interests are violated.

Natural monopoly occurs because the total cost for one individual enterprise to produce many different products is less than the total cost for many different enterprises to produce those same products independently. Natural monopoly usually occurs in the provision of public goods and services, such as water, power, transport, heating supply, and so on.[7]

Administrative monopoly is distinct from both market and natural monopolies in that it is established by the government through regulation and policy. Its purpose is to ensure the interests of the government and its locally affiliated enterprises, a phenomenon that is common in China during its gradual reform process.

By definition, corruption means that public officials abuse their entrusted power for private gains. We would like to emphasize that the "private" here cannot be understood narrowly to mean only public officials and their families. Rather, we must also take into account the interest groups that they are acting for or to which they belong. In a gradual transition economy such as China, some government departments try to block market competition via AM in order to protect their own interests or those of their locally affiliated enterprises. This is also a typical instance of corruption.

Causes of Administrative Monopoly

AM has occurred during China's transformation from a planned centralized economy to a market economy. Essentially, though, it is a problem created by the old system, in that it was a central characteristic of the centralized planned economy system because government's controls penetrated virtually all sectors at all stages of operation, from market entry to supply of raw materials, from price-setting to production output. Since 1979, when China began its reform and opening-up policy, the government has reduced and relaxed its control in many sectors, allowed competition, and thus enabled the gradual development of a market economy. However, in some sectors, such as those characterized by networks, the government's monopoly is still in place and often engages in anti-competitive activities through regulatory policies and administrative means, under the guise of sector management and maintaining market order. In this

---

[7] Natural monopoly can also provide a lot of opportunities for corruption – for example, people might offer bribes in exchange for a licence or a contract – but most such conduct pertains to administrative corruption.

game, the government is both the rule-maker, referee, and sportsman.[8] It thus becomes impossible to launch any meaningful campaign against monopoly that may result in "government failure."

One of the most difficult issues in China's economic reform is the "separation of the administration from the enterprise," under which government pulls back from all those areas in which a market-based system is more effective. In such a design, the government focuses on providing public goods and services. Certainly, it should be noted that after 20 years of reform, much progress has been made in this regard, with the government relinquishing direct interference in many sectors, and downscaling through institutional reform many administrative institutions that controlled those sectors. At the same time, it has transferred a lot of its power of coordination to those macro-management departments of the State. The SOEs have been gradually separated from the administration, and have become fully independent bodies competing in the market.

However, in those sectors that are traditionally not open to market competition and characterized by networks – for example, power, telecommunications, railways, and civil aviation, to name a few – the concerned supervising ministries still act on behalf of the sector interests and refuse to open them to market competition, with the excuse that these sectors are more suited to a natural monopoly. The reason behind this is that most of those monopolistic sectors are either solely state-owned or the State holds a majority of their shares, with the government retaining administrative control of management and personnel. Sometimes, they even promulgate policies that are inconsistent with the central government's development strategies.[9] Not only do these companies and sectors pay taxes, but they also make profits, and are thus a valuable source of revenue for the state.[10] Accordingly, the concerned ministries in the central administration act more on behalf of the interests of a few affiliated enterprises, rather than on behalf of the public's interest.

---

[8] Jeffery Sachs, Wing Thye Woo and Yang Xiaokai, Economic CID Working Paper, April 2000, available online at www.cid.harvard/.edu/cidwp/043.htm. *Reform and Constitutionalism Transition.*

[9] The prohibition by the Bureau of Civil Aviation in 2000 of price discounting in the civil aviation sector is apparently inconsistent with China's overall policy of expanding internal demand.

[10] China's Bureau of Civil Aviation plays two roles: it is both a sector regulator and a majority shareholders of many aviation companies. On average, it owns more than 85% of the shares in 10 aviation companies, which are recommended to be consolidated into one. It demands that all aviation companies buy air fuel from its joint venture subsidiary – Chinese Air Fuel Supply Company – which sells air fuel at a cost inflated by about 60%.

Since the beginning of economic reform, China has been undergoing a separation of financial power and administration power. Administrative powers for the local government have been expanded under the process of decentralization. Under this system, the operational performance of one region or one sector has a direct impact on the revenue of the local government. When local-owned or sector-owned enterprises become inefficient or loss-making, their direct superiors in the local government have frequently resorted to using their administrative powers to manage the market by restricting entry for other enterprises (for example, those not based in the region or with their primary activities in a different sector), rather than reforming the non-profitable enterprises so that they could compete in the market. Such incentives to pursue local or sector interests constitute a strong motivation for administrative monopoly, especially regional monopoly.[11] This phenomenon is explained below.

Main Forms of Administrative Monopoly: Regional Monopoly and Sector Monopoly

Regional monopoly is seen when local governments erect market barriers using their administrative power either (1) to restrict market entry for goods from outside into the local market, or (2) to restrict outflow of local goods, raw materials, and technologies from the local market.

Regional monopoly is harmful in many ways. First, it frustrates the emergence of a single national market and blocks its further development toward an open market system. Second, it directly disturbs market competition and rational or market-based allocation of resources. It produces rent-seeking opportunities and incentives for local government officials. Advocates for regional monopoly may argue that regional monopoly can protect the development of local enterprises, but in fact such a "development" may often be at the expense of the welfare of consumers in the region, or merely postpone the eventual reform or closure of the enterprise. A regional monopoly transfers the cost of inefficiency to consumers.

Sector monopoly is an outcome of the policies implemented by the central administration or some specific sector-governing bodies to exclude from competition or restrict entry to other sector players so as to protect the entrenched interests of a few sector players or affiliated enterprises.

We should bear in mind that AM has taken place in many sectors, outside of those frequently seen in sector and regional monopolies. AM in those

---

[11] For a discussion on the influence of decentralization on China's politics and economy, see Minxin Pei, "Does Decentralization Increase Corruption?" Presentation at "International Conference on Economic Reform and Good Governance: Fighting Corruption in Transition Economies", sponsored by the Carnegie Endownment for Peace at Qinghua University, Beijing, 11-12 April 2002.

monopolistic sectors – such as power, telecommunications, civil aviation, and railways – is surely remarkable and is finally receiving more attention. AM in higher education, medical care and sanitation, sports, culture, entertainment, publishing, tourism, and so on, should also be broken and these markets opened and competition allowed.

Features of Administrative Monopoly

According to Hui Yu,[12] the main features of AM can be summarized as follows:

- It mainly takes place in enterprises that are either owned by the State or whose shares are absolutely controlled by the State. In both cases, these enterprises are directly run by the government and subject to government control in personnel, distribution, and operation.
- The legitimacy for market monopoly comes from the administrational status of the enterprises, which are run by the government, and consequently from their compliance with the law or regulatory policies. Compared with other forms of monopoly, the most remarkable feature of AM is that the enterprises' monopoly status is ensured by the government with favorable rules or administrative regulations.
- Monopoly enterprises both pay taxes and turn in profits to the state treasury.
- Competition between monopolistic enterprises leads to an inefficient market.
- AM blocks market competition and leads to inefficiency of resources allocation.

Administrative monopoly is against competition because:

- It restricts market entry in those sectors not belonging to a natural monopoly.
- It applies discriminating treatment to different enterprises, especially private enterprises and enterprises non-affiliated to the government.
- The central government acts on behalf of enterprises to set up a cartel price.
- A monopoly of public resources is established; hence, only a few enterprises can have exclusive access to them.
- It establishes regional barriers by administrative means.

For a monopolistic enterprise, it is common that its demand curve shows demand that is equivalent to that of the whole society. Therefore, if it reduces the supply of its products or service, the price will be pushed up, while profits do not decrease and may even increase, despite fewer quantites sold. For society, however, this situation of relative scarcity will lead to an overall erosion of welfare.

---

[12] See Hui Yu, "How the Administrative Monopoly Will End?" *China Economy Times*, April 21, 2001

ESTIMATION OF LOSSES CAUSED BY ADMINISTRATIVE MONOPOLY

According to rent-seeking theory, monopoly distorts the efficient allocation of resources and causes two types of loss: loss of the net social welfare;[13] and the loss experienced by consumers – that is, the surplus is transferred from the consumers to the producers.[14] Research indicates that, due to a huge cost created by rent-seeking and rent-protection processes, the rent will finally dissipate and this will eventually lead to the loss of the net social welfare. Additionally, the loss of the net social welfare caused by monopoly is actually very small. Therefore, we will concentrate in this chapter on the loss of the consumers.

In China, the rent accumulated by the sector monopoly can be of two types. The first is the loss of social welfare reflected in the monopoly price; the other includes various illegal fees collected by those monopolistic sectors through various pretexts, upon which they transfer the costs of their mismanagement and their investments for future development to the consumers.

Table 2 sets out estimates of the loss of the net social welfare in China in the late 1990s caused by monopoly sectors setting monopoly prices.

Table 2 Estimation of rent in China's monopoly sectors, 1995–98/99

Monopoly sectors	Estimated rent created (billion yuan/year)	Percentage range of GDP (%)
Electric power	56-112	0.75-1.50
Transportation and post	74-90	1.0-1.2
- Post and telecom.	21.5-32.5	0.29-0.43
- Civil aviation	7.5-10	0.1-0.13
Medical care	7.5-10	0.1-0.13
Total	130-202	1.7-2.7

Note: *Calculated at present price; GDP is calculated as7.5 trillion.*
Source: Angang Hu (ed.), (2000), p. 61.

---

[13] Tullock, op. cit., p. 2.
[14] Ibid., p. 13.

Table 3 sets out estimates, based on official statistics, of the various illegal fees collected by the monopolistic sectors from 1998 to 2001.

Table 3 Estimation of illegal fees collected by the monopoly sectors, 1998-2001

Monopoly sectors	Year	Illegal income (billion yuan)	Proportion of GDP (%)
Illegal fees from power sector	1998-99	2.74	
Financial burdens on peasants by disunited living electricity price	2001	35	0.37
Illegal charges of telecom.	1998-99	2.17	
Financial burdens on patients by rectifying medicaments purchase and sale	2001	10.1	0.11
Other illegal charging cases	2001	3.15	0.03
Total		53	0.60

Source: Angang Hu, "A Huge Black Hole," Working Paper, April 2002, p. 7.

It is clear that sector monopoly has created huge economic losses. In fact, losses caused by AM are far greater than those caused by petty corruption, such as government officials taking bribes.[15] In addition to being one of the most severe types of corruption in present-day China, sector monopoly directly violates the consumers' interest and has thus become a focus of consumers.

However, despite consumer concern, until now, there has been very little study done on the economic loss caused by regional monopoly in China. In this regard, we find that the research done by Sandra Poncet, an economist from the Center for International Research and Development in Paris, quite

---

[15] According to Qingze Cao, who is the Deputy Secretary of the Central Discipline Supervisory Committee of the Chinese Communist Party, the amount of economic loss retrieved from 1.33 million cases, mostly concerned with petty corruption, from October 1992 to June 2001, is approximately RMB40 billion (around 0.75% of GDP).

inspiring.[16] According to one of her latest studies, the trade tariff between different provinces in China in 1997 was around 46%; a decade before, it was 35%. This means that the regional trade barriers within China are as high as those that exist between European Union countries, or between Canada and the United States. What is worse is that even in an environment where the import tariffs are decreasing, the inter-provincial trade barriers have been rising steadily since the 1980s. Poncet found that in 1997, Chinese consumers bought 21 times more goods produced in their local province than goods from other provinces, whereas in 1987 this figure was just 11 times. Chinese provinces' into international markets is already underway, but at the same time ironically, the domestic market is becoming increasingly discontinuous and fragmented.

Poncet's study shows that China's regional monopoly is not only very severe, but is becoming worse even as China integrates with the global economy. One can predict that "domestic market segmentation" will remain as one of the most important manifestations of AM for quite some time.

Dissipation of Rent from the Sector Monopoly

Rent sought by AM goes mainly on:

- bailing out the huge operational costs caused by mismanagement of monopoly sector enterprises;

- paying for employees' welfare in the monopoly sector or informal expenditures for the concerned government department; and

- providing profits to the state from the SOEs.

The presence of the monopoly rent makes it possible for poorly managed or poorly performing enterprises in the monopoly sectors to survive. Evidence bears this out, in that the efficiency of companies in the monopoly sectors is generally poor. According to Shujie Liu,[17] labor productivity in the monopoly sectors in China, from 1985 to 1996, was far below the average level in China. Despite this, the average salary of employees in the monopoly sectors is far higher than that of all other employees in China. Our research[18] has shown that, for the period from 1995 to 1999, employees in the power sector

---

[16] See Bruce Gilley, "Provincial Disintegration," *UNPAN Working Paper*, World Trade Organization, 2001

[17] See Liu Shujie (ed.), *Price Reform in Monopoly Sectors* (Beijing: China Plan Press, 1999), p. 7.

[18] See Hu Angang (ed.), *Fighting Against Corruption* (Hangzhou: Zhejiang People's Press, 2001), p. 58.

each earned RMB14,294 more than those in other sectors – that is, an additional RMB2,859 per year. Cumulatively, the power sector had to pay RMB7,910 million extra each year for employees' salaries. Numerous rents sought by the monopoly sectors provide abundant capital for keeping inefficient operations and high salaries possible in those monopoly sectors. Table 4 is an estimation of how the rent was spent on high salaries in the monopoly sectors in 2000.[19]

Table 4 Rent dissipated by salaries of employees in AM sectors, 2000

Sectors	Average salary of employees (yuan)	Average salary of the whole country (yuan)	Amount above national average (yuan)	Per employee (in 10,000s)	Total Rent dissipated (billion yuan)
Power, gas, and water supply	12,830		3,459	281.8	9.75
Post and telecom.	16,359		6,988	113.2	7.91
Civil aviation	23,454	9,371	14,083	11.7	1.65
Railway transportation	13,920		4,549	187.1	8.51
Total					27.82

Source: Statistical Yearbook of China (2001), pp. 116, 135, 140.

Tullock's research shows that rent will eventually be dissipated, and be converted into a net loss of social welfare. However, in the context of China's experience, we find that part of the rent is turned in to the State as the profits of the SOEs, and is not all dissipated. It seems there is a gap between the theory and the reality. But a further analysis proves that Tullock's conclusion is correct. According to Shujie Liu, for example, in 1996, when prices in the monopoly sectors increased drastically in comparison with those of 1985, and the increasing pace was much faster than the inflation rate in the same period, the profit rate of the power sector was only 7.33%; it went down 54.58% compared to 1985. At the same time, the deficit of the railway transportation

---

[19] This does not include other forms of income besides salaries for employees in AM sectors, such as prize money, subsidies, and non-money income.

sector was RMB1.38 billion, a decrease of 120% in comparison with its surplus of RMB6.4 billion in 1985. Also, the local telephone sector had a deficit of RMB3.56 billion; and the post sector lost RMB7 billion.[20] These statistics indicate that profit in the monopoly sectors is continuously declining, and thus support Tullock's observation on the dissipation of rent.

It is worth noting that the profits turned over to the State by monopoly sectors should include their return to the government's investment in the form of a capital investment. Also, in the past, the SOEs received substantial subsidies from the government and the return of income tax, as well as tax reductions, and so forth. Those enterprises in the monopoly sectors have not only dissipated a tremendous amount of rent, but have also absorbed huge financial incomes that should have been collected by the State.

From the above-mentioned analysis of the rent, we can find that much of it has been paid to enterprises' supervising government ministries, which became for them an important source of off-budget revenue used for extra expenditure, employees' welfare income, the construction of luxury hotels, guest houses, or training centers, domestic and international tourism, and so on. (More detailed studies can be found in Xiaobo Lu's paper on organizational corruption in China.[21]) All of this provides incentives for government departments to seek rent.

PROGRESS OF REFORMS ON ADMINISTRATIVE MONOPOLY SO FAR, AND A FUTURE VISION
Administrative Monopoly Has Become the Focus of Strong Public Concern

With the development of a market economy in China, many previous monopolies enjoyed by the SOEs have been diminished. Market competition is accelerating and ownership is becoming diversified. Competition is becoming more common, and thus consumers have benefited. In sharp contrast, the effort required to diminish the administrative monopoly in sectors such as power, telecommunications, railways, and civil aviation still remains a job for Hercules. It has also become the focus of public concern and of debates in the media: among the issues that have received attention are the excessive pricing of power in rural areas, the uneven telecommunications fees, the rising prices of railway tickets, and the ban on discounted airfares. Surveys (using

---

[20] See Shujie Liu (ed)., op. cit., p. 4.
[21] See Xiaobo Lu, "Booty Socialism, Bureau-preneurs, and the State in Transition: Organizational Corruption in China," *Comparative Politics*, April 2000, pp. 273–94.

questionnaires designed by us) of some local government officials and enterprise managers indicate that the sector monopoly is widely regarded as one of the most important type of corruption in China[22] (see Table 5).

Table 5 Level of corruption in various fields: The perceptions of local government officials and enterprise managers*

Ranking**	Local government officials		Enterprise managers	
	Sectors	Level of corruption	Sectors	Level of corruption
1	Monopoly sectors	4.30	Monopoly sectors	4.42
2	Customs	4.01	Customs	4.30
3	Revenue	3.22	Revenue	4.05
4	Judicial system	2.78	Construction	4.02
5	Construction	2.71	Judicial system	4.00
6	Personnel department	2.68	Political leaders and officials in leading positions	3.97
7	Financial system	2.58	Transportation	3.73
8	Political leaders and officials in leading positions	2.16	Personnel department	3.68
9	Transportation	2.16	Financial system	3.66
10	Banking and securities	1.97	Market management	3.64
11	Market management	1.92	Banking and securities	3.61
12	Supervision and party discipline system	0.53	Supervision and party discipline system	2.91

Notes: *There were 121 local officials surveyed in Yunnan province in March 2001; and 77 enterprise managers in Zhejiang province in April 2001.*
**The number "5" represents the most severe corruption and "0" represents the least severe corruption.*

Reforms are Under Way

Since the process of economic reform and opening up began in 1979, the reform of sector monopolies has remained marginal on the political agenda.

---

[22] See Angang Hu and Yong Guo, "How the Local Officials Estimate the Situation of Corruption in China," *CCS Working Paper,* No. 24, 2001, p. 7.

The rapid expansion of the sector monopoly, with the exception of that in the railways, in the economic reform has stymied any substantial plan to attack these "strong forts of the planned economy." In recent years, however, the media, on behalf of the public interest, has successfully highlighted and exposed the losses caused by sector monopolies. Now a strong public pressure has been mobilized and voices have been channeled into new pressures for further reforms. There is consensus among many social groups of the need to break the monopoly in those sectors and to replace it with competition. For this purpose, policy changes must come about.

At the Fifth Plenary Session of the Fifteenth Central Commission of the Chinese Communist Party in October 2000 a decision was made for the first time to diminish the sector monopolies in the power, telecommunications, civil aviation, and railways sectors. The reform was expanded to cover the public service sector in the Tenth Five-year Plan passed in 2001. At one press conference, Premier Rongji Zhu even openly criticized the sector monopolies and promised to promote further reforms in those sectors. At present, the priorities for further economic reforms for the Chinese government are to bring down regional monopoly and diminish administrative monopoly, and to try and establish a single and national market with fair competition and clear laws, and that is in keeping with market norms.[23]

China has enacted a series of law to ensure the operation of the market economy, among them the *Anti-Unfair Competition Law*, the *Bankruptcy Law for State-Owned Enterprises*, and the *Company Law*. A series of administrative ordinances for regulating the relationship between the government and the market have also been promulgated, such as the *Decision on Consolidating and Regulating the Market Order*, the *Decision on Prohibiting Building up Regional Barriers for Blocking Market Transaction*, and the *Notice on Further Consolidating and Regulating Taxation Order*. In 2001 alone, the State Department amended or abolished more than 1,100 domestic laws and rules that were inconsistent with the requirement of the rules or norms of the WTO.

China has recently made significant progress in curbing administrative monopoly. In the power sector and the railways, separation of the enterprise management and the operation of facility networks is under way. In the telecommunications sector, after two series of separations and recombination

---

[23] See Angang Hu and Yong Guo, "From Monopoly Market to Competition Market: A Deepening Social Reform," *Reform* (China), Vol. 1, 2002, pp. 17–28.

over the past years, competition is finally in sight. The civil aviation sector, undergoing another reorganization, has experienced both setbacks and progress toward competition. Some of the direct positive consequences of these reforms are apparent in the decreasing prices of the products and services delivered by these monopoly sectors (as a result of illegal fees being reduced), and improvements in the services and service quality. Even public hearings on the prices of products and services have been held. At the same time, regional monopoly has been brought under scrutiny. With the deepening reform of the economic system, the scope for monopoly rents is being drastically reduced. Administrative monopoly has accompanied China's economic transformation over the past decades, but it will gradually reduce with the conclusion of China's economic, social, and political transition.

Further Reforms to Curb Administrative Monopoly

China's reform can be divided into two stages. The first stage was characterized by policy changes and improvements within the existing political system that aimed to break down the highly concentrated planned economy framework and push for economic development. At that time, the incentive mechanism was introduced into the economy system, and a decentralization policy was adopted. In parallel to the state-owned economies, some non-state-owned economies were also allowed or tolerated. Hence, a "dual-track economy" or "transitional institutions" were established. This stage was characterized by adjustments to the existing system, and promotion of the emergence of new systems within the existing institutional framework.

However, with further reform of the economy, the institutional cleavages have surfaced. Simultaneously, China's economic reform has entered a second stage involving replacing old public institutions with new ones in order to build a new market economy. The core of such a transition is a transformation of the government functions. Because corruption is a manifestation of institutional failure during this transition process, it must be contained by institution-building and bulwarking.

The focus of the institutional reform is a reorientation of the State's role in the economy. An important driver for the emergence of AM was the desire of some government departments to control and monopolize public resources and exclude competition in the name of promoting sector development and maintaining social stability. This has brought about tremendous economic loss to the country and, consequently, the role of the State should be discussed and reorientated. Even though experts and officials have been calling for many years for "separation of the administration from the enterprises," such a situation has not yet been achieved and remains the source of many problems during the course of economic reform. Accordingly, we hold that the key factor in separating the administration from the enterprises is to reduce the government's interference in economic activities and allow the market to allocate resources, change the vertical monopolistic operation, and push for the reorganization of sectors and commercialization of enterprises. The State should promulgate policies to promote and institutionalize competition.

The goal in this process of institutional reform is "good governance," which is a new concept for state-governing.[24] The 1990s witnessed a rapid development and wide acceptance of the concept. According to the Committee of Global Governance, governance is defined as a combination of various means by which public- or private-sector persons or institutions are utilized to manage their common business. The key to governance is the participation of different sectors and stakeholders. Such a new definition brings a fundamental change to the traditional approach of government because, in the new framework, the government no longer enjoys a dominant position; instead, the market allocates resources, and civil society is allowed to participate in the decision-making process. Basically, governance is a process of public participation. It is a new interpretation of democracy. One key problem of institutional reform is how to transfer from "government" to "governance," and how to make the process of legislation and public policy-making more democratic, transparent, and legitimate.

China's institutional reforms must also be consistent with the norms and rules of the WTO. China's accession to the WTO in 2001 provided a good opportunity for further reform of the economic system. In order to secure membership of the WTO, the Chinese government made substantial concessions. One reason for this was that it wanted to take the opportunity to regulate the domestic market economies in the context of those commonly accepted international norms or rules, in the hope of diminishing sector and regional monopolies and building a proper legal framework on the basis of a review and adjustment of the existing legislation. However, there is still a long way to go before China's market system is fully consistent with the requirements of the WTO.

CONCLUSION
We have attempted in this chapter to identify a sophisticated phenomenon of corruption that has emerged in the context of economic transition in China:

---

[24] See World Bank, *The Quality of Growth* (Washington: The World Bank, 2000), pp. 127–215; Keping Yu (ed.), *Governance and Good Governance* (Beijing: Social Science Literature Press, 2000), pp. 1–15.

the administrative monopoly. Our findings show that administrative monopoly is one of the most severe types of corruption in China, and is distinctly different from that in other transition economies – in particular, in Eastern Europe and the former Soviet Union.

Administrative monopoly takes two forms – sector monopoly and regional monopoly – and is an outcome of the long-standing overlap of the functions of the government and enterprises. In the context of active rent-creating activities, government departments abuse their administrative powers and seek tremendous rents, which they provide to their affiliated enterprises. This not only causes huge economic losses, but also creates a huge burden at the expense of consumers. Administrative monopoly is a special form of corruption, emerging from the economic transition. However, with further development of China's economic and political system reform, further institution building, and accession to the WTO, the country is in an advantageous position to reduce the rents caused by administrative monopoly and to decrease its existence in the market. This can be a strong support for the gradual development of a new concept of governance in China.

Geopolitical
and
Regional
Relations

China 2002:
The Geopolitical Context

*Philip Bowring**

 For China, joining the World Trade Organization has been both the culmination of a long march begun by Deng Xiaoping almost a quarter of a century ago and a statement of intent about the future.

The corollary of the step-by-step liberation of China from the economic, social, and ideological shackles of the Mao Zedong

era was the gradual establishment if important economic relationships with the rest of the world, and the United States in particular. But the development of the bonds of trade, investment, and technology has also increased the complexity of China's own interests. Being a member of WTO should help to regulate some key aspects of those interests, hopefully guarding them against short-term political pressures within China as well as providing some protection against arbitrary actions by foreign partners.

WTO membership is both symbol and blueprint, as it is a significant factor in the four issues (in no particular order) which will dominate China's agenda in the first decade or two of the 21st century:

· economic modernization, particularly through enterprise reform;

· the future of Taiwan;

· the relationship with the United States; and

· China's Asian regional role.

Naturally, these issues have many inter-linkages. Keeping national interests balanced between them will be the central issue for any government in China. But there will also always need to be a strong sense of priorities, and of differentiating between short- and long-term aspirations. For example, however

* Philip Bowring is a columnist with the *International Herald Tribune* in Hong Kong.

strongly Chinese people may feel about the Taiwan question, over-emphasis on it could jeopardize the other three national priorities. At the same time, Beijing's policies on these issues must accommodate the desire of the Chinese people for recognition on the world stage. It was Mao who pronounced that, with the communist revolution, "the Chinese people have stood up." But it has taken trade- and investment-driven economic growth, plus strategic arms development, to translate Mao's slogan into something the rest of the world now acknowledges.

The links between the four goals can be expressed as follows. China cannot assert its place in the region and the world without economic modernization. Economic development is also necessary if the Communist Party is to be able to retain its leadership role. For the economy, sheer size is not enough. Technology that can compete with the United States and Japan is needed. Modernization and acquisition of technology – including military technology – cannot be achieved without foreign trade and investment which, in turn, requires a strong working relationship with the old-established capitalist powers, notably the United States. Recovery of Taiwan requires improving China's domestic economy and gradually altering the strategic balance in East Asia, reducing the dominance of the U.S.–Japan axis. Economic interaction with Taiwan helps that goal. Foreign trade emphasis inevitably means greater interaction with the trade-oriented countries of East and Southeast Asia, enabling China to expand its influence and emphasize its friendly neighbor status. In turn, that will enhance its strategic position and, hence, prospects for Taiwan reunification.

National goals must also exist within a domestic political framework in which the Communist Party is, and is likely to remain, the overriding factor. Shorn of ideology as it is, the Party is capable of the utmost pragmatism. But by the same token, lack of ideology can also lead to the triumph of corrupting forces more interested in personal power and enrichment than in pursuing a set of commonly agreed national aspirations.

The centerpiece of economic development is enterprise reform to create a structure of management and ownership that can respond dynamically to the challenges of a market economy. But divorcing economic power from the political power of the Party through the development of the private sector is easier said than done. Indeed, there are many in the Party who do not even want it in theory. Likewise, separating state enterprises from the Party and the managers from the policymakers is harder in practice than in theory. Political and economic power are hard to separate anywhere, particularly so given the nature and structure of Communist parties everywhere and of China's particular history of a centralizing bureaucracy whose reach has defined the

State. The role of state enterprises in the large corporate sector, and of quasi-public township enterprises at the lower level, is still overwhelming despite the rapid progress of small-scale private business, especially in services.

In a country the size of China, there will also be another battle – between the desire of the center to maintain its own authority over centrifugal tendencies which threaten national cohesion and economic order, and the entrepreneurial instincts and local interests of city and provincial economic players, be they private or public. The center has interests in common with foreign trade partners in WTO in curtailing internal barriers to trade and countering provincial governments that protect local interests at the expense of market-driven national forces. At the same time, the government continues to see a key nation-building role for major state-owned enterprises (SOEs) which may be at odds with the market principles of other major WTO players.

The Asian crisis may have taken the shine off the likes of the Korean *chaebol*. But the government in Beijing does see the need for a few major players to take a lead, to provide the nation with players in key industries combining size and excellence. Given that it will take many years for the local private corporate sector to develop the size and sophistication to be the leader in all but niche areas, the SOEs will continue to play a pivotal role to a greater extent than in most other major countries.

The other ever-present link between politics and economics is the problem of urbanization. Sixty-five percent of the population is still rural. Despite its advancement in a few areas, such as missile technology and IT, this rural predominance makes China more like India and Indonesia than Brazil or Iran. Urbanization is relatively slow despite high economic growth, because of restrictions imposed by the perceived need to keep urban incomes from suffering from too rapid an influx of rural labor into cities where unemployment is sometimes high due to layoffs of surplus SOE workers.

The rural/urban income gap issue may seem a purely domestic one. But WTO will also have an impact on farm incomes that will be both positive and negative. Although some farm prices in China are slightly above international levels, that is largely because production and export subsidies by advanced countries distort international prices and thus, indirectly, contribute to China's low rural income problem. The issue of farm subsidies is likely to be the most contentious at the forthcoming round of WTO trade negotiations. Although Europe, the biggest subsidizer, has at last agreed to discuss the issue seriously, the U.S. enactment of much-increased farm subsidies will make progress very difficult.

China's own farm output has been distorted by local as well as national grain self-sufficiency goals, as well as by restrictions on internal trade, illegal taxation, and so on. Overall, however, land productivity in China is high, though labor productivity on farms is low as many are under-employed or needed only seasonally. The farm situation also points up what for years to come will continue to be China's biggest single international comparative advantage: the low cost of its industrious, even if largely unskilled, workforce. There are still hundreds of millions of rural people who would probably prefer low wages in a sweatshop factory in a city to a hard life with minimal cash income and negligible educational opportunities for the family down on the farm.

Capitalizing on its comparative advantages, however, will only be possible if the global trade situation allows it, and if the central government is able to keep a strict limit on the amount of subsidy going to inefficient state sectors through bank loans or anti-market policies that keep some prices artificially high. Again, membership of WTO addresses itself to both these issues.

CHINA'S ECONOMIC GLOBALIZATION: FOREIGN AND LOCAL BENEFICIARIES

Membership of WTO has come about after years of wrangling, mainly with the U.S. over terms of entry. But far from being a predominantly adversarial relationship, the links to the U.S. have been absolutely crucial to the era of market modernization. That is not to say that the adversarial element will not increase as time goes by. The U.S.–China relationship has always been an unusual one marked by emotion and mutual fascination – a fascination not always backed by knowledge. For China, the U.S. has the twin faces of modernity and imperialism, the balance between the two varying depending on the era as well as on individual perception. Its current dichotomy could be summed up by the unsympathetic attitudes to September 11 revealed by Chinese Internet users, a huge group much attracted to U.S. technology as well as to McDonald's and Coca-Cola. Under Mao, the U.S. was the number one imperialist "hyena." In the earlier days of reform, the U.S. was almost uncritically admired as the fount of education, technology, trade, capital, law, democracy, human rights, and so on. Now, as China's own pride has swelled with success, admiration is tempered by old resentments, the Belgrade embassy bombing, and concerns that the U.S. now plans to thwart China's right to great power status.

The U.S., meanwhile, has long tended to approach China with missionary zeal as though the new power in the West had a manifest destiny to lead the old power of the East into a new era. Originally the message was Christianity and education. After 1949, it was to save China from atheistic communism. Since Deng Xiaoping began his reforms, the U.S. has offered China many opportunities for trade and investment in the belief that these would help lead it not only to a market economy, but to a free system based on law and democracy. The U.S. was idealistic – but not entirely wrong – in believing that trade led to development, which led to a more open and eventually more democratic society. At the same time, setbacks to the process, such as the 1989 Tiananmen events, easily led to disappointment and reactions that threatened the relationship. The two views of China – some held by the same people simultaneously – are reflected daily in U.S. newspapers: China the great growth and investment opportunity; and China the hotbed of human rights abuse and potential threat to its neighbors.

The missionary view of China has, of course, always been tempered by U.S. national interests. In the first decade of China's reform, a shared hostility to the Soviet "evil empire" was an important factor in the rapid development of relations. In practice, there may be little difference in U.S. policy toward China now, under a President who views China as a "competitor," than under President Clinton, who went from critic to talking of China as "partner." In different ways, both descriptions are true. Nonetheless, the importance that China and the U.S. attach to each may at times make the relationship both more intense and more difficult.

Trade links have become especially close. Including exports through Hong Kong, some 35% of China's exports go to the U.S. China now has a much higher level of dependence than other Asian exporters, and is approaching the U.S. market dependency levels once seen by Korea and Taiwan. This is partly the result of the ready access that China had through its most favored nation status long before it joined the WTO. The U.S. was more open – and earlier – to China than were other Western (or Japanese) markets. One result is that WTO entry in the short run should benefit the U.S. – and others – more than China.

In practice, other exporting nations such as Korea may benefit more than the U.S. from lower Chinese tariffs on manufactures such as cars and consumer electronics in which they are pre-eminent low-cost producers. But U.S. service industries see huge new opportunities in telecoms, trading, banking, and financial intermediation. Earning profits in China is, as many have found out, unusually difficult for a variety of reasons, and few U.S. investors boast of how well they have done there. But there can be no doubting the success – and, presumably, profits – of U.S. brand names such as Coca-Cola, Microsoft, and McDonald's and the role that U.S.-based auditing firms, management consultants, advertising agencies, and even lawyers have been playing in the development of modern institutions in China. Others see China as a vast new frontier that they cannot afford to ignore even if they are hesitant to project when it may become profitable. On other occasions, U.S. companies may have a reputation for thinking of short-term profits. But most of those who are now in China realize they are there for the long haul. Service providers such as accountants have been able to develop their mainland business from existing and already very profitable operations in Hong Kong.

China's reform process also had another dynamic which has increased the importance of the U.S. market for China. Opening up of special economic zones such as Shenzhen encouraged Hong Kong, Taiwan, and other East Asian exporters facing rising wages at home and, after 1986, pressed by the U.S. to have stronger currencies, to shift low-skill, labor-intensive manufacturing to the mainland. Their trade surpluses with the U.S. shrank rapidly, while those of China surged. The benefits to China may not have been as great as the trade numbers now suggest. Value added in China in labor-intensive industries is often low, sometimes below 20%. Thus, the bigger benefits have often accrued to component suppliers, factory owners, and trade intermediaries more than to mainlanders themselves. However, over time the development of ancillary industries on the mainland has greatly increased local value added. Taiwanese firms, for instance, started by simply using China for assembly operations but have gradually shifted many component manufacturing operations across the strait, either to meet their own needs or those of multinational clients who have themselves set up on the mainland.

The benefits of foreign investment have also been diluted by the generous tax holidays and other incentives offered. Although many of those incentives have expired, and most will now be outlawed by WTO rules, transfer pricing often allows profits to be reaped in Hong Kong or other offshore locations, thus avoiding paying taxes in China. Mainland, as well as foreign, firms have benefited from this process, which partly explains the huge negative "errors and omissions" item in China's balance of payments data.

Nonetheless, despite these drawbacks, the sheer scale of operations had a dramatic impact on China as a whole. The Shenzhen special economic zone started as an experiment by Deng Xiaoping and took a long time to achieve momentum. Success bred success, and what worked in foreign trade came to invigorate the domestic market. The transformation of much of coastal China was the result. This process is still going on and, indeed, has become a focus of cross-straits policy, with China trying to lure top Taiwanese semiconductor and other electronic hardware companies with offers of markets and protection, as well as cheap land and labor, while the government in Taipei has tried to hold them back to slow what it fears will be the hollowing out of local industry.

However, China's success in attracting most successful East Asian manufacturers – Korean and Japanese, as well as Taiwanese – to set up exporting plants on the mainland has also left both China and the U.S. with some very delicate economic issues. According to U.S. data, the trade imbalance in 2001 was US$83 billion. Worse, the ratio of exports to imports was five to one in favor of China. The U.S. data exaggerate the problem. Imports include not only those from Hong Kong – which is probably fair enough in that the special administrative region (SAR) itself now manufactures little – but also counts U.S. exports as fob while imports are cif. Nonetheless, it is a huge and precarious imbalance that is unsustainable if only because the U.S. current account deficit, now running at more than 4% of GDP, is generally viewed as unsustainable.

Much of what China exports is not produced in the U.S. anyway. If Chinese exports were disadvantaged, manufacturers would probably move to Mexico or India rather than back to the U.S. The U.S. is mostly interested in selling more capital goods and services to China than in blocking imports of consumer goods and electronic equipment. Nonetheless, a crucial question remains: what combination of U.S. recession, Chinese growth, currency realignment, and protectionism will be the means by which the U.S. current account deficit is reduced to sustainable levels? Given that China now has a bigger trade surplus than Japan, and a much bigger relative imbalance, there are clearly some rough waters to be navigated.

WTO membership will help protect China from arbitrary and selective actions. Generally, China is more vulnerable than any major country, due to the size of its trade surplus and the degree of its reliance on the U.S. market. Without WTO, China would be very vulnerable to vindictive action by a quixotic U.S. Congress were a U.S. recession to coincide with an event such as the Belgrade embassy bombing or the 2001 airplane incident off Hainan. But even so, China could well be hit hard by broad-based anti-dumping and other restrictive measures. When the U.S. announced punitive new tariffs on steel imports, China was quick to make common cause with the European Union (EU), Japan, Brazil, and others, even though the impact on China itself was likely to be small.

U.S.–CHINA RELATIONS: CURRENCY, GEOPOLITICS, AND REGIONAL TIES

If there is another major international currency realignment, as happened after the 1985 Plaza Accord, as part of an effort to reduce trade imbalances, will China be expected to revalue the yuan?

Most commentary has focused on the dangers to China of a very weak yen – and consequently weak won and NT dollar – forcing it to devalue the yuan and again set off currency instability in Asia. But a bigger problem may well be a sharp fall in the dollar, in which case China is likely to come under huge international pressure for a revaluation, or a gradual but marked appreciation of the yuan. It has been gaining global market share – and an increasing trade surplus – even during the period of dollar strength. China would be unpopular with its Asian neighbours, whose currencies would all appreciate in the case of a falling dollar, thus lowering their ostensible competitiveness on global export markets and especially vis-a-vis China. Regional relationships are an increasingly important input into China's overall policymaking. Certainly, China's current account surplus is large enough to withstand some yuan appreciation, although official thinking of the People's Bank of China at present is that liberalizing capital outflow would be preferable to currency appreciation, to slow the growth of foreign reserves.

These reserves are another complicating factor in U.S.–China relations. They now total some US$320 billion, a large proportion of which is held in U.S. government and agency securities. In theory, these holdings provide China with political and trade leverage in Washington. In practice, they are of limited use, as heavy selling by China would drastically depress their prices and that of the dollar.

In extremis, the U.S. could freeze these assets. But that would be the economic equivalent of using nuclear weapons. Both sides can, in theory, threaten dire things, but ultimately there is too much inter-dependence for such threats to be sustainable by either side. China needs the U.S. market for the dollars and employment it provides. It needs foreign capital and know-how for modernization and much of that comes because China has U.S. market access. Meanwhile, in the U.S., there is a huge commercial network dependent on manufacturing in and importing from China. All the big-name U.S. companies want to be in China seeing it as a last great frontier of expansion. They want to profit from its domestic market, as well as use it as an export platform. There are the Wall Street investment houses for whom China issues have been an important source of revenue, particularly at a time when much of the rest of Asia has offered thin pickings. The U.S. also genuinely and philosophically believes in the benefits of free trade and capital flows; thus, it is not easily swayed by the mercantilist argument that its openness to Chinese goods, and willingness to transfer capital and technology, is helping China rather than the U.S.

Both sides at times feel that the trade relationship has become too close for comfort given the difference in the two nations' systems and underlying distrust of each other's long-range, strategic goals. They never planned it to be so close. But the reality, and the mutual self-interest attaching to it, now acts as a restraint on other issues between the two sides.

So long as China gives priority to economic issues over political or ideological ones, it must try to keep relations with the U.S., and hence with the West in general, on an even keel. Meanwhile, the U.S., whatever its feelings about China's long-term strategic ambitions, cannot afford, just to spite China, to disrupt post-1945 global arrangements which have served it very well. China is now in the system.

But how do the two countries see each other's strategic situations and goals? And at what points do short-term interests clash with those goals? The George W. Bush administration has shown how the immediate issues can override others. That is evidently true for both sides, but perhaps more so for the U.S. given the perceived need in democratic societies to respond quickly to public or media opinion. The U.S. would have found it difficult to limit its response to verbal protests had one of its embassies been bombed by China "by mistake."

The skeptical, if not openly hostile, attitude toward China shown early on by members of the second Bush administration was dramatically changed by the events of September 11, 2001. China was soon being praised as a partner in the "war on terror." Though popular sympathy for the U.S. in China was less than resounding – at least, judging from the Internet – the official response was gratifying for the U.S. China played a role in persuading its old ally Pakistan to cooperate with the U.S. war effort. China acquiesced in the arrival of U.S. troops in Central Asia to bases not far from China itself. It not only paid lip service to hunting Islamic terrorists; it took the opportunity to link them to separatism in Xinjiang province, which provided good cover for a renewed crackdown on Uighur nationalism, although the links between the Uighurs, whose ethnic grievances are of long standing, and the Taliban are a matter of debate.

In Washington, the new focus on Islam, the Middle East, and old enemy Saddam Hussein provided a substitute for anti-China rhetoric and also overshadowed the fact that the U.S. continued pushing ahead with its missile defense program. President Bush was able to visit China in late 2001, in an atmosphere that was correct, though not warm. One year later, Jiang Zemin's visit to the United States, and especially his reception at President Bush's ranch in Texas, was much warmer and reflected a new geopolitical climate.

It is possible that the U.S. will be bogged down for a long time in the aftermath of September 11, and in the aggravation of its relations with all Muslim countries in the Middle East, regardless of their stripe. In which case, China may find it relatively easy to avoid overt friction over strategic issues. For now, China sees the U.S. presence in Central Asia as more likely to damage Russian interests than its own, and perhaps believes that the U.S. will find involvement in the region more trouble than it is worth. It will hope that the U.S. and Russia between them will help suppress Muslim extremism in the region so that China will gain benefits but not be blamed if the campaign misfires.

The sale of missiles and military technology to Iran and Iraq will continue to provide a source of friction with the U.S. but is not vital for China and can be turned off if the diplomatic price gets too high. The issue of strategic weapons sales and, possibly, the supply of nuclear know-how to Pakistan has long been a factor in U.S.–China relations. The U.S. believes itself to have a dual interest in pressuring China on these weapons issues. First, the spread of strategic weapons is seen as undermining U.S. global influence, as well as increasing the likelihood of a nuclear conflict. Second, its views of Iran and Iraq are heavily influenced by its close alliance with Israel. This explains why the U.S. is so concerned about Iraq's so-called weapons of mass destruction while Iran, which lost more than a million men to Western-backed Iraqi aggression against it in the 1980s, is not.

For China, cooperation with Pakistan has long been a cornerstone of policy toward South Asia. It has no desire to see India's relative position become too dominant. India may justify its nuclear capability by reference to China's own more advanced nuclear and missile capability. But for China the issue of a balance of terror on the subcontinent itself is more important. It sees Indian emphasis on China more as part of a desire – hard to fulfil – on India's part to gain equality with China on the international stage. But it lacks permanent United Nations (UN) Security Council membership, as well as equality in strategic weapons or economic clout.

The post-September 11 increase in U.S.–India cooperation – including military – is an additional complication for China. This may yet fall victim to other U.S. needs in the region. The U.S.–India relationship remains bedeviled by petty resentments. Nonetheless, with the old Delhi–Moscow link no longer a guarantee of cool Washington–Delhi relationships, India is now more of a background factor in U.S.–China relations than used to be the case.

One meeting point of Indian and Chinese interests is Burma. China's arms and aid support for the regime has given it much influence in Rangoon. Meanwhile, Chinese traders arrived in numbers, partly making up for the petty commercial sectors' loss of Indian traders expelled in the 1960s. China is believed to have listening posts in Burma to keep an eye on Indian naval activity in the Bay of Bengal. Burma–China and Burma–Thailand ties give China a theoretical access to the Indian Ocean which India resents (and of which the U.S. is suspicious) but has been unable to counter.

The issue of Chinese arms exports also links to the Korean question. China and the U.S. may agree on the need to prevent North Korea acquiring a nuclear capability that would threaten the stability of the peninsula. However, neither China nor South Korea is too concerned about Pyongyang's missile capability, which does not significantly increase the threat to the South already facing massed artillery and short-range missiles a few miles from Seoul. Again, the U.S. is more worried about missile sales because of its Middle East interests than its East Asian ones.

Looking beyond the repercussions of September 11, there are major strategic issues in East Asia. The U.S., together with its principal Asian ally, Japan, have what amounts to military hegemony in the region. China cannot for many years come close to competing even with Japanese naval power – restricted though its theater of operations currently is – let alone with the carrier battle groups of the U.S. While China's power has grown, it is still far from being able to offset the boost to U.S. dominance that was provided by the Soviet collapse. It has attempted closer relations with Russia. Both countries share a resentment of U.S. hegemonistic attitudes. They are concerned enough about Muslim fundamentalism and local nationalisms to have formed the Shanghai Cooperation Organization which embraces the former Soviet Central Asian states. However, Sino-Russian suspicions go deep, and President Putin's desire to seek an accommodation with NATO to concentrate on developing economic relations with the West has made Beijing uneasy. Nonetheless, the attractions of China trade for resource-rich Russia and Central Asia are considerable.

Through a combination of its own strength and appropriate alliances, China's ultimate goal is to supplant U.S. influence in the region with its own. This is a long-term strategy, and not one which need impact on more immediate issues of trade and investment. Generally speaking, policies of both the U.S. and China are driven more by short- to medium-term considerations than by distant goals. However, it is fair to say that China has a better-defined and integrated set of long-term goals, if only because it is not a global power with the myriad conflicting international and domestic interests which now flow from U.S. global dominance.

China does not have global power ambitions. It is strictly an Asian power – not one, like the Soviet Union, which had immediate interests stretching from the Bering to the Black seas, the Arctic to the Pacific oceans. However, it does possess a strategic nuclear capability – missiles that can reach the continental U.S. – which gives it global power status and bargaining chips which, in principle, could in future be used to press issues closer to home – for example, Taiwan or the South China Sea. U.S. dominance may seem overwhelming, but its future willingness to suffer significant losses in order to defend interests that do not directly threaten the U.S. is in doubt.

However, while it can continue to benefit from economic integration into the world, China will view its strategic advancement as being made possible by economic development, not as an alternative to it. The Deng doctrine that national strength grows out of economics, not ideology, is likely to remain at the center of Chinese policy – unless there is a 1930s-style breakdown of the world trading system.

Despite Taiwan, China has long tolerated, even assisted, the U.S. strategic dominance in East Asia because it was perceived as less dangerous than a revival of Japanese militarism as well as keeping the Soviets in check. The U.S. might want hegemony, but it was not after land. However, times change. China is becoming more powerful. An aging Japan looks more for comfort and security than expansion. Russia is on the defensive, at least in the Far East where Chinese commercial interests are growing. North Korea is too poor to be a credible threat to a prosperous South enjoying excellent relations with China.

So, China is looking to a day when the U.S. begins to pull back from its military commitments in the region. Can it afford so many carrier battle groups? Does it need 40,000 troops in Korea? Is the Okinawa base worth all the problems it creates for U.S.–Japan relations? None of these questions is on the current agenda, but could well be within the next five to 10 years. The need for the U.S. troop presence in Korea even came up during the Carter administration 25 years ago, when the Soviet Union was still in existence.

THE TAIWAN ISSUE

China naturally hopes that an eventual reduction in U.S. commitments in Asia, together with the development of its own naval and missile capability, will be the stick that persuades Taiwan to agree to a One-China formula which is acceptable to Beijing. However, there are several reasons why the Taiwan issue may remain exceptionally difficult, an international as well as a Chinese affair.

First, there is genuine sympathy in the U.S., and in the outside world generally, for Taiwan's right to self-determination. There are the historical links between the island and the Pentagon and the U.S. Congress which go back to the days of Chiang Kai-shek. The perception in the U.S. that China is a strategic competitor will strengthen those in Washington who want to keep the Taiwan issue alive as a counter to that. Commitment may fall short of being prepared for active intervention. President George W. Bush has verbally strengthened U.S. commitment to Taiwan's defense, but that seems more of a rhetorical statement than a change of policy. The basic U.S. position remains to maintain a policy of deliberate ambiguity which neither allows Taiwan to assume that it will be protected come what may, nor allows Beijing to believe that the U.S. will stand idly by if China either invades Taiwan or tries to strangle it economically.

U.S. ambiguity on the Taiwan issue is not just a policy. It is enshrined in formal commitments: on the one hand to China, as expressed in the Shanghai Communiqué and elsewhere, to support One China, and on the other to meet the demands of the *Taiwan Relations Act* to defend Taiwan.

In a sense, all of this is grounded in past, not present, realities – in the days before there was ever any talk of Taiwan independence and when the Republic of China (ROC) government in Taipei continued to claim that it was the legitimate government of all China. Democratic, post-Kuomintang (KMT) Taiwan now makes no such claims and bases its legitimacy on elections as well as the history of the ROC. But both Beijing and the U.S. cling to the notion that there can only be One China, rather than, as with Korea and previously also Germany, two legitimate governments of a temporarily divided nation.

Refusal to accept this, to continue to regard Taiwan as a renegade state, enables China to refuse to renounce the use of force to settle the issue. For now, the U.S. believes that China does not have the capacity to launch an invasion of Taiwan and that the provision of modern arms to Taiwan can keep the cost to China of a military solution too high to contemplate for more than a decade. If China shares this assessment, it will come to the conclusion that its best policy must be to maintain a military build-up while using a policy of dialogue to encourage better relations and dissuade Taiwan from large arms spending.

Strangling Taiwan economically by cutting off its trade remains a possibility. But ending trade just with the mainland would do huge damage to China's own economy. Trying to force foreign ships away from Taiwan might well invite U.S. and Japanese naval protection. Economic embargoes are usually slow to take effect and would only work if Taiwan was entirely lacking in friends. Despite China's power and prestige, that seems unlikely.

Taiwan is viewed by Japan and some Southeast Asian countries as a critical issue because of its strategic position at both northern entrances to the South China Sea – the Taiwan Strait and the much narrower Luzon Strait between Taiwan and the Philippines. For China, Taiwan is an integral province. For others it seems often a separate entity, settled by Chinese relatively recently and as close to the Philippines and the southernmost of Japan's Ryukyu islands as to the mainland. Its indigenous inhabitants – the majority until 200 years ago – speak Malay languages.

Thus, Taiwan is an important practical link to China's claims on the South China Sea. These are of crucial importance to Japan, because control of that sea means control of the main shipping lanes between East Asia and most of the rest of the world other than the Americas, passing Singapore, the Malacca Straits, and so on. Alternative routes do exist, but they are significantly longer. China's claims on the South China Sea cannot currently be exercised in the face of U.S. naval power and the opposition of most major countries to China's position on what they regard as international waters. But they do exist, and control of Taiwan is important to them.

Periods of tension over the Taiwan Strait, especially in 1996, have prompted increased Japanese awareness of this issue, appear to have strengthened U.S.–Japan cooperation, and have led to Japan enlarging the theater of potential operation of its "self-defense" navy. Japan has supported the U.S. program to develop a missile shield which, in theory at least, would provide continued U.S. strategic supremacy in the region, and could also be specifically designed to include Taiwan in its coverage. Even if the missile program does not achieve its goals, China can expect Japan to continue to build up its own independent defense forces, including the capacity to become a nuclear power with delivery capability at short notice.

For China, of course, the Taiwan issue is more a national than a strategic issue, the final end of its humiliation by foreigners. The mainland resents not just the separatist ideas of many Taiwanese but what it views as an overly sympathetic view by Taiwanese of their former colonial rulers, the Japanese. It particularly irritated Beijing that former Taiwan president Lee Teng-hui seemed more fluent in Japanese than in Putonghua. Japanese rule of Taiwan was mild compared with its behavior on the mainland in Korea and established an educational and public service infrastructure. Mainlanders are often remembered more for KMT oppression of Taiwanese sentiment and political activity after 1945. For Taiwan, this history has often overshadowed their Chinese identity. But for Beijing, these are details of history. Nothing should stand in the way of identifying culture and nation.

China originally hoped that the Taiwan issue could be resolved by gradually detaching the U.S. from Taiwan, and using its own economic reform to attract Taiwan into a compromise which would leave it with more autonomy than Hong Kong but within a single state entity.

This seemed a sensible approach. There was a surge of Taiwanese investment on the mainland, taking advantage not only of China's opening up but of specific incentives available only to compatriots. It seemed as though money plus cultural affinities could break down the political walls. However, this development coincided with the spontaneous upsurge in the liberal democracy movement in Taiwan. This amounted to a rejection of much that mainlanders, KMT or communist, stood for. It also meant that Taiwan was able to present itself to the outside world as a free and democratic society, rather than an authoritarian one run by history's has-beens. This was never remotely strong enough to overcome China's diplomatic weight and push Taiwan even close to international recognition as a separate entity. Nor, even after recognition of the two Koreas, did China ever contemplate conceding the possibility of two Chinas. Nonetheless, Taiwan gained kudos in the outside world for its de facto pursuit of democratic self-determination albeit under a protective American umbrella.

Beijing's past angry responses to Taiwan's separatist instincts and attempts to increase its international space rubbed salt into Taiwanese wounds. Verbal threats and missile tests played into the hands of Taiwanese such as Lee Teng-hui, whose KMT clothes thinly disguised a quasi-independence agenda. The overt mainland hostility had the effect of driving voters to back Lee, if not the openly separatist Democratic Progressive Party (DPP). It brought about a reaffirmation of U.S. military support. Aircraft carriers passed through the Taiwan Strait, and Congressional pressure on the administration to step up arms sales to Taiwan increased.

However, China appears to have learned from past mistakes that alienation of the Taiwanese is no way to advance unification. Elements in the military, and nationalist and anti-reform elements within the Party, emphasize the possibility of a military solution if Taiwan does not yield. At times, for domestic political reasons, no one wants to be seen to be soft on Taiwan or on its U.S. backers. However, there is now a better appreciation in Beijing of the nature of Taiwan's own politics. Ironically, this has probably been helped by the election in 2000 of Chen Shui-bian from the formally pro-independence DPP in place of Lee Teng-hui whose China-baiting met a predictable response from Beijing. Chen's actions as President have also underlined the central reality of Taiwanese politics: hardcore independence advocates, like hardcore pro-unification supporters, are on the fringe. Taiwanese mostly want the status quo of de facto independence and a balance between economic interests of closer ties to the mainland and political ones of maneuvering to expand diplomatic space and defense capability.

TRADE AS A TESTING GROUND FOR CLOSER RELATIONS

As a result, China, while keeping up pressure internationally and on the U.S. over Taiwan, has shifted policy toward the Taiwanese very much away from the threat of the stick to economic carrots and social contacts. The economic appeal of the mainland has long been there but has often been offset by abrasive political language. However, a softer tone from Beijing has coincided with an increased sense among the Taiwanese that they need the mainland market, as well as using it as a location for manufacturing. Recession in Taiwan in 2001 – an almost unheard of event – while the mainland economy continued to grow rapidly, increased the sense of vulnerability that Taiwan was too dependent on a narrow range of products and on the U.S. market.

This led to increased investment on the mainland in order to take advantage of higher growth and to improve the competitiveness of Taiwanese manufacturers in world markets. The shift of low-skill activities to the mainland has been going on for years, but China is now able to offer Taiwan higher skills and a broader base of IT support industries, particularly in and around Shanghai. The Taiwanese presence in that region has grown very quickly, with financial- and property-sector investors following in the wake of the manufacturers so that there are now several hundred thousand Taiwanese there, making a big contribution to the rapid improvement in the quality of services. They are also able to experience at first hand the liberal social climate that now exists in China's major cities.

The Taiwan government, under pressure from business interests, has had to liberalize its policies on the mainland. Banks, too, have been allowed to establish representative offices across the strait. Many investment restrictions had anyway long been evaded, which accounts for the fact that unofficial estimates put mainland investment at upwards of US$50 billion, or double the officially acknowledged amount. However, the Taiwan government has resisted the transfer of very large or technologically advanced investments. For example, although Taiwanese firms are involved in the rush to build semiconductor plants on the mainland, the most advanced technology is staying in Taiwan. The mainland plants will enjoy tariff protection in the local market, but it has yet to be shown that they are internationally competitive.

For China, attracting Taiwanese investors has a dual function. First, investments from Taiwan help build up know-how, particularly in the IT industry, so that China itself may emerge as a leader in some sectors of it, such as mobile phone applications. Through its transfer of technology, as well as the trade stimulus that it brings, Taiwan-based companies are a key factor in economic modernization. Second, it is leading to increased economic integration and social contact, particularly with Shanghai given that it is relatively advanced and offers Taiwanese a favorable view of the mainland. Eventually, it is believed on the mainland that this will filter into Taiwanese political perceptions and make it more accommodating.

For Taiwan, the mainland is a mixed blessing. It offers the most convenient location for low-cost manufacturing for third markets. It certainly offers investment opportunities that the Taiwanese can, because of language and cultural affinities, exploit better than foreigners. Taiwanese of mainland origin, especially from the Shanghai/Zhejiang/Jiangsu area, are rebuilding old family ties going back to pre-revolution times. Taiwan's financial sector can play a significant role as the mainland opens up to foreign investment. On the other hand, it is a threat to the less competitive parts of Taiwan's economy – which may suffer from Taiwan joining the WTO and having to open up to mainland exports. Over-emphasis on mainland investment could be against Taiwan's interest in continuing to develop as a global market leader in niche products, mostly IT-related. The most important keys to Taiwan's success are its close technology links to the most advanced players in the U.S., and to a lesser degree Japan, as well as to Western product markets. China may be a faster-growing market, but it is only one of several in the world. Much recent investment there has been driven by the needs of multinational companies setting up in China and wanting Taiwanese supplier firms to be nearby.

Although the mainland now accounts for some 25% of Taiwan's exports, much of that is components for exports to other countries, rather than for the domestic market. The value added in Taiwan is often higher than in China. Cross-straits trade grew very rapidly in the mid-1990s but in recent years has been barely faster than Taiwan's overall trade. It is now receiving another fillip from the WTO and the surge in Taiwan investment on the mainland. But the China market is still less important to Taiwan than the U.S. Although Taiwan's exports to the mainland are now slightly higher than those to the U.S., a large proportion of them are components for end products whose destination is the U.S. It is now estimated that half of the electronics/IT output of Taiwanese firms is carried out on the mainland. While this demonstrates the importance of the mainland in keeping the firms competitive and gaining world market share, it also underlines the dependence of China on the design, manufacturing, and marketing skills of the Taiwanese firms.

Cross-straits economic and political issues meet at the crucial issue of direct air, sea, and telecommunications links. The possibility of direct links has waxed and waned for a decade but still remains very contentious despite the establishment in 2001 of direct so-called mini-links between the mainland and the Taiwan-controlled offshore islands of Matsu and Qimen. Pressure from Taiwanese business leaders anxious to cut costs by avoiding transshipment of goods and people through Hong Kong has long existed and been especially strong over the past year. The issue again arose at the end of 2002 during the discussions over the possibility of direct air charter flights between Taiwan and the mainland during the Chinese Spring Festival holidays. However, direct links are seen, on both sides of the strait, to involve a key issue of political principle: the identity of the government in Taiwan. Is it separate but equal or, as Beijing argues, separate and subordinate?

Given the will, it is technically possible to have direct trade without resolving this fundamental issue. However, there is reluctance on both sides. Taiwan has security concerns. The mainland sees direct links – which would benefit Taiwan more than the mainland – as a bargaining tool in its effort to bring Taiwan to accept its interpretation of the meaning of One China.

This could change. The possibility has been aired of links being managed entirely by corporate entities with no formal official involvement. Definitions of One China can still be fudged or the niceties of direct links glossed over so that neither side deals officially with the other, just as negotiations, such as they are, are conducted through Taiwan's Straits Exchange Foundation and its mainland counterpart, the Association for Relations Across the Taiwan Strait, both beholden to their governments but not part of them.

But suspicion and reluctance remain. The mainland does not want to make the One China definition too fuzzy, at least while the U.S. continues to provide support for Taiwan's de facto independence. Shorter term, it also has some concerns about the negative impact on Hong Kong and Macao, both still suffering some lingering negative effects of reunification as well as of the aftermath of the Asian crisis. Loss of transit trade would not be as important now as a few years ago, when a higher proportion of China's export industries were located in the southern coastal provinces. Nonetheless, direct links would hurt Hong Kong trade and tourism and perhaps enable Taiwan's financial services to develop an axis with nearby Shanghai which would further weaken Hong Kong's position. From the Taiwan standpoint, although no one doubts the lower business costs of direct links, transit through Hong Kong and Macao has become so sophisticated that the commercial gains would be limited, particularly for IT products which move by air. The benefits of direct links would be mainly for Taiwan's service sector – finance, shipping, and aviation.

But it will take a while longer, and perhaps a more serious recession than in 2001, for Taiwan to stop paying some price for what its government believes is a need to keep a check on cross-straits traffic for fear of over-dependence on the mainland.

Meanwhile, Beijing's policy toward the island is significantly influenced by short-term political considerations as well as strategic goals. Periods of economic stress have caused doubts about the reform program to come to the surface. These find a home with nationalists, with some backing from military elements, who feel that too many concessions have been made to the U.S., to Taiwan, and to the outside world in general, in pursuit of economic goals. Surviving leftists resent the leadership's quasi-capitalist economic goals as well as the soft approach to Taiwan. Leadership struggles, should they occur, also have a potential to use being "tough on Taiwan" as a rallying point. There may be little difference in ideology, but as democratic politics in the West also show, factional and personal power struggles can exaggerate small policy and have results that are not in the rational national interest.

CHINA IN ASIA: FROM NATIONALISM TO ECONOMIC ENGAGEMENT

Today's Chinese nationalism is more a product of recent success than of the glories of an old civilization which the Communist Party mostly rejected anyway. As a result, so long as the economy and modernization continue to flourish under the impact of the outward-looking policy, the reactive elements, nationalist or leftist, seem unlikely to be able to challenge the consensus that Deng created and Jiang Zemin built upon.

But that poses both China and its Asian neighbors with questions about the role, goals, and priorities of the new China. Economics, ethnic issues, and territorial questions intertwine. Despite – or perhaps because of – its size and age, it has relatively little experience of dealing with foreign countries. Either they were nearby "barbarians," like the Mongols or later the Russians and Japanese, to be sometimes feared. Or they were small states on the periphery or across the South China Sea, which – as with the case of Vietnam– were occasionally punished for insubordination but could usually be ignored. Embassies of tribute from Southeast Asia were mostly to gain trading privileges rather than acknowledgment of fealty to the emperor in Beijing.

China's most obvious presence in Asia from the latter Ming period was indeed the reaction of entrepreneurial Chinese, mostly from remote southern provinces, against trade, migration, and consorting with foreigners. Large-scale exodus of Chinese was a 19th-century phenomenon, as Chinese sought work and trading opportunities in Southeast Asia as colonial rule brought mines, plantations and steamships, as well as political oppression.

But it is not just in Southeast Asia that demographic pressure and overseas opportunity has spurred the expansion of the Chinese people. China's self-image is of a self-contained, non-expansionist country. However, some neighbors see it differently, noting the relatively recent Sinicization of Taiwan, Manchuria, and latterly Xinjiang, through migration made possible by Beijing's political supremacy. The 20th century saw many twists in the relationship between China and its neighbors. The Japanese invasion led to an upsurge in overseas Chinese identification with the motherland, a process much encouraged by the Kuomintang. The overseas Chinese were themselves to suffer when Japan occupied much of Southeast Asia in 1941–42. Anti-Japanese sentiment also created a bond with Koreans and even Vietnamese. However, in Malay Southeast Asia there was some resentment that overseas Chinese were perceived to owe their loyalty elsewhere, and often too, if only for commercial reasons, to make common cause with the Western colonialists.

That partly changed after the communist revolution in China. In the anti-colonial spirit of the times, Chairman Mao urged overseas Chinese either to come back to China or stay where they were and be loyal citizens. However, Beijing's abandonment of its claims to the loyalty of overseas Chinese could not overcome the new perception that Chinese were now the spearhead for communist revolution in Asia, as demonstrated by their lead role in the Malayan insurgency as well as by China's direct participation in the Korean War. Suspicion of Chinese reached its zenith with the massacres of communists and their supposed sympathizers in Indonesia in 1965.

The Cultural Revolution removed any attractions China might previously have had to overseas Chinese in the region. There was no need to identify with China, which anyway was looking inward, and the U.S. provided an umbrella should it – or any other power – show aggressive intent.

However, the era of Deng Xiaoping – fortuitously beginning shortly after the end of the Vietnam War – opened a new chapter in China's relations with the region. It was seen as a new opportunity, and threat. On the one hand, China began to open its doors to trade and other linkages, and abandoned attempts to export revolutionary ideology. On the other hand, it became more assertive on issues of national and territorial interest. There was the costly war to "punish" Vietnam in 1979, and the advancement of its claims to the South China Sea through the occupation of some small islands, the build-up of naval capability, and the elaboration of claims to regard the whole sea as being part of its territory.

The past 20 years have seen a series of incidents, particularly involving Vietnam and the Philippines, as China has sought from time to time to advance its claims. There have been no overt disputes with Malaysia although it occupies some islands and China's claims reach to within a few miles of the coast of east Malaysia. Kuala Lumpur has been keen to play down the South China Sea issue while doing more than the other Southeast Asian claimants to build up its capability to defend the islands it occupies.

The whole South China Sea issue has troubled ASEAN, which has tried to find some common ground to engage China in dialogue on the issue. However, while being willing to discuss cooperation on scientific and economic issues, and to take part in so-called confidence-building meetings, China maintains that any formal discussions over boundaries, fishing and sea-bed rights, and so on, must be bilateral. The South China Sea is often seen as a struggle for its oil and gas resources. However, the potential for these has been greatly exaggerated. Commercial finds have been made in the shallow waters off Vietnam, Brunei, Malaysia, the Philippines, and China itself. But they are mostly small, at least by the standards of China's energy needs. Fishing is an issue, too, but again not critical. The greatest value of the sea is strategic – in particular, the sea lanes which link the Taiwan and Luzon straits to the Singapore and Malacca straits. Though the sea itself is large, due to its islets, rocks, and shoals the lanes for big ships are fairly narrow.

Particularly since the Asian economic crisis, China's stance on the South China Sea has been less assertive. That is not to say it is in any way retreating from either its claims or long-term goals. Time, it believes, is on its side. However, both China and its neighbors have given priority to enhancing their economic relationship. They see the benefit of increased economic cooperation, and China sees that its longer-term goals of expanding its influence in the region are best served through extending its economic and diplomatic reach, rather than suggesting to its neighbors that it desires to turn the South China Sea into a Chinese lake, or to supplant a distant U.S. hegemonism with its own. Whatever the political issues, there are natural linkages between the two. Southeast Asia has close trading and financial ties to the West and Japan dating to colonial times. Much of that business is in the hands of ethnic Chinese with ties to Hong Kong and Taiwan. So it was only natural that when China opened up, its regional linkages would expand along with its exports to the West. Chinese from Southeast Asia, as from Hong Kong, had emotional as well as practical reasons for investing, particularly in the southern coastal areas from which their forefathers mostly came.

The rapid growth of trade and investment had only a limited impact at the official level from 1997 onwards. The Asian crisis unfolded two years after

China had stabilized itself after the early 1990s' boom by devaluing its currency, ending the dual exchange system, and reining in inflation. When the crisis hit, Japan, preoccupied with its own problems and pushed around by Washington, was, despite its wealth and reserves, of little help to its neighbors. China, on the other hand, vowed to help by not devaluing its currency. The fact that its own earlier devaluation was one ingredient in the crisis and that it had no need to do so again was largely forgotten. China gained immense kudos internationally as well as in Asia.

Subsequently, while Japan has stagnated and other Asian countries have wrestled with the aftermath of the crisis, China's economy has steamed ahead remarkably. It has continued to gain market share around the world, and in the U.S. in particular, despite the advantages that the rest of East Asia gained from the 1997–98 devaluations, and in the face of a strong dollar, overcapacity, and falling prices. While other economies with dollar pegs struggled – as with Hong Kong – or like Argentina collapsed – China continued to pile up trade surpluses and reserves. The lure of China was further increased by the expectation, eventually fulfilled, that it would join the WTO.

LOOKING BEYOND THE VACUUM EFFECT

There is no question that China has been gaining market share to some extent at the expense of its Asian neighbors. Even in the first quarter of 2002, China's exports to the U.S. continued to expand at double-digit rates while other Asian exporters saw minimal growth. Behind this export boom is an even sharper increase in China's share of foreign direct investment (FDI). There are real concerns that in Southeast Asia it will continues to draw capital away from the region, and that its combination of low labor costs and high skill levels will drive many businesses elsewhere – in Southeast as well as Northeast Asia – to the wall.

The questions: is that true? And true or not, what should the response be?

The FDI trend is real but is partly one of cycles. Over-investment in Southeast Asia and Korea helped create the Asian crisis. It was naturally followed by a downturn. China suffers from overcapacity in many industries but has been able to attract new ones partly because of the strength of its Northeast Asian neighbors – Taiwan, Korea, and Japan – in what has been the great growth industry of the decade – IT. Add in the desire of multinationals to get a foothold in this huge market, regardless of cost, at a time when the WTO is opening up new avenues, and it is not surprising that China has done exceptionally well. But that does not mean it will continue to do so, at least once the multinationals have established their base.

China has anyway yet to prove it is competitive in non-labor-intensive industries. Its car industry, for example, is uncompetitive even by Malaysian standards, let alone Korean ones. Industrial fragmentation is much more common in a huge China with poor internal transport than in smaller countries whose major cities are mostly close to the coast. The export success is attributable more to FDI than to broader-based improvements in competitiveness. Foreign-invested companies' share of export has been rising steadily and some evidence now suggests that it is over 50%. There is nothing necessarily wrong with that, but it does indicate a vulnerability to the foreigners' investment decisions or ability to continue high rates of investment given widespread global overcapacity and weak profits. Korea and Taiwan were successful in challenging Japanese dominance in several fields, notably electronics, more because of the dynamism of their home-grown enterprises than because of lower labor costs. China has shown that it is a great location for foreign manufacturers, but its own firms have yet to make much of a mark or to suggest that they can compete with Taiwanese and Korean ones.

Overall, the region continues to benefit from the boost to specialization that China's opening has brought. The surge in regional trade is partly the result of this process. Value added may lag well behind gross trade value expansion and the end market may still be in the West. However, less noticed has been the huge expansion of China's two-way trade with Japan and Korea. Both countries now source many low-end finished goods such as garments from China while also using assembly plants in China as a way into the domestic market. Thus, while much of the world has been complaining about the ill effects of Japan's stagnation, its immediate neighbors have been making good gains in its market. Japan is still just ahead of the U.S. as China's largest trading partner and, despite high-profile rows over items such as garlic, the balance of trade between the two suggests that major trade problems are far less likely than with the U.S. The same applies to Korea, now China's third-largest trading partner.

Of course, neighbors in Southeast and Northeast Asia are reasonably concerned about implicit subsidies given to favoured companies through China's banking system, in addition to the system of administered pricing that creates unfair competition. Meanwhile, with or without the WTO, foreign access to local markets also runs up against local restrictions beyond the effective control of the central government. But the more measured view is that China is not about to overwhelm either the northeast in high technology or the southeast in market flexibility, openness, or level of institutional development.

The fundamental attraction of China is that it is increasing overall demand in East Asia. This includes primary commodities such as palm oil and rubber and tertiary industries such as tourism. Thailand, Malaysia, and Hong Kong, in particular, have hugely benefited from the surge in mainland tourism made possible by easier access to foreign exchange resulting from China's huge trade surpluses. Likewise, in looking to secure supplies of raw materials, China is looking to the neighborhood, where possible. Thus, for example, state enterprises such as Petrochina have been buying into Indonesian oil fields.

Not only has regional trade expanded on a broad base, but there is a growing realization that it will need to continue to do so. The U.S. market is widely viewed as approaching, or exceeding, saturation and the EU growth will be slow as it faces some of the same demographic hurdles and structural rigidities as Japan.

Regional integration, in which China is playing a pivotal role, is proceeding on two fronts: central bank cooperation and trade agreements. The first began in earnest following the Asian currency crisis. Agreements are now in place for swaps to guard against the kind of cascade effect seen in 1997–98. China, with its burgeoning reserves and reputation for currency stability, has played an important role in this. Whether the amounts involved are sufficient is another matter, but the growth of reserves and the reduction of short-term debts since 1998 has greatly reduced the likelihood of a generalized crisis.

However, regional cooperation is retarded by lack of trust between China and Japan. Moreover, Japan's own problems have prevented it from playing a leading role when it has both the largest reserves and a convertible currency. China, on the other hand, has a non-convertible currency and for now has pegged its exchange rate to the dollar, while neighbors such as Taiwan, Korea, and even Thailand and Singapore, have floating currencies and relatively few controls on capital flows. It seems likely that China will soon adopt a more flexible exchange rate regime in line with the regional trend, aiming for stability against a basket of currencies of its main trading partners. But full convertibility looks a long way off. The Asian crisis taught China lessons in the dangers of too fast capital account liberalization, particularly for countries with impaired banking systems. Although China's major banks, being state-owned, will not go bust, they remain probably the weakest part of the economy. China has recently given signs that it will allow some liberalization of portfolio investment – for example, through a form of Qualified Foreign Investor (QFII) certification, and vice versa through a QDII system. Hong Kong lobbying to allow mainlanders some access to its market may be successful. The authorities also recognize that, eventually, the A and B share markets will converge, in pricing and in fact.

But the bottom line of closer regional currency cooperation is that it must begin with the yen, which is already the biggest single influence on the won and the NT dollar, and a major influence on the Singapore dollar and Thai baht. China is reluctant to see Japan play a lead role, partly because of historical rivalry and partly because it has a greater dependence on the U.S. market and thus less need to think in terms of other currencies. However, over time, China will probably adjust. The extent of its acceptance and that to which East Asian currencies move toward closer cooperation, and thereby promote trade and investment flows and currency stability, remains to be seen. Much depends on changes in the international financial architecture, a subject much discussed since the Asian crisis but on which there has been scant progress. That, in turn, may hinge on the role of the U.S. dollar in international markets and the existence of major and rapid currency alignments similar to the shocks which ended the Bretton Woods system in 1971.

China and its neighbors have more control over how they manage their trade affairs. Parallel to its joining WTO, there has been much talk of regional free trade agreements (FTAs). Singapore has negotiated an FTA with Japan (as well as with other countries outside the region), and Korea has begun discussion of one with Japan. ASEAN already has its AFTA, which, for the original ASEAN six, has already reduced tariffs on most manufactured goods to very low levels. In a bold move in 2001, China and ASEAN set a 10-year timetable for an FTA between them.

That prospect scares some ASEAN countries, worried about their competitiveness, while others view it as more of a political gesture than a likely eventuality. Some believe that it would make more sense for AFTA to link first to Japan and Korea – although the high protection of agriculture in those countries is a huge obstacle given the importance of agricultural exports for most of ASEAN. (Singapore can easily sign FTAs, because it has no agriculture sector and scant protection of manufacturing.)

There has also been a suggestion for a China/Hong Kong/Macao FTA. Again, this would seem feasible because the two former colonial territories have no agriculture and even their manufacturing sectors are now small. Hong Kong would particularly like preferential access to the mainland's service sector. However, the definition of a "Hong Kong company" would be a major obstacle. China would not want Hong Kong to be a backdoor for foreign companies to get better access to its market than provided by WTO. At the same time, Hong Kong as an international center needs to be wary of giving privileges to Chinese nationals that are not available to other Hong Kong-based businesses.

How far and how fast these regional FTAs develop is uncertain. If world trade expands smoothly under WTO rules, the need for them may be limited. For now, however, they do provide some incentive for general liberalization of trade – in services as well as goods. In the event that world trade runs into huge new problems of protectionism – more episodes like the U.S. steel tariffs and farm subsidy increases – the regional agreements could form a basis for keeping regional trade expanding in the face of global contraction. At the very least, the regional trade discussions reflect how rapidly regional trade has advanced, in large part due to the role of China as both an import market and a location for regionally integrated manufacturing. Maintaining that momentum, perhaps in the face of major problems in the U.S. market, is a key not just to regional relationships and China's role. It is central, too, to the continuation of China's modernization and market-oriented reform.

That brings us back to the beginning of the story: WTO is the symbol of the economic issues at the center of China's enterprise reform process and of the primacy of medium-term economic issues in relations with the U.S., Taiwan, and the rest of Asia. In turn, those feed the modernization which is the road to the long-term political goals of national reunification and regional dominance.

China and the New East Asian Regionalism

Zhang Yunling[*]

INTRODUCTION

Regionalism is prevailing in today's world. With the great success of the European Union (EU), the ambitious plans for a Free Trade Area of the Americas (FTAA), and even the African nations' decision to move toward a union, the countries of East Asia have felt both pressure and the necessity to forge ahead with their own form of cooperation. The 2001 ASEAN Plus Three (APT) meeting (10 ASEAN countries plus China, Japan, and the Republic of Korea (ROK)) (also known as "10 + 3"), which was held in Brunei in November of that year, has drawn a great deal of attention. The East Asian leaders firmly committed themselves to the process of East Asian cooperation by further strengthening the mechanism of dialogue and institutional development. They studied the long-term vision of East Asian cooperation presented by the East Asian Vision Group (EAVG). Agreement was reached by the 10 ASEAN country members together with China on a free trade area (FTA) to be formalized within 10 years; and progress was made in talks between China, Japan, and the ROK aimed at strengthening their cooperation through starting a formal economic ministers meeting.

However, the process of East Asian cooperation will continue to follow the current framework (that is, "10 + 3") in the near future, rather than a clearly defined goal under an "East Asia" label. The current "10 + 3" movement is led by ASEAN. It seems that countries in the region still need some time to consolidate their long-term goals and determine an appropriate path toward real regional integration.

[*] Zhang Yunling is Professor, Director of the Institute of Asian and Pacific Studies, Chinese Academy of Social Sciences. Professor Zhang served as a member of the East Asian Vision Group, and was also a member of the China–ASEAN Economic Cooperation Expert Group.

THE EAST ASIAN CONVERGENCE

East Asian economic convergence, which began in the 1960s, could be said to have followed a "flying geese model" led by Japan and followed by the four "dragon" economies (ROK, Singapore, Hong Kong, and Taiwan), as well as some Southeast Asian countries and China. This model helped to build up a "vertical" chain through capital flows, technological transfers, and the supply of manufacturing parts, thus formulating a high-level intra-regional integration based on market exchange. Until the mid-1990s, intra-regional trade in East Asia accounted for more than 50% of trade in the region.

ASEAN started its Free Trade Area (AFTA) as early as 1992, but its role as a leader in facilitating FTAs in the whole of East Asia is marginal. The 1997 financial crisis was an important turning point, since it changed both the environment and structure of East Asian economic growth and integration.

Not surprisingly, as an aftermath of the financial crisis, there emerged a new push for regional cooperation, which led to the first APT leaders' meeting (at that time, 9 + 3) in Kuala Lumpur in November 1997. The aim of that meeting was clear: to achieve early economic recovery and prevent another such crisis. This is a very important historical event, since it opened the way for a real regional cooperation process based on regional interests and a newly defined regional identity – that is, East Asia.

This East Asian convergence goes beyond market integration by desiring governmental cooperation and institution-building.[1] East Asian regionalism finds its rationale not just in economic benefits, but also in political interests. Compared with other regions, East Asia is late in forging regional FTAs and other institutional establishments compared to other regions of the world. Aside from an intra-regional desire for a closer partnership, East Asia's new regionalism is also considered to be a rational response to the progress of other regions, especially to the establishment of the North American Free Trade Agreement (NAFTA).[2] By definition, East Asian economic integration started as early as the 1960s based on regional economic growth and only moving in tandem with the market operating independently while the process

---

[1] As argued by Shujiro Urata in "A Shift from Market-led to Institutional-led Regional Economic Integration in East Asia," Paper prepared for the Conference on Asian Economic Integration organized by the Research Institute of Economy, Trade and Industry, Japan, April 22–23, 2002, Tokyo, p. 1.

[2] It is considered that Prime Minister Mahathir's proposal of forming an East Asian Economic Caucus (EAEC) is a direct response to NAFTA. Peter Drysdale and Kenichi Ishigaki (eds.), *East Asian Trade and Financial Integration: New Issues* (Canberra: Asia-Pacific Press, 2002), p. 6.

of regional cooperation through regional institutional arrangements or formal governmental efforts began only in the late 1990s.

However, as a process of regional cooperation and integration, there are still many unfavorable factors. Political disarray makes many countries distant and distrustful. For example, it is still difficult for China and Japan to become real partners. Tensions existing on the Korean peninsula and across the Taiwan Strait have given rise to a situation of uncertainty and instability in the East Asian region. Economic convergence and regional cooperation will surely help to bridge the gap and create new trust, but political distrust may slow down or even obstruct the cooperation process.

The Progress of East Asian Cooperation

At the inaugural November 15, 1997 APT meeting, the main topics for discussion were: the prospects for the development of East Asia in the 21st century; cooperation between Asia and Europe; the Asian financial crisis; the deepening of regional economic ties; and coordination and cooperation on international economic issues. A considerable consensus was reached at the meeting on those topics, at which the leaders of the attending countries gave a clear political signal that cooperation in the East Asian region should be strengthened.

On December 16, 1998, the second meeting of the leaders of East Asia was held in Hanoi, Vietnam. This meeting accomplished concrete results, pushing East Asian cooperation in the direction of pragmatism. The main topics for discussion at that meeting were: strengthening regional cooperation; overcoming the financial crisis; the recovery of regional economic growth; and the promotion of regional security and stability. The participating Chinese leader, Vice President of the State Hu Jintao, put forward a concrete proposal for East Asian cooperation: that a meeting of vice ministers of finance and deputy presidents of central banks be held to discuss the issues of international financial reform and the supervision and control of short-term capital flows. All of the participating leaders of East Asia unanimously agreed to the Chinese proposal. This made it possible for the East Asian region to begin to have dialogue and consultation among high-level government functional organs for the first time, and to seek to establish a cooperative mechanism to deal with the major economic issues in the region.

The third APT meeting was held in Manila on November 28, 1999. The main topic for discussion at that meeting was how to promote cooperation in the East Asian region. The meeting was an important turning point and a new starting point for East Asian cooperation because it reached a consensus on the principles and key areas for promoting East Asian cooperation. For the first time, the leaders of East Asia issued a Joint Statement on East Asian Cooperation. This statement emphasized the leaders' determination "to realize East Asia cooperation in various fields." The leaders, moreover, "expressed greater determination to further deepen and expand East Asia cooperation and to work in the direction of laying stress on actual results, effectively improving the life quality of the people in East Asia and promoting the stability of the region in the 21st century." In addition, the statement listed a number of focal points for cooperation in the economic and social fields, as well as political and other fields, as follows:[3]

- *In the field of economic cooperation:* to accelerate trade, investment, and technology transfer; encourage technical cooperation in the area of technology and e-commerce; encourage cooperation in industry and agriculture; strengthen cooperation of small and medium-sized enterprises; launch industrial forums in East Asia; promote the establishment of East Asian economic growth zones, such as the development of the Mekong River valley; consider the establishment of an East Asian Economic Committee, and so on.

- *In the field of monetary and financial cooperation:* to strengthen regional supervision and control over the macro-management of economic risks, company management, and capital flows; intensify policy dialogue, coordination, and cooperation in such areas as the banking and financial systems; and strengthen the mechanisms of regional self-preservation and self-help in a framework of 10 + 3.

- *In the field of social and human resources:* to give impetus to the implementation of the proposal of ASEAN for the development of human resources and the establishment of a Human Resources Development Fund. Cooperation in the field of scientific and technological development, as well as in the cultural and information field, was also emphasized. Leaders also called for strengthened cooperation in development and to encourage sustainable development of the economy; to increase dialogue, coordination, and cooperation in the political and security fields and strengthen mutual understanding and trust; and to strengthen cooperation on transnational issues.

The fourth meeting of leaders, held in Singapore on November 24, 2000, worked out concrete measures for carrying out the focal points of cooperation decided upon in the statement of the leaders in 1999 and affirmed the "Chiang

---

[3] "Leaders' Joint Statement on East Asian Cooperation (November 28, 1999)", Manila, *People's Daily*, November 29, 1999.

Mai Initiative" reached at the meeting of ministers of finance in May 2000 on monetary cooperation. At the same time, it further decided on a plan of action on training in the financial sector and the development of human resources, and advanced a specific plan of action to speed up the construction of infrastructure in the Mekong River valley. In this connection, China promised to provide funds and technology for clearing up the waterways of the Mekong River and the building of the Kunming–Bangkok highway. In addition, the East Asian leaders promised to take joint actions on transnational issues, such as ways to deal with smuggling, drugs, and piracy. The practical working style and the positive posture oriented toward the future demonstrated at the meeting laid a sound foundation for the further, and deepened, cooperation in East Asia in the 21st century.

The fifth meeting of leaders was held in Brunei on November 5, 2001. The leaders gave continuing support to the East Asian cooperation process under the structure of 10 + 3. They discussed the vision report for long-term East Asian cooperation proposed by the East Asian Vision Group. The key recommendations made by EAVG are:[4]

1   To establish an East Asian Free Trade Area (EAFTA). In the long run, the Vision Group envisions the creation of an East Asian Economic Community.

2   To coordinate macroeconomic policy and financial market regulations, cooperate in monitoring capital flows, build self-help and support mechanisms, and work toward capital market development and eventual monetary integration in the region.

3   To promote coordination and joint action to combat common challenges such as drug trafficking, piracy, illegal migration, environmental disasters, money laundering, international terrorism, and other trans-border crimes.

4   To set up a regional organization, consisting of both existing national and regional scientific organizations, to identify and coordinate science and technology activities in the East Asian region.

5   To provide a strong mandate for the creation of an institutional mechanism for regional cooperation, with the ultimate goal of the establishment of a regional entity, the East Asia Community.

---

[4] *East Asian Vision Group Report*, Seoul, 2001.

The leaders did not immediately adopt the above key recommendations, but instructed the study group formed of senior officials from the 13 members to study the recommendations and work out a plan for implementation. In a special statement, the leaders also committed themselves to cooperate on anti-terrorism. In addition, the leaders of Northeast Asia – that is, China, Japan and the ROK – agreed to establish formal economic and trade ministers' meetings. This is an important step for the three countries in consolidating East Asian cooperation. However, the surprising news during the meeting was that China and ASEAN agreed on establishing a free trade and investment zone within 10 years.

Toward an East Asian FTA?
The agreement between the leaders of China and ASEAN on establishing a free trade area reflects closer relations between the two sides. In the past decade, China–ASEAN trade has increased rapidly from a low level: ASEAN's share in China's merchandise trade increased to 8.3% in 2000 from 5.8% in 1991, making ASEAN China's fifth-largest trade partner; while China's share in ASEAN's trade rose from 2.1% to 3.9% at the same time, making China ASEAN's sixth-largest trade partner. The establishment of an FTA between China and ASEAN will create an economic region with 1.7 billion people, a GDP about US$2 billion, and trade involving about US$1.23 billion (at present). According to the simulation conducted by the ASEAN Secretariat, a China–ASEAN FTA would increase ASEAN's exports to China by 48% and China's export to ASEAN by 55.1%. It would increase China's GDP by 0.3%, or by US$2.2 billion in absolute terms; and ASEAN's GDP by 0.9%, or by US$5.4 billion.[5]

The negotiation and conclusion of such an FTA between China and ASEAN will be hard work. Fortunately, 10 years allows time and flexibility to adjust and implement, and ASEAN has a ready model in the AFTA. The significance of establishing an FTA between China and ASEAN goes beyond economic benefits. There exist various disputes, and even conflicts, between China and ASEAN. A closer economic integration will contribute immensely to peace and stability between the two blocs. Of course, it will also contribute to peace and stability in East Asia, as well as in the Asia-Pacific region at large.

---

[5] *Forging Closer ASEAN–China Economic Relations in the Twenty-first Century*, Report by the ASEAN–China Expert Group on Economic Cooperation, Jakarta, 2001.

However, some people are still concerned about the impact such an FTA might have on the process of East Asian cooperation.[6] From a positive perspective, it may encourage Japan and the ROK to formulate a free trade arrangement with ASEAN; or it may press China, the ROK, and Japan to facilitate their closer economic arrangement, based on which an East Asian FTA (EAFTA) can be negotiated. In this consideration, a China–ASEAN FTA should be considered as a positive step in the process of East Asian cooperation. But due to the great divergence of the East Asian economies, a real FTA for the entire region is still a dream. Three major economies – Japan, China, and the ROK – will find great difficulty in agreeing on an FTA in the near future, although they already have a high level of integration forged by increasing business (trade and investment) among them.

The Goal of East Asian Cooperation

After several years of development, a general framework for East Asian cooperation has been established, which includes an annual leaders' meeting, regular ministers' meetings, and the senior officials' meetings. Along with the development of the process of cooperation, other mechanisms will be set up. East Asian cooperation has just made a start. At present, it is moving ahead on the basis of a "four wheels" process. The first wheel is the regular "10 + 3" – that is, cooperation in the entire area of East Asia. The second wheel is "10 + 1" – that is, ASEAN cooperation separately with China, Japan, and the ROK. The leaders' meeting of this group is synchronized with "10 + 3." The third wheel is "3" – that is, the cooperation between China, Japan, and the ROK; and the fourth wheel is the cooperation within ASEAN itself. The moving of four wheels at the same time conforms to the reality in East Asia at present. In the initial stage of East Asian cooperation, it is necessary to allow and even encourage the development of a multiple mechanism.

However, the integration of all tracks and the move toward an East Asian identity are of great importance. One approach is to enlarge ASEAN by encouraging other countries to join, so that ASEAN will cover the whole East Asian region. The system and form of the present ASEAN will be carried on. Due to the great weight of China, Japan, and the ROK, ASEAN will have difficulty absorbing them. Another option is to encourage the Northeast Asian countries to develop their own identity and to cooperate with ASEAN,

---

[6] It has been stated that the "challenge is to work out how they fit together in the regionalism portfolio." Christopher Findlay and Mari Pangestu, "Regional Trade Arrangements in East Asia: Where Are They Taking Us?" Paper presented at the PECC Trade Policy Forum symposium, Bangkok, June 12–13, 2001, p. 20.

eventually integrating into one organization for the East Asian region. The problem is that three major countries – Japan, China, and the ROK – will not easily forge a genuine community or FTA. The most feasible way is to create a regional organization in the early stage to coordinate the regional tracks. As a first step, a secretariat needs to be set up for "10 + 3" as soon as possible, followed by the establishment of a regional organization called the Organization for East Asian Cooperation (OEAC) before 2010.

Institution-building is crucial for the process of East Asian cooperation. OEAC will have a secretariat and functional committees. It will not only continue the current activities, but also develop new functions. The annual leaders' meeting will be, of course, a core activity. OEAC will not replace or unify other multi-layered arrangements in the region in the near future. However, efforts should be made in developing a framework and institutions on the regional level, such as the EAFTA, financial arrangements, and sub-regional development projects. Political and security cooperation should also be finally integrated into OEAC. Of course, OEAC's major role is organizing and coordinating, rather than mandating, regional affairs. Finally, OEAC should extend its membership to all East Asian countries.

The long-term objective of cooperation among the East Asian economies is for the region to recognize itself as integrated and with shared common interests and regional institutions. Viewed from a geographical position, an economic focus, and a practical angle, three large regions exist in the world today: The European Union, North America, and East Asia. The EU, starting with the establishment of an economic community by six countries, has now developed into a pan-European organization composed of most European countries, with a high-degree of economic and political integration. In North America, the United States, Canada, and Mexico have concluded a free trade agreement and established a free trade zone. In future, this free trade zone will expand to the whole of America to form a Free Trade Area of the Americas. In comparison, cooperation in the East Asian region lags behind. Although progress has been made in starting cooperation, East Asia still lacks a clear vision for long-term cooperation. It is in their own interests for the East Asian countries to strengthen cooperation among themselves. They should cooperate in a practical way and promote institutional building gradually.

Given the actual circumstances and possibilities at present in East Asia, economic and trade cooperation should be taken as the focal point in the initial stage of cooperation. The goal of economic and trade cooperation is to promote regional economic development through the establishment of regional free trade and investment arrangements. It may start with reducing trade barriers through trade and investment facilitation in areas such as customs procedures, trade disputes, personnel travel, and so on. At the same time, arrangements should be made to reduce and finally eliminate (obviously, step by step) the tariff and non-tariff barriers in the region in order finally to establish a free trade and investment zone.

Economic cooperation goes beyond free trade. Progress has already been reached in some areas; among other examples are financial cooperation, the development of the Great Mekong River Sub-region, the construction of the Europe–Asia railway, and cooperation in agriculture and food production, and in the development of human resources. Regional cooperative projects in the fields of energy, the environment, technology, and scientific research are already under way and can be further developed. Certainly, in this respect, the coordination of laws and regulations, and the links and collaboration in the planning of regional infrastructure – for example, the coordination of taxation and market rules and the connection of trans-regional communications – are also important. The main goals are not to establish engineering projects funded and managed by the governments of the various countries, but to create conditions through inter-governmental cooperation for enterprises and scientific research institutes.

For the long term, it is essential to develop cooperation based on institution-building. In areas such as regional monetary mechanisms, or regional funds, the door should not be closed. It is urgent that the regional swap arrangements based on the "Chiang Mai Initiative" be completed. Other areas, such as committees for trade and investment promotion, and for regional environment cooperation, should also be considered.

In view of the tremendous political differences among the East Asian countries, the objective of the political cooperation in East Asia may not lie in establishing a supra-national regional political organization and conferring upon it supra-national laws and administrative power, as in Europe, but rather to establish a mechanism of political consultation among the countries in the region, in order to strengthen political identification, and to alleviate and facilitate the settlement of contradictions and conflicts that have occurred or may occur. Through political cooperation, political understanding and trust among countries in this region will be increased and a mechanism for alleviating and settling disputes and conflicts will be established.

The focal points of the security cooperation are to strengthen consultation and dialogue, to stabilize the regional situation, to resolve conflicts, and to prevent the occurrence of conflicts, especially military conflicts. There exist among the East Asian countries various historical grievances and emerging differences and disputes. Without cooperation in security, economic and political cooperation will not succeed. It will be very difficult to establish a unified organization of common security in East Asia. However, East Asia should have its own security cooperation. In the future, it may be considered advisable to establish an East Asia Security Council for conducting consultation and dialogue on regional security. For example, meetings of defense ministers may be convened regularly, and links with other national or regional security organizations may be established through the regional security cooperation committee for conducting dialogue and cooperation. These can be developed along with other existing security organizations.[7]

In the area of security cooperation, an important focus should be non-traditional security issues, such as terrorism and transnational crimes (drugs, smuggling, illegal immigration, and so on), which have become increasingly serious. Because these problems are fundamentally regional in nature, it is difficult to settle them by relying only on the strength of a single country.

In East Asia, cooperation in the cultural and educational fields is playing an increasingly important role. Efforts should be made to promote the establishment of a regional cultural and educational committee, the creation of a regional cultural and educational fund, and the construction of a cultural and educational information network. As an important move to encourage and support the flow of personnel, measures should be taken as early as possible to encourage mutual recognition of academic credentials. Student exchanges in this region should be encouraged, through a regional cultural and educational fund, to engage in further studies or to study in the universities in the countries of this region. Positive measures should be adopted to encourage and support students to study and conduct exchanges in the East Asian countries.

East Asian cooperation is an open-ended process. If a goal is set too high at the very beginning, it may be counter-productive. Therefore, we should proceed from a lower profile with realistic goals and specific projects. Gradual institution-building remains indispensable. Any proposal to establish a real community immediately may lead to doubts and misgivings. This is because people might associate the idea of such a community with the European model – namely, achieving a high degree of integration or coordination of the different countries' economies, politics, and security. In view of the vast differences in East Asia, it is obviously impossible to establish that kind of community. The composition of the East Asian community should have its own characteristics.

---

[7] Simon Tay argued that due to the crucial role and direct involvement of the United States in East Asian security, any East Asian institutional identity will fail if opposed by the U.S. "A New ASEAN in a New Millennium," p. 232.

The establishment of an East Asian community should mainly aim at building up mechanisms of regional cooperation and resolving common issues for the region.

The 1997–98 financial crisis was a driving force for promoting cooperation in East Asia, but the crisis has itself created difficulties in doing so. Recovery from economic difficulties is a key concern for the countries in the region.

The process of East Asian cooperation is actually one with strong political dimensions. Unlike European integration, which had a clear political goal from the very beginning, the political will of East Asian countries is not so strong. Due to their great diversity, consensus-building among East Asian countries is always very difficult.

Great concern has been raised about the attitudes and roles of China and Japan in the process of East Asian cooperation. It is obvious that East Asia cannot be highly integrated without the active participation of these two countries, and more importantly, without a real trust and cooperation between the two countries.

The process of achieving East Asian cooperation will not be smooth sailing. It will encounter a variety of difficulties and setbacks on the way. It will require the efforts of several generations. While it took half a century for Europe to fulfil its dream of integration, it will take even longer for East Asia to achieve its goal of establishing a real community with its own character.

Japan and China -
A Competitive Partnership

Victor L.L. Chu[*]

 The Japan-China relationship is of paramount importance in the Asia-Pacific region, and indeed globally, and its importance will increase in the coming decade. Right now, that relationship is more coexistence based on geographical and historical reality than a true partnership, with focused inputs from each side. While we cannot ignore this reality, we need to be able to envision, and then work to create, a more lasting and meaningful relationship between the two countries.

A COMPETITIVE PARTNERSHIP

When all is said and done, Japan and China are likely to endure a "competitive" partnership in the foreseeable future. This is a special relationship where the two countries are partners, and yet competitors, at the same time. This is almost inevitable because, although Japan and China have many traditional values and social characteristics in common, the two countries have pursued different models toward social and economic development over the last 50 years. Historical factors, including differing interpretations of the past and its impact on the present, also intervene and shape the way the two countries relate to each other. Finally, current economic and global trading conditions present further challenges.

Notwithstanding all of this, the effective management of this partnership will have an enormous impact in sustaining the economic prosperity and stability of Asia in the long term. By "effective" management, I mean that while remaining competitors in some areas, China and Japan must look for mutually beneficial "windows" to enhance competitiveness for both.

---

[*]Victor L.L. Chu is the Chairman of the First Eastern Investment Group, Hong Kong

Many writers and economists have explored potential economic synergies between Japan and China. Many commentators will agree that the most significant and obvious of these include the relocation of Japan-based manufacturing and research and development to China as a low-cost production base and the development of new consumer markets in China by Japanese consumer brands. I would like to explore a few new possibilities.

CATALYST FOR COOPERATION OUTSIDE OF JAPAN OR CHINA

Currently, most of the attention in terms of trade and investment is focused on traditional bilateral trade and investments between the two countries. We should look beyond this, to the exciting new frontier in which Japan and China act as catalysts for each other in developing new businesses or projects in other emerging economies in Asia, and perhaps even in the Gulf Cooperation Council (GCC) area.[1]

For example, some ASEAN economies did not immediately seize the chance to invest and do business in China, and are now anxious to jump on the bandwagon and participate in the dynamic growth of China's domestic market. Meanwhile, Japanese companies have a wealth of experience in ASEAN economies as well as in China. They were among the first movers in ASEAN and China and are therefore well positioned to add value to Southeast Asian companies that are seeking a guiding hand or supporting partner. This is particularly the case now that the "ASEAN plus" FTAs[2] have finally arrived.

At the same time, China's accession to the WTO will put pressure on major Chinese firms to expand regionally and globally in order to mitigate increasing foreign competition in their domestic market. Japan's industrial companies, with global reach and expertise, are ideal partners for Chinese companies that are keen to expand overseas but are lacking in international experience and cross-border know-how. Of course, joint entry by Japanese and Chinese companies into Southeast Asia needs to be well framed, so that it does not arouse unnecessary tensions. Southeast Asian countries are already

---

[1] The Gulf Cooperation Council seeks to strengthen cooperation (in areas such as agriculture, industry, investment, security, and trade) among its six members: Bahrain, Kuwait, Quatar, Oman, Saudi Arabia, and the United Arab Emirates.

[2] The idea of a free trade areas built around Asean has been mooted by numerous countries in the region, particularly in 2001 and 2002. Among those under consideration are "Asean+1" which refers to a free trade area between Asean and China, and "Asean+3", which includes Asean countries, China, Japan and South Korea.

aware that their export-driven economies are in some instances threatened by competition from China. The impact of adding a Japanese element must be portrayed in the right light.

The ongoing restructuring of Japan's corporate and financial sectors will also present Chinese companies with a unique opportunity to invest in Japanese businesses in order to tap Japanese marketing, production, and management expertise. Some Chinese companies have already begun to take advantage of this: for instance, the electronics maker Haier has inked deals with Sanyo for joint production and marketing products in China and Japan; it has similar deals with the Taiwanese electronics company Sampo. We should see a growing momentum of *two-way and three-way* cross-border merger and acquisition activities in the coming years.

The GCC countries represent another area of potentially huge significance. China has until now regarded these countries primarily in the context of establishing its energy security for the next period of growth. Japanese companies have also regarded East Asia as a first portal for investment and operations expansion. The Gulf area countries, meanwhile, harbor not only huge financial investment potential but also deep knowledge on tapping natural resources and the environment, and providing niche-service operations. Japan and China, representing different strengths, could approach this area of the world jointly.

CROSS-STRAITS ECONOMIC COOPERATION

We should also look at the growing potential that lies in the increasing economic ties between mainland China and Taiwan. This begins with investment from Taiwan into the mainland, which is believed to have exceeded US$100 billion already. Electronics and IT products receive much publicity, but trading and investment ties also exist for a wide array of products, such as footwear and toys.

It now seems possible that the so-called "Three Links"[3] between Taiwan and mainland China may be resumed in the foreseeable future after a suspension of 50 years. Taiwanese companies have already taken advantage of the mainland as a place to do business. In the fullness of time, progress on the "Three Links" could create the same opportunity for Chinese companies to do business in Taiwan. This would mean a tremendous inflow of Chinese direct investments into Taiwan across all the major business sectors. This could be a golden opportunity for Japanese companies to position themselves

---

[3] "Three links" refer to direct trade, postal and transport services across the Taiwan straits.

as strategic partners for Chinese companies as two-way cross-straits investment flows take off in earnest.

STATE-OWNED ENTERPRISES

Another dimension worth exploring is in the area of China's ongoing state-owned enterprise reform and the financing of private enterprises. Regarding SOE reform, the bottom line is that China's banking system needs to be radically reformed before time runs out. The root of the problem is the inefficiency of Chinese state-owned corporations. To perform surgery on the state-owned sectors, a properly funded social safety net must first be put in place so as to avoid potential social chaos. The funding of that social security system will partly rely on the sale of the State's holdings in these enterprises (effectively privatization), more than 1,000 of which have already been listed on the Chinese stock market.

Japan has had some success in unlocking and reducing the cross holdings among major listed companies. This expertise will be of tremendous value to China as it searches for different options for unloading the vast state holdings in listed companies without permanently damaging the stock market. On the other side, Japan's experience in building and maintaining a living social security system should also be of value to China as it searches for options.

A CHINA BOARD IN JAPAN?

Another interesting window of opportunity for Japan is the possibility of creating a market for successful *private* enterprises in China to seek international equity funding. Because of its internal priorities and regulatory considerations, China has yet to authorize the formal launching of a second board or an exchange catering to private enterprises wishing to go public. Private enterprises routinely identify the lack of access to capital as one of their primary hurdles in developing their businesses. And because of the large number of private enterprises that are already qualified for listings, there will be a capacity constraint even when a second board is introduced or a more fluid process for listings on the main board comes into being.

The Hong Kong Stock Exchange has captured the market for SOEs to access international capital markets, and at the same time, the Singapore and Shanghai stock exchanges have entered into partnership. Neither of these is targeting private enterprises, despite the need and potential. This may be a good opportunity for the Tokyo or the Osaka Stock Exchange to consider creating a China board to capture the best of these dynamic companies. Of course, a clear and sensible framework is needed for this to occur, and Japan could consider the H share program on the Hong Kong markets.

However, this could bring long-term strategic benefits to Japan's competitive partnership with China. Japanese investors will be able to participate in the rapid growth of some of the best companies in China, while these companies will be drawn much closer to Japan because of their listings here. Their listings will in turn stimulate exchange, business cooperation, and two-way knowledge sharing with Japanese companies both in Japan as well as regionally. Lastly, the listing of Chinese companies in Japan could also inject new attention and investment into the markets in Japan, where we should note steadily declining turnover and a decreasing number of new listings.

A RELATIONSHIP OF PARAMOUNT IMPORTANCE
I would like to conclude with one thought. China's economic growth has been, and will remain, spectacular – the combined result of the economy's size and the speed of its growth. The three strategic relationships that are most likely to impact on China's long march toward becoming an economic and geopolitical powerhouse are its relationships with Taiwan, with Asia, and with the United States. The Japan–China relationship is a nexus at the heart of all of these, and the countries are already among each other's top trading partners. At such a time of critical change for both economies – Japan seeking new alternatives for recapturing its growth, and China seeking new partners to sustain its growth – it is now time to further develop this special partnership and explore new angles.

Part 3
Views from the
Government

Looking Ahead Past WTO Entry

Chen Jinhua[*]

 In 2002, China was ranked sixth in the world in terms of total economic output and seventh in terms of the volume of foreign trade. These are indications that living standards in China have improved. Entering into the 21st century, China is actively implementing the third step of its strategic objective in the drive for modernization, that of striving to reach the level of the moderately developed countries in the world by 2020, and by 2050 basically realizing modernization of the economy. During the course of this modernization process, there will be tremendous business opportunities. During the Tenth Five-year Plan alone, China needs to import US$1.5 trillion-worth of products from all over the world.

China's entry into the World Trade Organization (WTO) marks its participation in economic globalization at a higher level and with a wider scope. It indicates a greater and deeper involvement of Chinese companies in global markets, in terms of cooperation and competition. It also brings about a higher and deeper level of competition of foreign players in the domestic market, and as such the major factors of competition in the international market will become component parts of competition domestically. To meet these new challenges, Chinese enterprises have been speeding up reforms, increasing productivity and efficiency, instituting more standardized forms of governance and management, and generally improving their overall quality.

We have our work clearly cut out for us with regard to WTO entry and we have already moved beyond the initial stages in absorbing our commitments. For example, in terms of investment, in early 2002 the government revised and promulgated the *Directory of Industries Opening to Foreign Investment*, which expanded the number of sectors open for foreign investment from 186 to 262, and expanded the allowable proportion of foreign shares in other

* Chen Jinhua is Vice Chairman of the Chinese People's Political Consultative Conference

industries. It has, in line with the spheres, quantity, business scope, share requirement, and timetable committed to by the Chinese government, further opened up service areas such as banking, insurance, foreign trade, tourism, telecommunications, transportation, accounting, auditing, and legal affairs. The new directory also further promotes foreign investment in the western regions of the country. The process of implementing these policy measures has already injected new vigor into the opening-up program. In the first 10 months of 2002, contracted foreign investment increased by over 35% as compared with the same period the previous year, and foreign investment utilization has also remained steady despite the downturn in the global economic climate.

The momentum of economic growth in China, coupled with the new stimulus of entering the WTO, the continuing flow of foreign investment, and the beginnings of more domestic private investment, enable us to have confidence in China's good prospects for continued development in terms of its economy and society. In formulating the objective of a 7% economic growth rate for 2002, the government based its estimates on a zero growth rate due to the grave international environment, in geopolitical and economic terms, at that time. Although the international situation has hardly improved, or at least has remained constant, our exports have continued to grow, exceeding our original forecasts. This has provided a new positive element for the realization of a 7% economic growth rate in 2002.

Nevertheless, China continues to face various problems, some of which could be difficult to solve. However, we are committed to the idea that development speaks for itself and in fact bolsters our ability to confront serious situations. This has been proven by the process of reform and opening-up in China over the past 20 years, during which the national economy has surmounted steeper and steeper challenges, and this trend will continue in the future. Needless to say, it continues to be important to study and promote active discussion of the prospects and problems faced by China after WTO entry and in view of the changing regional and international situations. Only through such exchanges of views can we spread knowledge and build upon past experiences to achieve even greater progress.

The history of mankind has proven that change is a tremendous dynamic for progress. Every great new era requires changes and will eventually bring about the changes demanded by its communities. Chinese entrepreneurs are willing to join with their international counterparts to discuss the widespread impact of the current era of changes, and to explore ways of sharing the fruits of those changes. I am convinced that, with our joint efforts, China's growth will continue to meet its current and future challenges and create further opportunities.

Accession to the WTO:
New Opportunities and Challenges Facing China's Socialist Market Economy

*Peng Sen**

We are at the beginning of the new millennium and looking into the future. I should like to take this opportunity to briefly review the course of China's reform and opening up.

China's economic restructuring started in 1978. Since that time, the way of thinking of over one billion Chinese people has profoundly changed. The reforms have also changed China's economic structure and social outlook. Many world statesmen have regarded reform as China's second Long March in its modern history; it is also said to be one of the most significant experiments for mankind in the 20th century. As a result of sustained efforts and arduous exploration, China has gradually achieved a significant transition from a planned economy to a market economy, and the basic framework of a socialist market economic system has taken initial shape, mainly with the following features.

Owing to a comprehensive adjustment of the ownership structure in the national economy, the proportion of the state-owned economy in terms of industrial output value has dropped to less than 30%, from 80% at the commencement of the reforms. Collective, individual, private, and foreign-owned companies are now able to compete on an equal footing under market conditions.

China's commodity market, capital market, and labor market have developed rapidly. Market forces play fundamental roles in fields such as pricing and allocation of resources. Prior to the reform, the state controlled the price of almost all commodities and the factors of production, whereas now it controls the price of only 13 commodities and services.

An initial framework of macro-regulation and a control system compatible

---

* Peng Sen is Vice Minister, State Council Office for Restructuring the Economic System.

with a market economy has taken shape, based mainly on financial and monetary policies.

Much progress has been achieved in the reform of state-owned enterprises (SOEs), with a focus on establishing a shareholding system, assets restructuring, and bankruptcy of unprofitable SOEs.

A new social security system has been put in place. A pension scheme, medical insurance, and unemployment insurance have been developed, with both a social pooling and individual account combined together.

An all-embracing opening-up pattern covering various levels and fields has been adopted throughout the country. China has taken an active part in international exchanges. So far, it has approved the establishment of 380,000 foreign-funded enterprises with agreed investment of US$726 billion and actual investment of over US$380 billion.

Reform and opening up have tremendously emancipated social productive forces, promoting China's impressive economic growth. During the past 23 years of reform, China's GDP has achieved an annual growth rate of 9.5%, and the overall import and export volume of foreign trade grew by 15.3% annually. China is now the world's seventh-largest economy in term of GDP and the ninth-largest in terms of the volume of foreign trade.

The world economy has slowed significantly in 2002. Some major economies have fallen into recession. International trade has declined by a significant margin. Under such circumstances, the Chinese economy has also been affected to some extent. To cope with this new and difficult situation, the Chinese government has adopted an expansionary policy to boost domestic demand. Meanwhile, efforts have also been made to expand exports and attract foreign direct investment (FDI). As a result, China's economy has continued to maintain a good momentum of growth. A growth rate of 7.4% is estimated to be achievable for 2002. Foreign trade will grow by 6%, and FDI will increase by over 20%. At the time of writing, China's foreign exchange reserve had reached US$203 billion.

Despite remarkable achievements made in the course of its reform and opening up, China still has some deep-rooted, unresolved problems. There still exist structural obstacles restricting the sustainability of its economic growth. The main problems are the lack of effective demand, irrationality of the industrial structure, the relatively low quality of economic growth, the backwardness of management systems, and the increased pressure of unemployment. In order to tackle these problems, further efforts must be made to deepen the reforms and to open the country wider to the outside world in order to improve China's socialist market economic system.

After 15 years of hard negotiations, China was finally accepted as a full member of the World Trade Organization (WTO) at the Doha conference held in the third quarter of 2001, I am convinced that China's accession to the WTO marks the beginning of a new stage in its economic restructuring and opening up. It will provide a new impetus for China's economic growth.

There is no doubt that the WTO accession will exert a great and far-reaching impact on China's economic development and social progress. In essence, China will strictly follow market rules, open further to the outside world, and integrate its economy more closely with the world economy. Needless to say, the WTO accession will also bring about grim challenges apart from opportunities. As the Chinese philosopher, Zhuangzi, once said: "Safety and danger sometimes exchange roles; sorrow and happiness sometimes come along in company." Pressure might be turned into strength; from challenges come opportunities. As far as China is concerned, we not only need to embrace and grasp opportunities, but also to learn how to cope with challenges. Only by so doing can we put ourselves in a better position in the volatile and highly competitive new century.

BOOSTING STRENGTHS AND GRASPING NEW OPPORTUNITIES

The Chinese government will continuously push forward economic reform and strictly follow the basic rules of the WTO so as to provide an environment for stable and rapid growth.

- It will further adjust its legal system governing international economic activities, and revise or abolish regulations that are not in conformity with the WTO rules. In line with the requirements of an open market economy, China will strive to put in place finally a unified, open, and transparent legal system conforming to common international practices.

- It will speed up the reform of its public administration and change government functions. Further, it will reduce government red tape, standardize its approval process, enhance the legal supervision mechanism, and conduct administration in strict accordance with laws.

- It will deepen the reform of the SOEs and accelerate the strategic adjustment of the state sector. It will encourage large and medium-sized state enterprises to adopt a shareholding system through standardized public listings, Chinese–foreign joint ventures, and cross-shareholdings. It will speed up the pace of reform in monopoly sectors such as the power, civil airline, railway, and telecommunications industries, by introducing competition and establishing modern regulatory systems.

- It will continue to enforce market rules by cracking down on sham and shoddy commodities, strengthening the protection of intellectual property rights, abolishing regional barriers, and breaking up monopolies, with a view to creating a unified, open, fair, and orderly market environment.

UPHOLDING COMMITMENTS TO THE WTO

China will strictly honor its solemn commitments in acceding to the WTO. It will implement trade and investment policies based on openness, transparency, and equality.

· It will further reform the foreign trade management system by replacing the foreign trade approval system with a simple registration system, implementing unified and transparent foreign trade policies, and accepting WTO examination of China's trade policies.

· It will continue to open up service sectors such as banking, insurance, telecommunications, foreign trade, commerce, transportation, construction, tourism industries, and intermediary services. It will explore new ways of using foreign capital more effectively, and encourage foreign investors to establish Sino-foreign joint ventures, Sino-foreign cooperatives, or wholly foreign-funded enterprises in the above fields in accordance with relevant Chinese laws and regulations.

· It will lower tariffs to the average level of developing countries. By the year 2005, the overall level of China's tariffs will be reduced to around 10% from the current level of 15.6%. Meanwhile, it will reduce and abolish such non-tariff measures as licenses and quotas for imported products.

· It will implement open, transparent, and equal trade and investment policies, continuously improve the investment environment, encourage fair competition, and grant national treatment to foreign investors. All this is conceived to be able to help strengthen the confidence of foreign investors in doing business in China.

PROMOTING SUSTAINABLE DEVELOPMENT OF THE ECONOMY

The Chinese government will continue to focus its efforts on promoting sustained, rapid, and sound development of the national economy in order to improve the living standards of its people. China is a big developing country with a population of 1.3 billion. Its development will require long, unremitting, and arduous efforts. The next five to 10 years are of crucial importance in China's economic and social development. Starting from 2002, China has entered its Tenth Five-year Plan period. The Chinese economy is expected to grow at an annual rate of about 7% in that period. By the year 2010, China's

GDP is estimated to reach US$2,000 billion. With its rapid economic growth, China possesses a huge market potential, thus offering tremendous trade and investment opportunities for foreign investors. We believe that China's economic growth will also benefit the world's economic development.

Currently, China is implementing a "Going West" strategy for development of its mid-west regions. With its abundant resources and cheap labor, the mid-west regions can provide foreign investors with unprecedented opportunities.

China is vigorously pushing ahead with strategic adjustment of the economic structure and industrial upgrading. This will be achieved mainly through making full use of technological progress and innovations. This undertaking effort might also offer foreign investors good business opportunities and broad market prospects. China has compiled an investment catalogue intended for foreign investors. Foreign-invested enterprises are welcome to set up research and development centers in China, to invest in high- and new-tech industries, and to participate in the technical upgrading of conventional industries.

China welcomes foreign investors to participate in its SOE reform. The Chinese government is studying ways to transfer property rights to SOES to foreign investors. China is willing to explore the appropriate means and ways to enhance cooperation with foreign investors in various forms, such as equity participation, leasing, sales, and cooperative production.

Beijing will host the 2008 Olympic Games. This will greatly boost China's economic growth, advance its infrastructure development, and promote its economic development toward the direction of modernization, legalization, and internationalization. The Olympic Games will bring about tremendous business opportunities.

Mankind has entered the new millennium. Economic globalization continues to be intensified. High- and new-tech industries are developing vigorously. Meanwhile, many new situations and problems have also emerged. The first year of the millennium has witnessed volatility and uncertainties in world political and economic situations. Transnational business operation has become riskier, the cost of international business transactions has increased significantly, and the process of economic globalization has become more complicated. Faced with this challenge, national governments around the world have strengthened their macroeconomic regulation and control internally, while seeking to expand cooperation externally. The APEC meeting held in Shanghai in October 2001 was very successful. The WTO agreed at its Fourth Ministerial Meeting to launch a new round of multilateral trade negotiations. China and the ASEAN nations have jointly decided to establish a free trade zone among them. These efforts will further contribute to closer cooperation among the world's nations.

We are convinced that peace and development as the main themes of our times will remain unchanged. The development trend of multipolarization of the world will continue. China will continuously pursue its market-oriented reform and opening-up policies. China's economic development needs the world, and will also at the same time contribute to a more prosperous world economy. China will stick to its current course. While managing well our own affairs, we would also like to take an active part in the process of economic globalization, and seek to strengthen international economic cooperation. A stable, developed, and forward-looking China will certainly contribute more to world peace and development.

The Outlook for China's Monetary Policy

*Wu Xiaoling**

 China has been continually reforming its financial regulatory system. Monetary policy has played an important role in the stable development of the national economy.

Confronted with challenges from the Asian financial crisis and from changes in supply and demand in the domestic market, the government has taken measures to stimulate domestic demand since 1998. In line with the proactive fiscal policy, the People's Bank of China (PBOC) has adopted a sound monetary policy. In order to prevent and dissolve financial risks and improve loan quality, the PBOC uses various monetary policies and increases the money supply in a proprietary manner. Since 1998, the PBOC has lowered the RMB interest rate nine times, the foreign currency deposit interest rate over nine times, and the required deposit reserve ratio three times. The PBOC makes open market expenditures and adjusts the credit policy, all of which ensures a modest increase of money supply and loans. Between 1998 and 2001, broad money (M2) grew at 15.4%, 14.7%, 14%, and 14.4% per annum, respectively. Loans of financial institutions grew by RMB1.15 trillion, RMB1.08 trillion, RMB1.33 trillion, and RMB1.29 trillion, respectively. Sound monetary policy has played an important role in containing deflationary pressures and sustaining economic growth.

USING POLICY TO PROMOTE ECONOMIC RESTRUCTURING

The PBOC has instituted policies and regulations to encourage banks to increase consumer credit, export credits, loans to the agriculture sector and

---

*Wu Xiaoling is Deputy Governor, People's Bank of China.

to small and medium-sized enterprises (SMEs), particularly in high-tech sectors, as well as stock-pledged loans, to support structural adjustment and national economic development. Between 1998 and 2001, loans to finance infrastructure construction and technology renovation increased by over RMB1 trillion. Consumer loans also increased rapidly, to RMB699 million, which is 40 times more than in 1997. Meanwhile, loans to non-state-owned enterprises, mainly targeting SMEs, increased to RMB4.8 trillion yuan by the end of 2000, accounting for 48% of the total commercial loans. These trends are all good departures from past practice and have provided a good basis for further reform and restructuring.

The PBOC has also been actively implementing a program to stabilize the financial sector. This includes establishing four asset management companies (AMCs) to acquire and dispose of non-performing loans (NPLs) of the wholly state-owned commercial banks; consolidating small and medium-sized financial institutions; and supporting and coordinating with the Ministry of Finance to issue RMB270 billion of special government bonds to recapitalize the four wholly state-owned commercial banks and increase their capital adequacy ratio. At the same time, it has strengthened financial regulation. These measures will enable financial risks to be resolved gradually.

A NEW BASIS FOR BANK REGULATION AND MONETARY POLICY MANAGEMENT

In 1998, the PBOC removed the credit ceiling on commercial banks and introduced asset and liability ratio management. Since then, the PBOC has reduced the required reserve ratio, increased possibilities for refinancing, expanded rediscount and open market operations, and made steady progress in interest rate liberalization. Open market operations have now become the main tool for the PBOC in the daily operations of monetary policy. Over several years' development, open market operations can now effectively control the liquidity of commercial banks and base money aggregates, and affect the interest rates in money markets. In this way, the PBOC has gradually shifted its regulation from direct to indirect in nature.

The moderately tight monetary policy pursued since 1993 was effective in containing inflation and bringing the economy to a soft landing. Responding to the deflationary tendency in the wake of the 1997 Asian financial crisis, China adopted a proactive fiscal policy. On the monetary front, we have chosen a sound, or stable, monetary policy, instead of a proactive one. There are several reasons for this choice. The SOEs were highly indebted and demand for lending was sluggish, and in turn, commercial banks, historically weak in self-discipline, already had high NPL ratios. Moreover, the root cause of deflation was structural imbalances within the economy and not insufficient money supply. An overly expansionary policy against such a backdrop would do no good in addressing deflation; rather, it would harm the remaining pillars of soundness of the economy.

The goal of monetary policy in China is to preserve the stability of the value of our currency in order to promote economic growth. With money supply as the intermediary objective, we use many monetary policy instruments to indirectly regulate base money. As financial reform progresses, there have been more discussions on the choice of intermediary objective. Some people have questioned the fitness of money supply as such an objective. Since money supply is still closely related to output and price changes and can be adjusted through interest-rate movements, central bank lending, and open market operations, this remains a proper intermediary instrument for China at our current stage of development.

Meanwhile, we shall also look at other indicators and study the range of intermediary objectives in light of new developments – in particular, the leveraging role of interest rates in macroeconomic adjustment. In addition, we shall proceed steadily with interest rate liberalization, using interest rates to guide the flow of funds. We shall further develop the money, bond, and paper markets, and make full use of the resources-allocating function of the market. We shall increase the band by setting a minimum lending rate or a ceiling for deposit rates. Finally, we will form a market-based system of interest rates in which financial institutions will decide interest rates according to money market supply and demand, based on the interest rates of the central bank and with money market interest rates as intermediaries. At the same time, we shall coordinate local currency and foreign currency interest rates. While foreign currency rates shall move along with international market rates, the RMB interest rates will have to follow domestic economic developments. Open market operations will have a larger role to play and their efficiency will be improved.

Imbalance in the national economic structure has been a big barrier to smooth economic development in recent years. The PBOC will continue to leverage credit policy and guide commercial banks to expand and increase their credit to fulfil the reasonable needs of the economy in these areas. By increasing credit, we shall further support agriculture and SMEs, especially private high-tech companies; improve the guarantee system for SMEs; encourage companies to use foreign currency loans to import advanced technology and machines which are badly needed at home; and expand consumer loans.

THE RMB EXCHANGE RATE AND THE NEED FOR INTERNATIONAL COOPERATION

China adopted the managed floating exchange rate regime in 1994, and long-term stability of the RMB exchange rate is conducive to stability and economic growth in China, in Asia, and the world at large. The RMB is not likely to come under excessive upward pressure if the pent-up demand for foreign exchange is gradually released. Confronted with the challenges of our WTO membership, we will improve the RMB exchange rate mechanism and increase the floating band appropriately. We will coordinate both local and foreign currency policy and enhance monetary cooperation regionally and internationally.

As a result of WTO accession, intensified international capital movements will increase the pressure on capital account convertibility. We need to watch closely these movements, the changes in international payments, and the influence that they have on money supply and the money policy transmission mechanism.

STRENGTHENING FINANCIAL SUPERVISION AND PROMOTING BANK REFORMS

Efficient mobilization of saving in the form of deposits and reallocation of these among other regions, sectors, and enterprises are made possible through bank intermediation. Commercial banks are essential in the transmission of monetary policy. However, if state-owned commercial banks cannot adjust their operations according to the monetary policy of the PBOC, the monetary policy cannot be effectively transmitted. As such, reforms of wholly state-owned commercial banks must be further accelerated. The focus here is on how to transform wholly state-owned commercial banks into financial institutions that operate on a truly commercial basis while improving their liquidity, stability, and profitability. Efforts should be made to improve corporate governance and enhance internal control and performance. Prudential accounting, the five-category loan classification standard, as well as loan-loss provisioning and writing-off will be implemented. The ratio of NPLs of wholly state-owned commercial banks should be reduced by three percentage points every year. Capital adequacy should be increased to international standards through government funds injection and ownership reform on the basis of lowering risky assets and internal control.

In the coming years, the environment for monetary policy will undergo significant changes, including the scope of regulation, goals, instruments, and effects. For example, the content of monetary supply will change; the scope of regulation will be expanded to foreign banks; and the influence of capital market development on monetary policy will increase. So, we shall strengthen our research into and study of monetary policy, along with information collection, and improve the financial statistics system, the monetary policy framework, and at the same time, the transparency of monetary policy decisions.

A Vision for Venture Capital in China

Cheng Siwei[*]

 Venture capital is a high-risk, portfolio, long-term, equity, and professional investment. It plays a critical role in increasing the fruits of industrialization and commercialization of research, stimulating the development of high-tech industries, and providing us with an effective investment tool. Realizing technological innovations and high-tech industrialization through venture capital will facilitate China's striving to become a "brain" country in the age of the knowledge economy, able to produce knowledge and own intellectual property, rather than a "body" country which can only use knowledge and import technology.

The United States is not only the first country to develop venture capital, but also the largest nation in terms of size. Its experiences can be summarized as follows:

· Limited partnership is the basic organizational form of venture capital companies.

· An effective incentive system is the key to the success of venture capital.

· Venture capital should support start-ups and the development of high-tech venture enterprises.

· Initial public offerings (IPOs) and sell-outs are the major exits of venture capital.

· The government should create a favorable policy and legal environment for venture capital development.

[*] Cheng Siwei is Vice Chairman of the National People's Congress.

After more than a decade of exploration and preparation, the venture capital industry in China began to move forward rapidly in 1998, and has gradually shown its importance in the transformation of scientific fruits and industrialization of high-technologies. To date, the aggregated venture capital investments in China have amounted to US$800 million. However, the size of venture capital investments is yet to be expanded, and relevant laws and regulations are yet to be stipulated or revised. In addition, more understanding of venture capital's characteristics, its focal areas and potential difficulties, is needed across more sectors of society. In addition, venture capital investments need to be standardized, and instances of great success are few. Private participation is also inadequate.

I have studied venture capital investments in China from three aspects: the macro system (systems and mechanisms), the micro system (including organizational form of venture capital companies and operating mechanism), and practices.

The target of venture capital development in China is to establish a comprehensive venture capital system within 10 years, with the annual venture capital investments up to RMB10 billion. To this end, we suggest a three-step development strategy. The first step is to establish venture capital consulting and management companies which evaluate and recommend venture capital projects for investors at home and abroad, manage the projects for the investors, and, if conditions permit, establish venture capital investments according to the Company Law. Currently, there are over 160 venture capital investment companies and over 180 venture capital consulting and management companies in China. It seems that Shanghai, Beijing, and Shenzhen will be the most promising cities in terms of developing China's venture capital industry.

The second step is to establish venture capital funds and formulate relevant regulations and management rules to attract capital both in and outside China. The legislative process on the law of investment fund is progressing smoothly. The participation of foreign investors in the venture capital investment fund is under consideration. In China, the capital market is not well developed, and bank savings exceed RMB12 trillion, of which two-thirds are personal savings and one-third institutional savings. Therefore, the development of an investment fund has great prospects.

The third step is to establish a comprehensive venture capital system that will support the venture capital industry and provide it with an exit. The government must develop measures to support the venture capital industry through legislation, including investments, grants, guarantees, interest-rate subsidies, tax reductions, and regulations covering mergers and acquisitions and IPOs of small enterprises funded by venture capital. Eventually, rules and regulations should be promulgated for venture capital intermediaries, and the second board of the stock market, for growing enterprises, should be constructed.

To realize the above strategic target and tasks, consistent efforts must be exerted to create several fundamental conditions: a group of entrepreneurs with innovative products, a number of outstanding venture capitalists, sufficient capital support, exits, and a favorable policy and regulatory environment.

System innovation in venture capital in China shall facilitate the creation of venture capital professionals, support innovators to become entrepreneurs, and attract investors to make venture capital investments. Limited liability companies could be the major organizational form for venture capital companies at the present stage, but shall gradually be transformed to limited partnerships. Project managers must have more decision-making power, and a flat and semi-autonomous learning organization must be created. Investments in venture enterprises shall be made by a soft commitment method by which the investment shall be in line with the percentage of equity shares and can be transferred among shareholders who invest directly in the venture enterprises. An incentive system, including salaries, welfare, bonus, equity shares, and stock options, must be established in venture capital companies.

The primary responsibility of venture capitalists is to select suitable projects, based on distinct business models, mature technical bases, promising market prospects, solid economic benefits, feasible satisfaction of capital requirements, and reasonable pricing of technologies.

To develop venture capital in China, we must draw on international experiences and come up with a way with Chinese characteristics. We believe that venture capital will certainly become the big engine propelling the wheel of innovations toward prosperity, as long as we adhere to the spirit of observing carefully and not being afraid to try new methods, and avoid pointless debates marked by dogma.

China's Entry into WTO:
What Does It Mean for the Global Economy?

*Long Yongtu**

China's entry into the WTO has had a major impact on the global economy. This is driven by two fundamental truths: first, it is the world's largest developing country entering into the circle of international trading nations; and second, it is simultaneously the entry and start of the integration of the world's biggest potential consumer market with global markets.

China is a developing country. This fact is acknowledged by the United Nations, the World Bank, and the International Monetary Fund and has never been challenged. During the negotiations on China's WTO entry, a small number of the group's major members refused to acknowledge this fact, with the excuse that China had already become one of the world's top 10 trading countries, based on evidence from China's global GDP rank. In doing so, they aimed both to impose the responsibilities of developed countries on China and to mitigate against what they perceived to be a possible imbalance of rights given to developing countries and the developed countries.

China has never given in on this key issue, for several reasons. First, we rest on economic fact: China's annual per capita income is still below US$900. Second, it is a political choice – namely, that China as a developing country has always adopted a foreign policy based on consolidating its relations with other developing countries. This is of critical importance when we examine the impact of China's WTO entry on the world economy. It strengthens the position of developing countries in a joint effort to change the old international economic system that was built up and predicated toward the interests of developed countries, and to build a new international economic system. It will strike a balance of interest between the developed world and the developing world in international economic and trade relations.

* Long Yongtu is Chief Trade Representative and Vice Minister of Foreign Trade and Economic Cooperation.

This new balance of interest will be mutually beneficial for both developed and developing countries in the world. It will help to boost prosperity and growth for developing nations, which will in turn inject a new vitality into the world economy. The developed nations, whose economies have been in stagnation during 2002, will clearly benefit due to increased demand, cross-border flows including in finance and tourism, as well as other areas. One should also note that the realization of this new balance of interests would strengthen the authority and credibility of the WTO.

The current debate on Trade-Related aspects of Intellectual Property (TRIPS) and public health issues during the new round of WTO multilateral trade negotiations can provide grounds on which to showcase a shared seeking of interests among developing countries. China and other developing countries already share many major concerns.

First, they are all against the abuse of anti-dumping measures which is a killer weapon used by developed countries to offset the advantages that developing countries can derive from their labor-price competitiveness. These measures are also harmful to consumers in developed countries, as they are deprived of accessing the most competitively priced goods.

Second, they are all against the biased and unscientific technical barriers frequently used by the developed countries to block the imports of agricultural products from the developing countries. It has been documented many times that despite much rhetoric of support for the poor in the developing world, industrialized nations' subsidies and protections on agriculture far exceed the average subsidies in the developing world. This not only raises prices for consumers in the West, but also hurts the poorest citizens of developing nations, the farmers.

Third, they are all for the free movement of persons, a major precondition for the developing countries to provide labor services in the developed countries. This means that developing countries can unite in their opposition to barriers enacted to close the borders of developed countries.

Fourth, they are all searching for a balance of interest in the two areas of the protection of intellectual property and the promotion of technology transfer. China has also tried to negotiate this difficult path, by boosting protections for intellectual property while trying to ensure openness and fairness in access. Finally, developing nations are united in their desire to see the rapid and effective implementation of the WTO clauses that are beneficial to them, in the interests of mitigating the risks of entering the global trading system.

China's entry into the WTO can promote the development of these key issues that are vital for the interests of the developing countries. WTO is an organization that sets and enforces the rules, and the global trading system is filled with problems and imbalances, especially between the developed and developing countries. Progress of rule-making in these areas is not an attempt to drive a wedge between these two groups, but instead to strike a balance of interests and thereby create a win–win situation that enables all to benefit.

The second major implication of China's entry into the WTO is linked to the fact that China is the country with the world's biggest market potential. The significance of China in this regard is linked to three basic characteristics.

The first is, of course, population. With 1.3 billion people, sheer size will make China the world's largest or among the largest markets in a wide range of goods. This is already becoming apparent in the fields of mobile phones and computers, for instance. To a strong population basis, we add China's economic growth rate, which determines the speed with which an economy is able to transfer market potential into market reality. In the last two decades, China's consistently high growth rate has been unique in the history of economic development. The projected continuation of this high growth rate reinforces the momentum for China to become the world's largest market.

Lastly, China's economic and trade policies are decisive factors that assure its contribution to the global economy. The Chinese government during the last two decades has been persistently carrying out the policy of reform and opening to the outside world. China has been consistently seeking the import of goods, capital, technology, and expertise, to reinforce and enhance its own economic development. These factors have helped China to advance significantly, and have also enhanced the quality of its growth.

WTO entry builds on this by ensuring that China's own economy becomes more and more integrated with the global economy. Thus, the world stands to benefit from China's vitality at a critical point in the global economic system.

Of course, China's development is set to bring about more competition, not only for developed nations but also for developing countries. In fact, this has even been referred to as a "China threat" in some areas of the world. However, we should also admit that there would be no market economy in its real sense without competition, and that this competition could provide a positive impetus to the reform and restructuring of industries in other countries, regardless of where they stand on the scale of economic development.

In addition, if competition is managed correctly, it could be transformed through the spirit of cooperation. Good management of competition in the global economy is the responsibility of the WTO. It is only with the right system of rules that it becomes a win–win situation in the global economic development. Meanwhile, China is keen to turn its competition with other countries, especially with the developing countries, into cooperation.

The negotiations for a free trade area between China and ASEAN, which started in 2001 and received further support in 2002 from both sides, aim to frame trade and investment cooperation between China and the ASEAN countries. The creation of the single market between China and ASEAN can turn competition into cooperation and yield benefits for both sides.

In summary, I wish to re-emphasize that the WTO has two basic functions: to set up the rules of the game of international economic relations, and to promote the opening up of the global market.

As the world's largest developing country, China's entry into the WTO will enable the WTO rules to better reflect the balance of interests between the developing countries and the developed countries, to better promote global economic development, and to contribute to the establishment of a new international economic order. The entry of China as the world's largest developing country will enlarge the scale of the world economy. And China's opening policy will underscore and further contribute to the establishment of a more open global trade system.

Development Strategies for Big Cities

*Li Yuanchao**

Economic development in China has entered an "Age of Cities." In the past five years, 70% of the wealth newly added in China was created by cities, which accommodate only 30% of the total population.

Chinese cities can be classified into three categories. The first category is the international metropolis, whose population exceeds 10 million and GDP exceeds RMB280 billion. There are two cities belonging to this category on China's mainland: Beijing and Shanghai. The second category is the big city, whose urban population exceeds one million, total population (including the rural population) exceeds five million, and GDP exceeds RMB100 billion. Sixteen mainland cities belong to this category, including Nanjing, with a population of 3.4 million in the urban area, 6.2 million in total (including the rural area), and GDP of RMB115 billion. The third category is the medium- or small-sized cities whose population is under one million.

A DEVELOPMENT STRATEGY FOR A BIG CITY: NANJING

Like other big cities in China, in the past five years, Nanjing has maintained a rapid economic growth. There has been an increase from RMB28.4 billion to RMB46.6 billion in industrial added value, from RMB4.456 billion to RMB5.875 billion in agricultural output, and from RMB28.264 billion to RMB53.807 billion in added value in commercial and service industries. GDP rose from RMB67 billion to RMB115.4 billion, an annual growth of 11.8%. Fiscal revenue rose from RMB7.879 billion to RMB20.477 billion, an annual increase of 21.4%. The urban per capita disposable income increased from RMB5,603 to

---

* Li Yuanchao is Party Secretary, Nanjing Municipal Government and Deputy Party Secretary, Jiangsu province.

RMB8,848, and rural per capital income increased from RMB3,128 to RMB4,311 for farmers.

The high-speed development of Nanjing since 1997 has benefited from the following five development strategies.

1   *Renovation of large-scale state-owned enterprises (SOEs) through incorporation* – this has improved the market competitiveness of large enterprises and guarantees over 50% of the tax revenues.

2   *Cooperation of foreign investment with the existing state-owned stock assets* – the Chinese electronics industry base has been reconstructed with foreign investment. Through technology and products updating and joint ventures, the Panda Group doubled its output in three years.

3   *Expansion of construction scale using state infrastructure construction loans* – Nanjing has made use of the domestic demand expansion policy to expand investment in and advance its infrastructure construction.

4   *Cultivation of commercial and electronic markets by taking advantage of the domestic demand* – Nanjing has built concentrated areas for electronics, in addition to a commercial area which in 2001 achieved an output of over RMB10 billion (despite the impact of the September 11 tragedy).

5   *Rapid expansion of higher education* – the number of university students increased from 150,000 to 300,000 during the period, proving that the city is capable of providing high-quality, low-cost professionals.

The situation for the next five-year period will change in some respects:

•   The world economy has slumped rapidly since September 11, 2001. (The slump is estimated to last a period of three to five years.) International capital is seeking low-cost investment.

•   The global production of technology will increase and product life cycles will shorten. The speed of updating industrial technology, especially electronic technology, will accelerate.

•   China has entered the World Trade Organization (WTO) and will further participate in the global division of work. The rules of the Chinese market economy face major changes.

In response to these changes, Nanjing has formulated development strategies centering on the improvement of the city's comprehensive competitiveness. They include:

Overall Development Objectives

- *A city with a dynamic economy* – develop the chemical industry, electronic and automotive bases, and commercial, science and technology, and information centers.

- *A city with cultural distinction* – develop a famous historic and cultural city, a famous modern science and technology city, and a famous cultural business city.

- *A city with a superior residential environment* – develop the best residential city, the most secure city in the country, and a national environment-friendly city.

Speeding Up Economic Growth

- *The plan to double industrial output within five years* – establish four major industrial development zones and expand the input. Realize the concentration of resources in competitive industries, the concentration of assets in competitive enterprises, and the concentration of capital in competitive products. Speed up the technological upgrade.

- *The plan to double the rural economy within five years* – realize agricultural industrialization. Develop the rural industrial parks. Accelerate the urbanization process, with 2% of the rural population to be urbanized every year.

- *The plan to double the tourism economy within five years* – double tourist numbers and tourism revenue.

- *The plan to expand commercial services within five years* – establish a regional logistics center and develop new business and financial centers.

- *Encourage housing, automobile, and tourism consumption and double the amount of consumer loans.*

Speeding Up the Opening-Up process

- Engage actively in the global division of industrial production. Downsize the city industries and transform them into processing bases of the world's chemical and electronic industries.

- Formulate preferential policies to speed up the acceptance of international capital. Double the attraction of foreign investment within five years.

- Cooperate with multinational companies to introduce state-of-the-art information technology and pharmaceutical technologies.

- Introduce foreign universities and research and development institutes by following the WTO provisions.

Speeding Up the System Reform

- Speed up the reform of state-owned enterprises (SOEs) by incorporating large enterprises and privatizing small enterprises, with priority being given to joint ventures.

- Commercialize infrastructure construction by implementing the reform of *Operating the City* and encourage corporate or private investment in infrastructure facilities.

- Reform the government administration system by extensively curtailing the government's approval rights and build a service-oriented government.

- Reform the managers and officials recruitment system by "socializing" the recruitment of management of SOEs and "democratizing" the recruitment of government officials.

Improving the Modernization Level of the City

- Expand the city construction input to realize the city's expansion in the form of "Three Concentrations and One Dispersion."

- Develop the new city and preserve the old city by learning from Pudong and La Defence. Invest RMB60 billion to develop a new commercial and residential area equal to the size of the old city.

- Establish a new-style urban area by learning from Cambridge and Harvard. Build a new urban area integrating the university town, high-tech zone, and the commercial and residential areas.

- Reform the household registration system by accepting investments from immigrants to advance with the city expansion.

It is calculated that by following the above-mentioned development strategies, through 2001, Nanjing's GDP growth can be maintained at around 11.5% (4% higher than the national average), and per capita income can increase approximately 7% (1.5% higher than the national average). Within 10 years, the size of the developed urban area will have doubled and the urban population will have increased by one million.

Part 4

Executive

Roundtable

Reviewing Progress and Looking Towards the Future

This chapter brings together diverse views from the business community on China's economic past, present, and future. Though not meant to be comprehensive, the chapter offers a contrast to the "expert" and government views of the previous two parts of the book.

Fortune, *Forbes*, *Businessweek* and other business magazines have loudly proclaimed the success and riches of China's entrepreneurs, millionaires and young stars. While one should hesitate to absorb this gold-rush mentality at face value, one also cannot deny that there is great potential in China. The business community is right to ensure that at least some of their investment and planning are focused on China even while they weigh the risks, dubious facts, and current problems.

Entrepreneurship—in many forms— is the source of the new dynamism that has revitalized the domestic business environment and made it a new global destination. Entrepreneurship is always identified as a factor of success for the overseas Chinese in Hong Kong and Southeast Asia, and pure entrepreneurship is now spawning thousands of new businesses in China. An example is Zhang Yue, who founded Broad Air Conditioning in his hometown of Changsha, Hunan, which is now a leading innovator of cooling technology in China. Wang Wei, left a lucrative career as an investment banker to found his own mergers & acquisitions advisory company, long before m&a's were the preferred way to solve the SOE problem.

Entrepreneurship has found a natural partner in technology, due to the up-to-date knowledge needed, low-start up costs and lack of geographical limits. Thus, Edward Tian and James Ding were able to found AsiaInfo while in the USA as graduate students, and then bring the company to China to become one of the country's fastest growing IT supplier companies. Another example is Jack Ma, who abandoned a career as an English teacher to found

Alibaba.com, the one of the largest (profitable) online product sourcing sights. Cyrill Eltschinger is one of the few foreign entrepreneurs in China, who has set down roots by creating IT United, a small technology services and consulting company.

Entrepreneurs are also found in state-owned companies, and they reveal themselves in their openness to new ideas and tenacity in implementation. Edward Tian now runs China Netcom Corporation, a state-owned telecommunications supplier. Zhou Lin leads Shenzhen Development Bank, which has become one of the first and few state banks to gain foreign shareholding from Newbridge Capital. Jiang Jianqing runs China's largest bank, ICBC, in a way that seems inimical to the image of the stodgy indebted state-giant.

All of these entrepreneurs—regardless of the size of their companies—have in common the ability to look beyond their immediate situations to view opportunities on a wider horizon. That means networking both within one's industry and outside of it, in the international community and amongst people from all sectors. One notes that they have all participated as discussants in World Economic Forum activities because they see the long-term benefits.

There they are likely to meet foreign business people who are also interested and involved in China's economy, and who also are exhibiting entrepreneurial spirit in their approach to China. Peter Lau of Giordano has had a particularly difficult task in ensuring that Giordano's business was not derailed by the disputes between the company's founder and the Beijing leadership. Today, Lau's methodology has paid off, and Giordano is fully exploiting the opportunities in both manufacturing and selling into China. David K.P. Li had the challenge of orienting Hong Kong's largest family-owned bank toward the mainland whilst maintaining its solid base in Hong Kong. Hironori Aihara and Richard Edelman have both been challenged with the need to integrate the mainland market into global business plans. Both have carved their own paths, Aihara through the Global Information Infrastructure Commission and other industry groups, and Edelman more directly as a member of the International Advisory Council of the Mayor of Shanghai.

This roundtable brings together all these views to reflect on China's progress in the recent past, and look toward the future. They are drawn from each of the groups that is changing China: foreign and local investors, state and private companies, small and large organizations, and a variety of sectors. The participants, once again, are (in alphabetical order):

Hironori Aihara, President and Chief Executive Officer, Mitsubishi International, USA
Richard Edelman, Chairman, Edelman Public Relations, USA
Cyrill Eltschinger, Chief Executive Officer, I.T. UNITED China, China
Jiang Jianqing, Chairman and President, Industrial and Commercial Bank of China, China
Peter Lau, Chairman and Chief Executive Officer, Giordano International, Hong Kong SAR
David K.P. Li, Chairman and Chief Executive, Bank of East Asia, Hong Kong SAR
Jack Ma Yun, Chairman and Chief Executive Officer, Alibaba.com, China
Edward Tian Suning, Chief Executive Officer, China Netcom Corporation, and Vice Chairman, China Netcom Group, China
Wang Wei, Chairman, China M&A Management Company, China
Zhou Lin, President, Shenzhen Development Bank, China
Zhang Yue, Chairman, Broad Air Conditioning, China

1. China is Big. How Can it Grow Quickly?

Jiang Jianqing:
In 2001 and 2002, despite the slowing down of the world economy, China managed to keep its rapid pace of growth, with GDP increasing by 7–8% in both years. China is now a US$1 trillion economy, and ranks sixth in the world in terms of total GDP. However, due to our huge population and regional differences in cultural and natural conditions, the GDP per capita is still rather low. We need to maintain a fast pace of economic development in order to raise living standards, and this can be done in the following three ways:

- *Continuing with economic restructuring:* China's reform and opening-up process over the past 20 years has paved the way for its rapid economic development. Reform and restructuring will continue to be important as China continues its economic transition.

- *Raising internal demand:* By increasing domestic demand, the dual powers of consumption and investment will ensure that a fast pace of economic development continues. To ensure this, we need to increase the income of both urban and rural inhabitants and cultivate their purchasing power, as well as maintain the pace of Treasury bond investment in order to raise the overall investments in fixed assets. Lastly and most importantly, we will carry out the Western development strategy in order to coordinate and distribute development among all the regions of the country.

· *Promoting exports and attracting foreign investment, upon China's entry into the WTO:* A recovery in the world economy can be an opportunity for us to promote exports and attract foreign investments. However, even in an environment of weak global demand, China has excellent competitive advantages in manufacturing, which can make exports and external demand an additional powerful engine of China's economic development.

Zhang Yue:

Maintaining fast growth is the biggest challenge today for China. However, the government's behavior is still far from becoming normalized to meet this condition, in comparison with other countries. For instance, in determining investment priorities, government officials at all levels regard this as an opportunity to exercise administrative control and power. They make significant efforts to maintain this control. As a result, until now, through domestic and overseas investment, the state-owned enterprises have been key drivers of the country's economic development.

However, given big changes in the competitive environment in China, especially after China's entry to the WTO, it is hard to tell how long this status will last. Increasingly, the private sector in China is playing a significant role in ensuring the sustainable and steady development of China's economy through a steady expansion of manufacturing and other outputs, the creation of jobs, and the introduction of top management methods and innovations. I believe the private sector will become more important in the future.

Edward Tian:

The power of information technology has placed us at the beginning of a period of growth that will enable us to leapfrog the West. This is based on three strengths.

· market growth, which places China as the number two worldwide in Internet growth;

· the effect of technology in terms of business process reengineering which will increase the efficiency and dynamism of Chinese companies; and

· the shift of foreign manufacturers to China which is building a world-class manufacturing industry in the country.

The slowdown in the Western markets is further propelling growth in China – and our reengineering now is similar to the same processes in the U.S. and Europe during the 1980s. For us, at China Netcom Corporation, it is a chance to go abroad.

What China lacks now is research and development skills. We need to work together with India and Silicon Valley to build up our capacities in innovation and entrepreneurship. We will have to develop the patience to foster innovation, but in time, and with the right efforts and partners, Chinese companies can become great innovators.

2. What Are the Best Practices for Driving Change in State-Owned Enterprises?

Wang Wei:
Management buy-out and mergers and acquisitions are the best ways, and both require drastic change to the financial system. The system must be structured to evaluate and provide financing to capable managers and entrepreneurs. Right now the system does not provide any support, and this is a remnant of the past. The same situation exists with the Go West campaign, which is still using the old planned economy mentality: using government power to push enterprises to change their resource allocation and structures. Of course, the government should continue to use the usual incentives such as tax and credit to support this. But in principle, I think the best position for the government is not to be directly involved in management and not to compete with the private sector for funding and benefits from enterprise reform.

Zhang Yue:
The necessary condition for reforming SOEs is corporate governance, and one of the best ways to achieve good governance is privatization. The enterprise should be in the hands of the most capable managers who stick to the path of good governance. Only consistent, high-efficiency good governance can produces profit for these enterprises. This has been demonstrated in the private sector and this should be considered as an option for the SOEs.

3. What Is the Most Effective Way to Institute Corporate Governance in Chinese Enterprises?

Zhou Lin:
The Western type of corporate governance puts emphasis on the relations between the shareholders and the management. However, due to economic, social, and cultural differences, different countries have different practices of corporate governance. As its economic reforms are going on, China is striving to bring in some good economic management practices from Western countries, among them corporate governance. At present,

problems still exist in China's practice of corporate governance, namely the absence of ownership, the lack of incentives for managers, the lack of internal operational independence, and so on.

The key lies in Chinese banks' capability to adapt to internationally accepted practices. The government should back out of its role as the biggest investor. Diversification of shareholding should be realized. Management authority should be returned to those with the expertise and interest in running the company. The present situation, where the highest decision-making authorities are nominated by the government, should be changed. An organizational structure comprised of the shareholders' congress, the board of directors, the board of supervisors, and the management, should be improved. The three mechanisms of decision-making, executive, and supervising should be separated and enabled to restrain each other. The incentive mechanism should be improved. An effective evaluation mechanism vis-à-vis the management should be established. Managers' income should be in accordance with the bank's revenue and the annual return to the shareholders.

A healthy legal system ensures the realization of corporate governance. A healthy legal system, impartial prosecution of criminals, and civil accountability should be established to prevent any abuse of power. Protecting the interests of the small and medium shareholders is also a critical part in the development of corporate governance in China.

David Li:
That's an interesting question, seeing as it is exactly the same question investors are asking about major U.S. corporations. I think the answer is the same for both: it is absolutely necessary to make senior management of publicly listed companies more accountable to shareholders.

In China, that can be done by expanding share ownership and reducing the share held by the state to a minority interest. I would also like to see the growth of a strong institutional investor community, willing to be outspoken in defense of shareholders' rights. The role of independent directors needs to be expanded – ideally, more than 50% of directors should be independent non-executives.

Another leg is a strong and independent business press. On this score, however, China's journalists have already shown themselves to be every bit the equal of their U.S. counterparts. After all, it was a Chinese business journal that first blew the lid off the Euro-Asia Agriculture fiasco.

Jiang Jianqing:

Although China's opening-up has achieved significant success already, we are still in the process of trying to achieve a central goal of reform, which is to transform and restructure the state-owned enterprises. The SOEs should become economic entities with legal person status, which manage and are accountable for their own initiatives, operations, and profits and losses. After years of practice and exploration, China has found the right way to reform these enterprises – that is, by establishing a modern enterprise system with clearly established ownership frameworks, well-defined rights and responsibilities, separation of the enterprise from the administration, and management techniques based on science instead of politics.

Under this system, through diversifying the investors and ownership base, and separating the ownership from the legal property rights of the enterprises, an effective governance mechanism will be established. It will be able to perform the needed system of checks –and balances so as to make the company's shareholders general meeting, board of directors, board of supervisors, and the management board independent. All must be distinct, with clear boundaries between their rights and responsibilities, thus forming an incentive and control mechanism.

At the National Financial Working Conference held in early 2002, it was decided that the state-owned commercial banks should be transformed into modern financial enterprises with good corporate governance, clear operational goals and systems, sound financing, and increased international competitiveness. This is consistent with the requirements for establishing the modern enterprise system. We at the Industrial and Commercial Bank of China are endeavouring to meet these challenges, with the goal of transforming ourselves into a publicly listed bank within the next five years.

Peter Lau:

In my view, good governance is about long-term profit. Long-term profit is what is needed for a firm to survive. Therefore, profit, or short-term profit, should never take priority over good governance. The real issue is, "What is good governance?"

Most of the corporate governance concepts and behaviors have come from the West and may not have given sufficient consideration to other cultures. For example, Japanese firms are criticized by Wall Street for being bureaucratic, inflexible, and unwilling to "reengineer," therefore making them less efficient than their Western counterparts. The so-called Asian values held by many firms in Asia, including Japanese firms, include looking after the welfare of their members. Decisions are not always made based on optimization of profits.In the West, profit optimization is expected by Wall Street and the system of capitalism, and accountability to one's shareholders, is one's first and foremost priority. In the East, however, accountability to society at large has greater importance. The concept of good governance differs between cultures and this fact cannot be ignored.

Should "good governance" behaviors come into conflict between the East and the West, which one should take priority? The answer is different for each company and culture.

4. What Lies Ahead for China's IT Industry?

Cyrill Eltschinger:
The Chinese government has outlined a bullish five-year plan for specific projects within China's IT industry. This includes nine to 10 major development projects for integrated circuits. In addition, total software sales are expected to reach RMB250 billion, with the proportion of Chinese software within global sales rising from 1.2% to 3.1%. The share of the domestic software market is expected to reach over 60%. Exports are expected to reach between US$1.5 billion and US$2 billion.

In addition, the plan outlines a push to bring the output value of communications products to RMB350–400 billion (US$42–48 billion) by 2005 and export earnings to more than US$20 billion. Chinese companies will also be looking to increase their share of the computers and network products market. At present, foreign players – both at the domestic and international level – dominate this market. The objective is to bring the home market share up to 50% and to increase exports. In short, the idea is to make computer and network products a pillar of China's electronics and information industry.

If this agenda is kept, Chinese technology could potentially leap-frog legacy technologies that still exist in the West. Chinese people may enjoy certain new technologies before they are exported to other countries. Mobile phone ownership already outstrips landline installations in certain rural areas of China. As 3G mobile technologies begin to take hold, China may find itself at the cusp of the technology wave, as a consumer as well as a producer

Jack Ma:
We have seen Internet-based commerce grow very rapidly in 2002, even in the midst of global recession. From 1999 to 2001, for instance, we had one million new members, but in the first half of 2002, we have had 400,000 new members. It's a sign that people are starting to understand the advantages of

Internet commerce. We are attracting buyers from around the world to China, and our surveys show that over 70% of import/export companies are sourcing through our site, Alibaba.com. The keys to this are quality control and customer service. We are constantly checking the quality of the suppliers who are on our site, and the site maintains quality records so that new buyers can verify potential suppliers or customers.

Moreover, I-commerce is truly two-way: not only do Chinese manufacturers sell to abroad, but foreign companies are also using the Internet to sell into China. Initially, we didn't think that the potential could be this significant. At the same time, we always have to remind ourselves that we are not an "IT company" per se. We are a business services company that uses the Internet to serve our customers. This is one thing that some early technology-based companies neglected to realize – that really, business is about serving your customer, even if you use technology or the Internet to do so.

5. In the Coming Five Years, What Will Be the Makeup of China's Financial Sector, in Terms of State, Joint Venture, and Foreign Companies?

Jiang Jianqing:
China joining the WTO in November 2001 means, for the financial sector, a ste-by-step opening up to foreign investors during a five-year transitional period. By the end of this period, all foreign financial enterprises will be able to provide Chinese customers with the full scope of financial services. In the insurance and securities sectors, however, there will still be a limit on the proportion held by foreign investor in joint ventures.

Because of this, the next five years – of which we have already completed one – will be a period of restructuring for China's financial industry, with considerable and significant changes. Currently, the wholly state-owned financial institutions and those in which the state holds the majority stake have the greatest market share in terms of assets, loans, customers, and business products. For instance, the assets of the four state-owned commercial banks account for 60% of the total assets of all the commercial banks in China, while foreign banks account for only 2%.

However, foreign banks are developing at an amazing speed. Their total assets at the end of 2001 were 2.4 times higher than in 1995. Given such a high speed of development, joint ventures and foreign-funded financial institutions will comprise a considerable part of China's future financial sector.

In the coming five to seven years, I estimate that wholly state-owned financial institutions and those in which the state holds the majority stake will see a reduction in their market shares, but will continue to maintain their status as the largest market player. Joint ventures, foreign-funded, and privately owned financial institutions will all significantly increase their shares.

The Industrial and Commercial Bank of China (ICBC) is the largest commercial bank in China and also one of the top 10 banks in the world. We are undergoing a full and far-reaching restructuring. In addition to maintaining our present market share, ICBC is seeking to be innovative in its technology, management, and mechanisms so as to offer high-quality services to our customers and clients in China and all over the world.

Zhou Lin:
The state-owned banks – that is, the four major banks – will continue to occupy a dominant position in China's financial sector in terms of scale of assets, capital and deposits, as well as regarding their network coverage and number of employees. This situation won't be changed in a fundamental fashion in the next five to seven years, although shareholding-oriented structural reforms will be carried out.

The financial joint ventures, including banking, stock exchange, insurance, credit and renting businesses, will be further developed. By attracting experienced foreign banks to actively take part in operations and management, Chinese banks could learn much from their Western counterparts in terms of management expertise, marketing capabilities, and new technologies, and adapt themselves to international norms.

The privatization of small –and medium-sized banks would be speedily carried out. Private-owned banks would emerge like the tip of the iceberg in China's banking sector. The government will terminate its role in these small –and medium-sized private banks. Their shareholders would in future be private or collective in nature. Of the private sector, by the private sector, for the private sector – these characteristics would inject new life into the private banks.

Foreign banks, including other foreign-owned financial enterprises, would be operating in China in accordance with our commitment to the WTO. The entry of foreign banks to the Chinese financial market would introduce brand-new management concepts, operation styles, and financial products on the one hand, and have a negative impact on the other – that is, as a result of the brain drain and loss of clients. However, we firmly believe that we would learn very quickly from our competitors and, accordingly, our domestic banks would develop even more rapidly.

6. What Challenges Does China Face in Education and How Should it Deal With These?

Peter Lau:

China's public education system has been chaotic and decaying due to a lack of funding. Over the past decade, the Chinese government has devoted a mere 2.4% of GDP to public education, far lower than the average 4.1% in other developing countries. The national budget is mainly spent on urban universities and colleges, rather than on the over 200 million primary and secondary school students. Since the mid-1990s, lower tiers of government have been expected to foot their education bill with taxes from their localities. However, many local governments are crippled by debt and on the verge of bankruptcy, and this in turn hampers the local education system. It's a problem replicated around the country.

The funding gap between big cities and rural areas is huge. In some rural areas, the average annual spending per child is less than US$1. Authorities have responded by neglecting maintenance, employing unqualified teachers on lower pay rates, increasing class sizes, and levying an array of fees. The central government's strategy for overcoming the chronic under-funding of education is to encourage schools to "go into business." Also, due to China's residency laws, migrant children are barred from local schools. In respond to that, self-funded (by teachers and parents) schools have sprung up across China.

For the affluent group, the solution to the decaying public education system has been to enroll their children in private schools or send them overseas. But for the mass of the country's workers and peasants, they have no choice but to put their faith in their government to improve the education system. According to the Education Blueprint, over 95% of the Chinese population will enjoy nine –years of compulsory education by 2010. Education at the level of senior middle school will be greatly developed, which will be enjoyed by the majority of young people in cities and economically developed regions. For counties that cannot wait until 2010, one of the solutions would be to rely on foreign funding or donations.

Jack Ma:

Someone can have a great education from the best schools, but he or she won't be a good employee unless they have values. This is of critical importance for the company today and why we at Alibaba have created a structure of nine core values – built around teamwork and serving our customers – for employees. It may seem like a basic thing, but it's critically important. We spend virtually no money on marketing, but RMB5 million on training for our 580 employees. If someone has no values, we lay them off; on the other hand, we have only a 10% staff turnover rate, which I'm proud of.

The global environment has been important in developing my own view of this "other side" of education. At the annual meeting of the World Economic Forum in New York in early 2002, the most important things I learned were about leadership, values, and mission. Leadership is not a position or a job – it's about direction, actions, and values. Leaders have to be concerned about creating values within their company if they want to succeed in leading people.

7. What Are China's Main Human Resources Challenges?

Cyrill Eltschinger:

Economic success in Europe and the United States has been predicated on a flexible labor force. Firms often hire contractors just for the duration of a contract. China will need to adopt a more flexible employment market if its firms are to become successful. This will allow firms to be more responsive to their clients as they hire appropriate professionals, instead of always being stuck with the same unprofitable skill sets. The IT industry, in particular, will benefit both from greater human resource flexibility and from leveraging blue-collar programmers.

More highly educated and experienced managers with a technology background will also increase competitiveness. Managers who have experience and training from the United States and Europe are valuable here. However, China now has the economic opportunity of training its people domestically. The rise in the number of multinational companies doing business in China means that trained managers can rise through the ranks without undergoing education or training. In addition, top universities such as Tsinghua and Beijing are producing formidable talent.

If Chinese companies are going to successfully compete in Europe and the United States, greater emphasis should be placed on improving the standard of English in the professional community. This will involve increasing the numbers of native English speakers available in China to teach and/or work in predominantly Chinese firms. In addition, encouraging the broadcasting of foreign television programs and printing/importing foreign news media and contemporary literature will also help.

Jiang Jianqing:

With a population of nearly 1.3 billion, or one-fifth of the world total, China is the most populous country in the world. This has given it abundant human resources in terms of quantity. Its comparative advantage built around the labor force in recent years has attracted businesses around the world to invest in China, particularly in the manufacturing sector. Globally, this has promoted realignment of some industries and the efficient allocation of resources.

However, with the development of China's economy along with science and technology, new challenges have emerged regarding human resources, and this can be seen in the irrational structure of human resources in China. Nowadays, most Chinese working people remain at a fairly low level of knowledge and expertise. The supply and demand for manpower in the job market don't match very well. The lack of well-educated and trained employees restrains the growth of some industries that require advanced technologies and techniques. To address this problem, the Chinese government has formed the strategy of "to revitalise the nation through science and education" as one of its fundamental state policies, with the purpose of improving the quality of Chinese workers through long-term efforts.

The Industrial and Commercial Bank of China has laid great emphasis on human resource issues. In the past two years, ICBC has significantly downsized our headcount and carried out reforms in HR management. Since 2000, ICBC has laid off 130,000 staff and in the meantime launched a comprehensive training program in order to update ICBC staff's knowledge structure. In 2001, ICBC provided training programs for staff at different levels. Altogether, 1,044,219 incidences of training were offered to its employees – that is, on average, each employee received 2.4 incidences of training. Having realized that in the near future the competition in China's banking sector will eventually result in a competition for talented people, ICBC is committed to restructuring and optimizing its HR portfolio, so as to guarantee its leading position among its competitors.

Peter Lau:

China's main human resources challenges lie not in the private sector, but in the public sector. China's civil service has to be modernized, not only in form but also in substance. There are two very important hurdles here. First, the overall pay scale in the civil service must be upgraded. Although the government is going in that direction, it is not fast enough to develop a new generation of civil servants with an appropriate world outlook as well as the skills to deal with a market-driven economy. The brightest and the best are attracted to multinationals and private business. The skills gulf between the private and public sectors would retard the pace of economic advancement in China.

Second, the underlying attitude of governments – which is to "govern," rather than to "facilitate" business – must be changed. We still find a lot of roadblocks and arrogance in many industry-related departments such as the

Commerce Bureau, the Customs and Excise, and the Tax Departments.Officials there have yet to understand the positive role the government could adopt in order to help legitimate businesses prosper. Their "regulator" mentality creates unnecessary animosity and hostility between businesses and the government. Foreign firms, in particular, are finding the task of dealing with government officials a necessary evil that causes inefficiencies in business systems. More educated younger staff must be attracted to government jobs with respectable pay levels if the quality of the Chinese civil service is to be upgraded.

8. How Will Growth Regions such as the Pearl River Delta and the Yangtze River Delta Impact on National Development?

Zhou Lin:

The Pearl River Delta, centered on Hong Kong, Macau, and Guangdong, has made great contributions to China's reform and opening to the outside world, and has now become a mature, active, and highly cooperative economic zone in East Asia. Comprised of a great number of domestic, foreign, and joint ventures, as well as research and development institutes, a new production zone is being established built around the high-tech sector. This has become a brand-new driving force for the regional economy, with three metropolitan circles under formation all within 100 kilometers of each other: Guangzhou–Foshan, Hong Kong–Shenzhen, and Macau–Zhuhai, which in turn form a triangular economic zone.

With China's accession into the WTO, this economic zone is playing the role of an engine in economic development, because of its sheer size, economic power, flexibility, and connections with the international community through Hong Kong and Macau. Its effects radiate outwards into the surrounding regions, including the backward western regions.

The "Yangtze Triangle," led by Shanghai and joined by Nanjing and Hangzhou, with over 200 kilometers separating the three cities, has amassed a large number of Taiwanese, foreign, and private-owned ventures, and has been among the most active economic zones in China. In the near future, a super-metropolitan group can be envisaged in the area. We can see that the Pearl River and Yangtze triangles, together with the Beijing–Tianjin–Hebei region and the Central China region, will eventually become the four driving engines in China's economic development.

David Li:

Uneven development is a fact of life. Both the Pearl and Yangtze River deltas are blessed with easy access to world markets and a thriving hinterland from which to draw strength. Both these areas are attracting a discordant share of the foreign investment entering China; both are putting that investment to good use, and leading the way for China's future development.

These areas will continue to draw the lion's share of investment; they will be the leading centers, drawing talent from the rest of China. This is not at all unusual. For most of the last century, major centers in the U.S. have drawn people off the land and away from smaller communities. In the U.S., it has only been over the past 10 years or so that we have seen a minor reversal of this trend, as people long for an alternative to the big city. I daresay that, in China, the bright lights of Shanghai, Guangzhou, and Shenzhen will remain a strong lure for many years to come.

Peter Lau:

The Pearl River Delta is emerging as an economic powerhouse in Asia, as well as one of the world's largest manufacturing basins. Since it was one of the areas that was first allowed more autonomy in external trade and investment, it has already attracted a number of Asian companies as well as multinationals to invest in the region since mid-1980s. The delta is now unsurpassed as a production base for exporting to overseas markets and for the Chinese mainland. Today, the region produces about 35% of China's exports. Although it may not be providing the cheapest costs, it has already achieved internationally recognized quality and process standards. Moreover, companies in the Pearl River Delta have already fostered a group of local middle management that has the experience of working at multinationals, and who are in great demand today. Therefore, despite Shanghai and its neighboring cities challenging the Pearl River Delta's role as the gateway for investment in China, it will still enjoy its first mover advantage in the near term. In the meantime, local authorities are forging ahead with vast infrastructure projects and granting more latitude to foreign investors in order to attract even more capital. Hence, the Pearl River Delta's robust growth seems to be unstoppable for the moment and its important role as a major exporter will be sustained, especially with the rapidly developing ports such as the Yantian ports.

In the meantime, the Yangtze Delta is emerging as another gateway for foreign investment, overshadowing the economic importance of the Pearl River Delta. Tertiary services in finance, retail, and tourism are flourishing in Shanghai. The city's industrial development appears to rely increasingly on high-technology research and development that requires access to a wide range of top professional, scientific, and technical expertise, and excellent communications and international transport systems. Trading and distribution businesses will be further enhanced with the recently developed transportation network. Together with its easy access to the four major ports, the Yangtze Delta can offer a range of competitive international distribution options. In addition, with the entrepreneurship of residents in the region and local government's tax incentive, the region had competed away a lot of foreign investment as well as talent. In the medium term, the Yangtze Delta is likely to evolve into a super-powerhouse in Asia.

Wang Wei:
Unlike the enterprise cluster centered on associated industries in a mature market economy, China's economic zones is mainly a product of system transformation. The "high-tech zone" or "free trade zone" is a typical example. More conspicuously, there is the so-called delta phenomenon. "Delta" is also a product of system reform.

At the beginning of China's economic reforms, the Pearl River Delta was the zone where enterprises clustered whose core businesses were trade, tax-free, and the preliminary service industry. Its economic boom resulted on two basis: one because the central government didn't have time to control it, directly, and thus allowed trade to go on unhindered, and two, because the government exchanged the lack of political control for the economic rewards shared by the zone. At the same time, foreign investors also made use of the cheap resources and the market environment to promote Orignal Equipment Manufacturing (OEM) in this area. The experiment of the Pearl River Delta gave Chinese consumers and policymakers a special observation angle. It showed that the market economy was not necessarily the opposite of a planned economy, and could be a pleasant supplement to it. It also provided a platform for international investors to enter the China market and build up their confidence.

Yangtze River Delta is a product of the shrinking central government control in the process of market economy development recently. The market-oriented product development, marketing system, service standard and planned production organisation, management and employment formed a special combination. Foreign investors also upgrade their business from trade to manufacturing and then financial service industries. Many multinational companies even plan to list in China's capital market. The organised market economy in parallel with planned economy becomes the main stream of this area. Large state owned enterprises (in Shanghai) and advanced private companies (in Jiangsu and Zhejiang) coexisting and supporting each other becomes the characteristic of the region.

Furthermore, in the coming years, we will see that the enterprises in the two region differentiate in the direction of associated industries under the pressure of global competition, forming new enterprise clusters such as clothing industry, manufacturing industry and chemical industry, etc.

9. How Should China Develop its Urban and Inland Areas?

Hironori Aihara:
The people's government of each city is aiming to create a total plan for city development projects and the induction of foreign investment that will please everyone.Foreign investors are looking for the specific merits of each region and require Chinese cities to create proposals which highlight their advantages, such as their natural resources, culture, climate, and so forth.

Zhang Yue:
China's economic growth has become concentrated in the east and south. In the future, with the Go West campaign, the disparity between the coastal regions and the rest of the country will be eased. The Go West campaign will also be significant in terms of the energy sector, in particular by developing the natural gas industry. The investment in this huge construction project could return profits for 30–50 years. It is a bright prospect, indeed.

Richard Edelman:
I can't claim to offer a strategy for all of China's cities or provinces, but I can speak on the development of one – Shanghai – based on my knowledge of other urban centers wuch as New York, where I live. I strongly believe that Shanghai is a model for what other cities in China can achieve through the WTO. It is already one of China's most vibrant and progressive places and now it has won the right to host the Expo 2010. It should build on this to communicate its aspirations, somewhat in the manner of the "I love New York" theme.

Shanghai is already considered to be the country's financial center; it could add more colors to this image by considering something like an Asian trading wall like the Nasdaq sign in New York. A key component in building up as a financial capital is, of course, access to information and the media. In line with this, Shanghai could consider developing its media industry much more intensively, to make the city a true capital of news. This would include encouraging the broadcast and online media to make the city their Asian headquarters, in addition to cultivating and building relations with the international media. Lastly, world-class cities have arts and culture. Shanghai could also consider hosting a major film festival, or design or arts competition. Even a major sports competition could help to communicate its image as a cultural capital. The WTO is not a magic bullet that guarantees immediate prosperity, but it opens up the chance for Shanghai, and other cities in China, to review and renew their campaigns for excellence.

10. How Does China Invest and Do Business Abroad?

Hironori Aihara:
We can think of four patterns for China's investment abroad:

- From the economic point of view, Chinese companies invest in countries that have lower costs, such as Vietnam, Laos, and the rest of Indochina.
- From the political point of view, China invests in countries to help support local economies that need it, such as in the African nations. China may develop its foreign relations as a result.
- From a political and security point of view, China can invest in countries where future business developments or oil or energy security can be expected, such as the Central and Latin American countries, and the Middle Eastern countries.
- China can invest in order to develop its trading relations. For instance, to offset a huge trade imbalance, China may invest in the United States.

Chinese companies have also begun to purchase small and medium-sized Japanese high-technology companies that were in danger of bankruptcy. This is only one part of an increasing trend of Chinese companies buying into Asian companies, in high-tech and other fields, in the future.

Richard Edelman:
Entry into the WTO will raise expectations greatly at home and abroad. There is a real potential for disenchantment, with unrealistic hopes dashed by harsh realities. Two major consequences are the expectation that China will now have to exhibit compliance with international norms on items such as intellectual property and shareholder rights. At the same time, China will be much more scrutinized by the international media and also may be criticized by outside forces, including "green" or human rights groups, foreign labor unions, and politicians. All of these mean that China must adopt a new model of persuasion, move from decree to dialogue, and adopt much more an approach of speaking to multiple stakeholders in a consistent fashion.

A key part of this is engaging the global media, as a key part of "going abroad." China must provide stories beyond politics and business: including art, culture, and people. It needs to take its story to the key media markets, including New York, London, and Tokyo. Many people in the international community already have a very rational interest in China based on economics and politics. Now China needs to help them have an emotional connection with the country. This will foster more understanding and build allies.

At the same time, China should recognise that civil society – both at home and abroad – cannot be ignored. Edelman's research has shown NGOs to be the new super brands – in fact they are now the Fifth Estate in global governance. Maybe non-government organizations should be invited to Shanghai to meet and/or to work with the government in benchmarking best practices in the environment, labour, or other aspects of social development. A key part of China's international media strategy should be the promise of transparency and openness. Thus, "going abroad" for China should be based not only in investment but also in communications and the media.

11. How Can China and Southeast Asia Achieve a Win–Win Relationship?

David Li:
China's emergence as a major world trading partner and its growing economic strength will have a major impact on Southeast Asia. How well Southeast Asian countries adapt to China's economic power will dictate whether they turn China's strength to their own advantage, or are overwhelmed by it. During the past year, most Southeast Asian economies benefited from China's surging exports. Their own exports surged in parallel, supplying inputs to China's export manufacturing industries.

In future, there will be many new opportunities for Southeast Asian countries. For example, tourists from the mainland will visit Southeast Asia in increasing numbers. Southeast Asia is rich in resources, and China will increasingly turn to Southeast Asia for the raw materials and semi-finished products it cannot produce at home. Established companies that are major players in their domestic markets in Southeast Asia will have a new outlet for expansion, as China is a raw and underdeveloped market. The key for Southeast Asia is to exploit the new market opportunities presented by China.

Hironori Aihara:
Asian countries, especially the ASEAN countries, are losing competitiveness domestically in certain industries. They might shift those

areas to China, where the labor cost is still low. And by concentrating their resources on more value-added industries, this division of layers of industries among countries will create a balanced coexistence.

Peter Lau:

The emergence of China as a major economic player should be no surprise to anyone. It is futile to try to compete with China, as it would not be a win–win result. Southeast Asia should seriously look at the "comparative advantage of nations." The big question is how to get the cash earned, or to be earned, by China recalculated throughout Southeast Asia. There are three key areas to look at: (1) foreign direct investments (FDI) from China to Southeast Asia; (2) supplying China with the raw materials that it lacks; and (3) providing high-value-added services to China.

·   *FDI:* It is both politically and economically beneficial for China to recalculate her wealth back to Southeast Asia. China has a good motive to do so. It is up to the Southeast Asian nations to open their doors to foreign investments, including from China. Overseas Chinese have always had a tradition of spreading their risks, and mainland Chinese are no different. Like any investors, Chinese investors are also looking for transparency and the rule of law to protect their investments overseas. Given the full cooperation and friendly policies of the host countries, the mainland Chinese could be extremely creative and entrepreneurial investors, helping their host countries to thrive.

·   *Raw materials:* China lacks many raw materials with which to fully exploit her anticipated status as the world's "workshop." Rubber, petrochemical products, pulp and paper, steel and other building materials, to name a few, must be imported from outside. The Southeast Asian nations could be the main suppliers of these raw materials for both Chinese manufacturing and infrastructure building.

·   *High-value-added services:* More and more Chinese are traveling abroad. Southeast Asian resorts are major attractions for Chinese travelers. Chinese are thirsty for better education for their children, and Southeast Asian educational institutions are generally preferred (although in competition with American universities) to mainland Chinese universities. Furthermore, most Southeast Asian countries are more conversant with the English language. Special language schools catering to Chinese of all ages wishing to upgrade their English skills would be a tremendous business opportunity.

12. What Will China's Competitive Edge be Globally in Five Years' Time?

Hironori Aihara:

China stands to benefit immensely in terms of its vast, cheap, young, and comparatively high-standard labor force. They will maintain this advantage for at least another five years.

Cyrill Eltschinger:

With a population of 1.3 billion, China's greatest existing asset is its human capital. Couple this with its emerging, rapidly developing market status and you begin to build a picture of the huge global role that China is gaining as a producer and consumer not only across industries, but also in the service sector.

In terms of software outsourcing, major trends predict that China will surpass India. The most profitable form of this outsourcing will probably be contained within the offshore market. Firms that will grasp how to take advantage of the human capital in this way will enjoy more success than those that attempt to approach the China market with Western strategies.

David Li:

When looking at China, it is important to remember that it is a continental economy, with strong domestic demand. Until now, the one factor that has hindered the growth of major Chinese brand names has been the poor distribution network. It simply was not physically possible to move goods reliably and cost-efficiently.

As the transport bottlenecks are eliminated, and as companies expand with new plants in strategic areas, Chinese companies are building major domestic brands. Quality is improving all the time.

At present, most of China's exports are shipped out under brand names owned by U.S. and European firms. With a strong home market and a proven export capability, Chinese companies will increasingly compete in international markets under their own brand names. In just a few short years, we have seen Chinese companies take over the lead in supplying DVD players to the U.S. market. Other products from other industries cannot be far behind.

Edward Tian:

China's competitive edge will first be built around a world-class manufacturing base that serves the world. It's a win–win strategy for both sides, in that China can provide global companies with a low-cost, efficient, and reliable production base. Many Western companies are already taking advantage of this, by moving parts of their global supply chains to China.

One other country with which there is still a lot of potential for partnership is Japan. We have had no major dialogue with Japan, and yet our economies are economically complementary. We need to begin to develop this relationship more deeply, perhaps through a Northeast Asian forum. Japan has much knowledge and patience for innovation, which is why its companies lead the world in these categories. Here, in China, we have not developed those skills yet. It's a major opportunity.

Part 5
Conclusion

CONCLUSION

In the final analysis, it is difficult to predict the course of China's development path. The editors, together with the contributors and participants in the roundtable, can only hope to shed light on specific aspects that feed the country's growth. Even for the government, situations change, new realities come to light, and the impacts of policies ripple outwards.

Nevertheless, we can, based on the contributions herein, envision a situation in which China pursues and accomplishes what it already knows it must, which is to overcome current contradictions, inequities, and stumbling blocks in order to achieve a "best case" scenario. The leadership knows this, and the business community has already started to push forward. In 2002, China achieved the scale of a US$1 trillion economy, and at its current growth rate it is on its way to becoming the world's largest economy in about 20 years. Government, domestic business, and foreign investors will all contribute to this success.

Such a development means a dramatic transformation of the world power balance, resulting in new models and frameworks for international organizations, trading blocs, and regional and global governance. This is even more true in the midst of a slowdown in the economies of the world's heavyweights, such as the United States and Japan, and the overall decline in global trade and foreign direct investment flows. With China's economy past the threat of deflation and progressing steadily at GDP growth rates of 7–8% a year, the country is positioned to increase its influence on the global trading floor. Chinese companies have already poured an unprecedented amount into foreign ventures, carving oil deals in Southeast Asia and entering global markets with both cheap goods, such as toys and shoes, as well as high-tech gear such as wafer chips, televisions, and telecom switching equipment. More Chinese tourists have ventured abroad, and tourism officials predict that by 2010, China will be one of the world's largest sources of tourists. China could even assume the mantle of a real global growth driver. Indeed, no country could possibly dream of replacing the United States in this role. While many things could derail the Chinese economic miracle – and we have tried to ensure their discussion through this book – it is worthwhile just to envision what China as a "first among equals" economic power would mean.

Until now, the globalization debate has been characterized by the so-called north–south divide. The industrialized countries of the north were accused by the poorer countries of the south of exploiting globalization to their advantage. Now, however, China has reframed that dichotomy by becoming the first "poor" country to gain from globalization without the boom-bust cycle seen elsewhere in the developing world. Although China is still a developing country, the pace at which it has absorbed the main facets of globalization has been stunning. Simultaneously, the looming liberalization of key sectors of greatest "globalization-tension," such as agriculture and financial services, should make us question the assertion that globalization merely creates a larger divide between the rich and the poor.

Some may see China's embracing of globalization as being at the expense of its fellow developing countries, creating a south–south divide to replace the north–south divide. For instance, companies such as Toshiba have moved their production lines from Southeast Asia to bigger plants in China. Also, India has filed numerous anti-dumping cases against China, and has accused it of rerouting international finance and investment from the Subcontinent to China. The case for a looming south–south battle as the new offspring of globalization seems strong.

Why should one believe that this is not the case? Because to do so would confuse short-term dislocation with a lasting paradigm change.

The seeming flight of manufacturing to China is merely one step in a longer chain of productivity enhancement and comparative advantage. But it is not a zero sum game, and replacements are not absolute. The demand for core competitiveness and a niche advantage has always been the prevailing law of business survival. The only way that companies and economies have prospered over time is by honing their competitiveness and efficiency in identifiable markets. Singapore is not the first economy to adapt to this law by trying to establish strengths across selected industries, and the same is true for Taiwan. If economists agree that "China cannot manufacture everything for everyone," then they will agree that this is doubly the case for small economies with limited manpower, natural resources, and investment.

One cannot deny that there is dislocation and pain in communities that are experiencing the so-called flight of manufacturing to China. The task for these countries is to view these as freed resources that should be put to alternative uses. At the same time, companies that gain in productivity will invest back into economies, thus completing the cycle. This may be an idealistic view, but it is one that carries the credence of the history of trade and investment flows. It is also being mimicked domestically within China.

Many have already commented that, while China contains some of the fastest-growing regions of the global economy, its impoverished inner regions help to deflate the myth of the dragon-in-waiting. Many of the country's new leaders have already acknowledged the need to close the income gap in China, which is already wide and forecasted to become even wider, without drastic policies and actions in the short term. The process of economic movement among the provinces, and the shuffling of key "rising stars" among the major provinces in the west and east, is an indication that this gap is being taken seriously by the leadership. In addition, many in the business community are very aware of the existence of not only income gaps between different geographical areas in China, but also of divides in terms of education, health, technology, and other areas. They also see it increasingly as their duty to contribute to rectifying these gaps and playing their full roles as corporate citizens. China's civil society is still in its infancy, and in contrast to countries in which non-governmental organizations often stand against government, in China's case the NGOs will likely stand alongside government. This is especially true for one of China's most urgent tasks, poverty reduction. The new government has many programs and plans, and these will all see China move ahead in a steady way, together with the economy's evolving groups of stakeholders, including business, civil society, and the media.

In short, China has reframed the logic of globalization by domesticating it and proving that poor countries need not be losers. The task for China remains that of sustaining its growth, while making its growth sustainable in the long-term, in terms of industry, the environment, and social development. This is good for the stability of the country, and for the global economy. Only continued growth will ensure that the current challenges are met.

It is still an open debate as to how the developed and the developing worlds will deal with the new driving force of globalization. It should be clear that China is not the Trojan horse of the industrialized world – its government officials, entrepreneurs, and consumers have saddled this racehorse themselves. The process of globalization will continue – and as such, all stakeholders, from government, business, and civil society, should jointly work to mitigate its risks. China has already made an important contribution to the globalization debate. It will also add an important dimension to the concept of sustainable growth.

China is entering a new era of changes, and its economic globalization is ensuring that its growth is infused with elements from a wide range of sources, both Chinese and foreign. Multiple forces are converging on China as it transforms itself, bringing truth to its existence as the "middle kingdom" as befits its name. And, with the exception of decline in the 19th and parts of the 20th century, China has always been a central power with the force of 5,000 years of civilization and history behind it.

China is already the most populous country in the world and the third largest in terms of area. It is en route to becoming one of the world's largest economies. To quote Napoleon: 'China is a lion. Once it is awakened, it will shake the world'. China has not only awakened, it is now shaking the global trading system and the paradigms of the international economy. It is clear that the world has to redefine the parameters of its relations with it if the full economic and political potential of this country is to be brought to fruition.

Index